Games Businesses Play

Cases and Models

Pankaj Ghemawat

The MIT Press
Cambridge, Massachusetts
London, England

This book was set in Palatino on the Miles 33 typesetting system by Graphic Composition, Inc.

Printed and bound in the United States of America

The paper used in this publication is both acid and totally chlorine free (TCF). It meets the minimum requirements of American Standard for Information Sciences— Permanence of Paper for Printed Library Materials, ANSI Z39.48-1984.

Library of Congress Cataloging-in-Publication Data

Ghemawat, Pankaj.
    Games businesses play : cases and models / Pankaj Ghemawat.
      p.   cm
    Includes bibliographical references and index.
    ISBN 0-262-07182-7
      1. Management games—Case studies.   2. Industrial organization—Case studies.   1. Title.
HD30.26.G47   1997
658.4'0353—dc21   97-7564
                                                                                  CIP

To AMG I and AMG II

Contents

Foreword

by Daniel F. Spulber

The field of management strategy studies how managers design organizations, compete in the marketplace, and cope with legal and regulatory constraints. Developments in economics of the last decade or more, notably the application of game theory to the study of industrial organization, provide a new set of tools for understanding strategy. Game theory has much to offer management strategy, both as a guide to analyzing how managers compete and as a method for devising competitive actions. Pankaj Ghemawat's *Games Businesses Play: Cases and Models* provides an innovative application of game theory to understanding management strategy that is well-grounded in the study of business cases.

Case studies have long been at the center of management education, providing teachers with a convenient way of framing lessons about business policy and giving students a chance to test their skills against a set of market conditions and observable outcomes. Although they are of great value in the classroom, case studies also have been notoriously long on history and short on analytic content. This need not be so. Business decisions are replete with challenges for economic researchers. Pankaj Ghemawat's analysis remedies this shortfall by bringing game-theoretic analysis to bear on a well-chosen set of case studies.

The case studies in the present book are a culmination of a long tradition of business cases pioneered at the Harvard Business School. Case studies are now being developed in many universities and are a regular feature of management teaching. The application of economic reasoning to business cases took a great leap foward with Michael Porter's crafting of industrial organization techniques to address strategy questions. Porter helped create a growing field of economic analysis of strategy, including an innovative series of books by Ghemawat (1991a), Milgrom and Robert (1992), and Brandenburger and Nalebuff (1996). Pankaj Ghemawat's present book moves things foward by bringing game-theoretic techniques to bear on case studies.

Two of Pankaj Ghemwat's studies of Nucor steel, which form the basis of a chapter in this book, kicked off the publication of case studies in the *Journal of Economics and Management Strategy* (JEMS). While industry studies have long been a part of industrial organization, case studies of the organization and strategy of *individual* firms have been rare. Yet empirical researchers are inevitably aware of how differences between firms affect the results of their studies, but they have often lacked the tools for exploring the consequences of those differences. An examination of how individual firms act both complements and enriches industry studies. It was a wish to further the application of industrial organization economics to business problems that led me and a distinguished group of coeditors and editorial board members to found JEMS. The journal remains dedicated to the proposition that economics has much to contribute to business decision-making and that the study of microeconomics can be greatly strengthened by the consideration of practical issues in mangement strategy. Since its inception, the journal has emphasized rigorous modeling using economic theory and econometric analysis. At the same time many articles in JEMS include intuitive explanations and examples applied to specific industries and individual firms. The journal's success among researchers and managers, and the evident inclusion of business issues in other industrial organization journals since its founding, are testimony to the relevance of microeconomic analysis for business decision-making.

The value of case studies published in JEMS and other outlets is in the questions raised by a detailed and systematic examination of the considerations involved in management decisions and the consequences of the managers' organizational and competitive actions. There are those who will assert that case studies are essentially anecdotal and by their very nature limited to one data point. However, case studies not only provide a wealth of technical details, more important, they create a bridge between managerial strategy-making and economic analysis. Case studies provide insights into company strategy-making that can serve as an important guide to theoretical modeling and empirical estimation. Case studies can be valuable in several ways: First, case studies are useful for testing and developing the theory of the firm. Second, case studies provide a means of understanding and extending empirical work on industries. Finally, case studies allow the development of strategy recommendations by identifying the effects of alternative strategies in specific situations.

The question of firm heterogeneity lies at the heart of important debates in both industrial organization and management strategy, for related reasons. In industrial organization, the issue is whether the market power and profits of firms are due to market concentration, barriers to entry, or to firm differences in efficiency. In management strategy, the issue is whether firms can obtain market power and profits by reliance on entry barriers or by developing and taking advantage of unique resources such as organization, management skill, or technical knowledge. It becomes apparent that the best way to address the question of whether firms differ is to begin by examining the characteristics of individual firms. There is therefore a need for case studies in economic analysis. Case studies present a detailed examination of the firm: its organization, its market actions, and the effects of public policy constraints on its activities.

Case studies of individual firms are particularly valuable not only in recognizing firm heterogeneity but in identifying the effects of firm differences on economic performance in a systematic way. By taking the firm as the unit of analysis, case studies can compare the relative effects on the firm's market success of organizational forms, incentives, pricing policies, innovation, and other activities. Empirical research on the organization and competitive strategies of individual firms is most successful when it leads to a reexamination of existing models of competition.

In this book Pankaj Ghemawat focuses on the strategic role of commitment. When firms can make credible commitments to particular actions, they can influence the outcome of the competitive game, contingent on the strategies of other players. The cases analyzed run the gamut from short-term pricing strategies to longer-term strategies of capacity investment and reduction, product and process innovation, and entry strategies.

Pankaj Ghemawat's institutional descriptions show an in-depth concern for essential industry details without being exhaustive. In the General Electric case, for example, game theory is useful in narrowing the focus to pricing and capacity choice, with companies facing backlogs as they produce to order. This raises questions about how firms choose between producing to

stock and producing to order, and the many institutional conditions and strategies that determine such choices. In addition the
interplay between pricing and production decisions stands out
in relief because of the substantial cost of producing large turbine generators. He considers one-period and multi-period
price-setting games that suggest that the large firm will price
high when backlogs are low, and he confirms this prediction with
regression analysis. This fascinating analysis raises questions
about capacity investment and entry decisions in the generator
industry that go beyond the scope of the present study. Moreover
the interplay between pricing and backlogs bears examination in
the context of other industries.

The capacity investment questions are pursued in the Du Pont
titanium dioxide case and in the chemical industry with Ethyl's
lead-based antiknock additives and Allied Chemical's synthetic
soda ash. Again, the analysis integrates a discussion of firm-level
data with presentation of innovative game-theoretic modeling.
The Du Pont case examines capacity growth, explicitly accounting for differences in size between competitiors, rather that one-
size-fits-all modeling. Similarly the chemical processing industry
cases show how the closure/shrinkage of plants can depend on
firm size as well as plant-level differences in efficiency.

Consideration of investment extends to product and process
innovation, respectively, in the study of Intecom's private branch
exchange (PBX) development and Nucor's enterprising adoption
of thin-slab casting of steel. Intecom's introduction of the first
voice-and-data PBX is examined in the context of competition
between an incumbent monopolist (AT&T) and upstart entrants.
The steel industry case contrasts the technology adoption decision of a smaller-scale successful entrant (Nucor) with that of a
large-scale traditional producer of steel (U.S. Steel). These cases

highlight the effects of firm differences on competititve strategies in a theoretical context as well as in specific innovative contests.

The detailed case studies conclude with the war of attrition between British Satellite Broadcasting and News Corporation's Sky Television for the satellite TV market in the United Kingdom. A game-theoretic model of the war of attrition that explicitly accounts for player beliefs is used to explore the effects of strategic uncertainty in the bruising competition between the satellite broadcasters.

In sum, Pankaj Ghemawat has set out to demonstrate the applicability of game-theoretic reasoning to problems in management, and the book is highly successful at this task. Each chapter presents an empirical case study focused on a single firm, carefully sets out a game theory principle, and then examines the applicability of that principle to the case at hand. The book demonstrates the difficulties and rewards from confronting game theory principles with firm-level data. It carefully asks questions about specific company actions, such as whether observed backlogs in the large turbine generator industry could be explained by strategic choice of buffers by firms in the industry, or whether capacity expansion in the titanium dioxide industry was a preemptive strategy. Such an approach will be useful for teaching students about the basis of game theory while introducing them to the application of strategic reasoning to business problems.

Pankaj Ghemawat's approach also will be valuable for researchers in industrial organization because it will stimulate them to conduct case studies of companies as a means of testing ideas about strategic interaction. The blend of game theory and case studies in the book will enrich both areas, bringing realism and novel problems to game theorists and analytic methods to business strategists. Thus the games businesses play will prove to be enlightening as well as entertaining.

Preface

This book is motivated by a puzzle. Over the last thirty years business strategy has increasingly come to be influenced by theories of competition. Over the last twenty years industrial organization (IO) economics has played a leading role in shaping business-strategic reasoning about competition. Yet many business strategists are quite skeptical about whether IO has much more to contribute to their field.

This skepticism seems closely related to the shift in IO economists' attention from cross-industry empirical analyses to game-theoretic analyses of competition in individual industries (new IO). Business strategists are rather less certain about the benefits of trading in old IO for new IO. In particular, many of them question the usefulness of game theory for business strategy.

A number of attempts to address this question on purely conceptual grounds have been made but seem to have left predispositions largely intact. This book takes a different tack: It explores the uses and limits of game theory on the basis of detailed case studies of different types of commitment decisions. In doing so, it makes the important methodological point that while the case method is often disdained, particularly by IO economists, it seems uniquely well suited in many instances to the task of confronting game theory with the real world of business.

The research cases on which this book is based have been compiled over the last fifteen years. Although much of the interpretative material is new to this book, most of the individual cases have already been published in rather different form in scholarly journals. Seminar audiences at more than two dozen institutions, and several dozen colleagues, have helped shape my interpretation of them. I am particularly grateful to Adam Brandenburger, Anita McGahan, and Barry Nalebuff, who worked with me on the material that underlies three of the chapters in this book, although they should not be assumed to agree with the way in which I have chosen to present that material in this book. Richard Caves, Jerry Green, Arnoldo Hax, Richard Meyer, Jan Rivkin, and Mike Scherer read an earlier draft of this book in its entirety and supplied a host of helpful comments. Clayton Christensen, David Collis, Tarun Khanna, Elon Kohlberg, Marvin Lieberman, David Salant, and Arthur Schleifer, Jr., were of great help with individual chapters in this book. Patricio del Sol assisted me with the citation counts that are reported in chapter 1, and my father, Dr. Mahipal Singh Ghemawat, with the thankless job of proofreading. In addition executives at more than a dozen companies, some of which are cited in the chapters that follow, helped keep the effort grounded in reality.

My biggest debt, however, is to the Harvard Business School. I can think of no other institution that would have been as unstinting in its support and encouragement of a research effort that has spanned so many years and taken me well off the academic beaten path. I hope that in some small measure, this book will add to the general appreciation of the School's tradition of detailed investigation of individual cases.

Finally I would be remiss if I did not note that the integration of the individual cases into this book coincided with an expansion of the size of our family unit. This book is dedicated to my wife and daughter for their patience and good humor over the last two years.

Games Businesses Play

1   Game Theory and Business Strategy

This book is motivated by a puzzle. Since the late 1970s industrial organization (IO) economics has been revolutionized by game theory: the study of rational choices by actors—in this context, usually firms—whose payoffs depend on each other's actions and who recognize that fact. Yet this game-theoretic revolution has not made nearly as much of an impression on the applied field of business strategy as did the "old" (pre-game theoretic) IO studies, despite some obvious affinities between evolving business-strategic concerns and game-theoretic contributions.

While this disconnection can be rationalized in several ways, the premise of this book is that it is due, in large part, to a missing empirical link: Game-theoretic models have not lent themselves to conventional large-sample tests to an extent that would, if the results were positive, persuade researchers in business strategy of their utility. This book therefore proposes more attention to detailed analyses of individual cases as a way of exploring both the uses of and limits to game-theoretic reasoning on business strategy. The rest of this chapter expands on these ideas.

1.1   The Promise

In late 1994 the Nobel Prize in Economic Science was awarded to three game-theorists, John Nash, John Harsanyi, and Reinhard Selten. This award, on the fiftieth anniversary of the publication of John von Neumann and Oskar Morgenstern's (1944) path-breaking book, *The Theory of Games and Economic Behavior,* marked an affirmation by the economics profession that game theory had finally come of age. Game-theoretic research is now rampant across the entire field of economics.

Industrial organization (IO) is probably the field of economics most strenuously cultivated and successfully captured by game theorists. Exhibit 1.1 summarizes the results of my content analysis of IO articles published in the five most cited general-interest economics journals—the *American Economic Review, Econometrica,* the *Journal of Political Economy,* the *Quarterly Journal of Economics,* and the *Review of Economic Studies*—and indicates that there was an upsurge in the use of game theory in IO in the late 1970s (see appendix A for details). Since 1980, about 60 percent of all IO articles published in these general-interest journals have focused on developing or testing game-theoretic models. The ascendancy of game-theoretic models and methods may be even more marked when one looks at journals that specialize in IO: The leading specialist journal (at least through the 1980s), the *RAND Journal of Economics,* is sometimes referred to as the RAND Journal of Entry-Deterrence for its fascination with a particular class of game-theoretic models. Authoritative texts such as Tirole (1988) and Schmalensee and Willig (1989) corroborate the fact that IO economists currently see little alternative to game-theoretic analysis, except in the special cases of perfect competition, monopolistic competition, and pure monopoly.[1]

---

1. Consult, in particular, Peltzman's (1991) review of Schmalensee and Willig (1989).

Exhibit 1.1
Game-Theoretic Articles in Industrial Organization

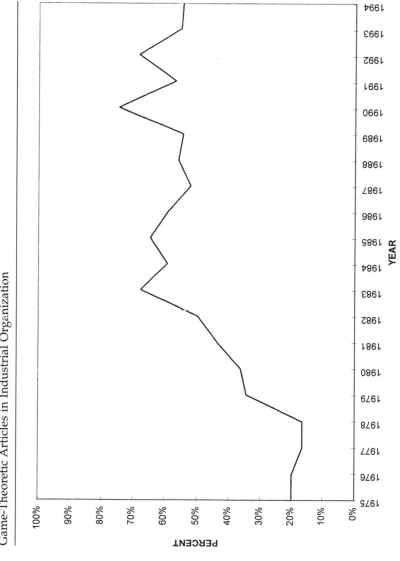

IO economists' enthusiasm for game theory spills over to the field of management that is most closely connected to theirs— business strategy. Given the ways in which game theory has changed IO, and the directions in which the strategy field itself has evolved over that period, the expectation that game theory would transform business strategy would seem, prima facie, to be reasonable. Consider these changes one by one.

The Evolution of IO

Old (pregame-theoretic) IO has had a significant influence on the field of business strategy. Porter's (1980) classic book, *Competitive Strategy*, has proved particularly important: Its IO-based principles for distinguishing "good" (profitable) industries from "bad" ones are widely used by practitioners as well as in the MBA classroom. One might expect game-theoretic IO's prospects for influencing business strategy to be even better since it bridges some of the differences that Porter (1981), among others, identified as driving a wedge between old IO and business strategy:

• *Public welfare versus private profits.* Attention to developing profit-maximizing strategies for playing nonzero-sum games has tended to shift the focus of IO analysis away from public welfare and toward private profitability. The "policy implications" section of the typical old IO paper used to dwell on public policy; discussions of the implications for business strategy are now much more common.

• *Average profits versus profit differentials.* When old IO did focus on profitability as its performance indicator, it concentrated on average profitability at the industry level. Game-theoretic IO, in contrast, allots much more attention to the structural and strategic bases of sustained profit differences among (actual and potential) competitors in the same industry. Business strategists are, by and large, more interested in the latter than in the former.

• *Similarities versus differences across industries.* Unlike old IO, which attempted to uncover structural regularities that applied across all industries, the new game-theoretic IO is sensitive to industry idiosyncrasies. Attention to the respects in which industries differ from one another is explicit in the emphasis on careful work at the level of individual industries.

• *Structural determinism versus endogeneity.* While old IO often invoked structural determinism, game-theoretic IO recognizes that the elements of industry structure cannot be treated as exogenous; instead, they are considered to be endogenous to firms' strategies (read conduct in the context of the old structure-conduct-performance paradigm). This obviously expands the action implications of the theory.

• *Static versus dynamic analysis.* Finally the game theory revolution has injected some dynamism into IO. Its manifesto, after all, has been that history matters. While there is some debate about whether game theory has done enough in this regard (e.g., Porter 1991), the point being made here is that it has helped rather than hurt.

For all these reasons an economist might reasonably expect business strategy to follow in the footsteps of IO and be in the grips of its own game-theoretic revolution.

The Evolution of Business Strategy

A second set of reasons for expecting game-theoretic IO to have a significant influence on business strategy is related to changes in thinking about business strategy over the last ten years. These changes have basically involved a shift in focus, from the product market activities that competitors perform to the durable, firm-specific factors that underpin differences in their product-market opportunity sets. While a few strategists continue to insist that product market activities are primordial (see chapter 6 for additional discussion), the revealed preferences of strategy researchers supply direct evidence that a substantial shift of opinion *has* taken place. Additional detail can be found in the rash of recent manifestos to this effect (e.g., Grant 1991, Peteraf 1993, and Teece and Pisano 1994).

From an IO perspective, such a shift would seem to be welcome: experiments, mental and actual, with contestability theory (Baumol, Panzar, and Willig 1982) suggest that interesting product market imperfections—ones capable of leading to sustained profit differences among competitors—generally rest on factor market imperfections.[2] Factor market imperfections are the leitmotif of recent contributions to strategy despite debates, motivated to some extent by commercial considerations, about whether to couch such imperfections in terms of firm-specific resources, competences, or dynamic capabilities.[3]

Game-theoretic IO is not only consistent with "new" strategy's focus on firm-specific resources and other factor market imperfections but would also seem to be well-positioned to contribute to our understanding of them. To see this, consider the simple framework in exhibit 1.2, which distinguishes firms' capabilities or opportunity sets from the choices, factor- and activity-related, that they make but lets those choices feed back into firms' future menus of opportunities. Business strategists, particularly ones who focus on dynamic capabilities, have hitherto concentrated on the feedback loop from activities or processes; the feedback loop from factor commitments, in contrast, has commanded relatively little attention. Fortunately commitments to tangible and intangible factors are precisely what occupy center stage in much of the game-theoretic IO literature (e.g., Shapiro 1989)! The potential for complementarity between new IO and new strategy should be clear.

---

2. For additional discussion, consult Ghemawat (1991a, ch. 2).
3. Consult, for instance, the debate in the pages of the *Harvard Business Review* between Prahalad and Hamel (1990) and Stalk, Evans, and Shulman (1992) about whether core competences are distinct from capabilities.

Exhibit 1.2
Capabilities, Activities, and Commitments

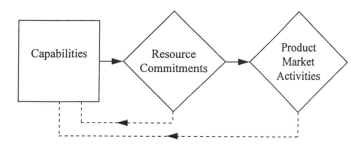

1.2 The Problems

These priors about the potential for game-theoretic techniques of the sort that pervade IO to influence business strategy as well have not, however, been borne out. Once again the most direct evidence on this score comes from content analysis of the articles published in the most-cited journals—in this case the *Academy of Management Journal*, the *Academy of Management Review*, the *Administrative Science Quarterly*, the *Harvard Business Review*, and the *Strategic Management Journal (SMJ)*. Based on a relatively expansive definition of articles that involve the use of game theory, I counted fourteen over the period from 1975 to 1994, or one article every seven journal-years (refer, once again, to appendix A for details). While these numbers are too small to permit systematic trend analysis, there *was* a relatively recent peak, with a grand total of four such articles published in 1991—on which more below. I would also guess that the use of game theory was even rarer in management journals that ranked lower on the citation sweeps (with the possible exception of *Management Science*, which was edged off the top five list by the *Harvard Business Review*).

The limited diffusion of game-theoretic IO models, and game-theoretic techniques more generally, into business strategy tends to evoke different responses on different sides of that divide. On the supply side there is some amazement that despite the work of von Neumann and Morgenstern (1944), Schelling (1960), and their successors, the sorts of "strategic" (self-consciously inter-active) considerations emphasized by game theory have not reso-nated more with strategists who must anticipate business competitors' moves. There are also mentions of diffusion lags and mutterings about obtuseness and obscurantism.

Looking at the demand side, there would seem to be some particles of truth to these characterizations, even the less polite ones: At academic seminars one still runs into business strate-gists who believe that IO concentrates on perfect competition or that game-theoretic IO is confined to zero-sum games. But there *are* thoughtful business strategists who understand game-theoretic models, and have even made up ones of their own, who nevertheless have significant reservations about this analytical apparatus. Rumelt, Schendel, and Teece's (1991) introduction to the *SMJ*'s special issue on "Fundamental Research Issues in Strategy and Economics" is a particularly good example, partly because of who wrote it and partly because that special issue contained three of the four articles on game theory published in the leading management journals in the "peak" year of 1991.

Rumelt, Schendel, and Teece (1991, pp. 18–22) cite several spe-cific problems, from a business-strategic perspective, with game theory. First, knowledge about the strategic phenomena to be studied is outside the scope of game theory and game theorists are (asserted to be) generally unwilling to learn much about business, leaving a leading role for scholars (presumed to be strategists rather than economists) who identify phenomena worth studying. Second, game-theoretic analyses focus on ex-plaining the possible existence of interactive effects rather than assaying their practical importance, which hurts predictive power. Third, game-theorists model strategic phenomena piece-meal, in a way that focuses on a minimal number of economic variables to the exclusion of others—psychological, political, or-ganizational, technological, and even economic—which limits both scientific testability and practical utility. Fourth, game-theoretic equilibrium may be an unreasonable outcome to expect to observe in practice because of the information and the degree of rationality required to get there. Fifth, while game-theoretic models of industrial organization focus on external interactions, the roots of competitive advantage may be internal. This last point is a bit confusing, but is elaborated later on in the same issue of the *SMJ* by Williamson (1991), who asserts that interfirm efficiency differences are generally a more important influence on observed outcomes in business than are pure interactive effects.

These and related points have been debated extensively. The debate has not had much of an effect on predispositions: Schol-ars trained in game theory tend to be in favor of it, and others to be against it. Additional debate in the abstract about the merits and demerits of applying game theory to business strategy seems unlikely to alter this pattern.

A more satisfactory approach is suggested by the observation that the importance of each of the problems flagged by Rumelt, Schendel, and Teece is, ultimately, an issue that can only be re-solved by empirical work. And empirics is precisely where game-theoretic IO is weak compared to old IO, which was un-dergirded by thousands of interindustry studies. This weakness can be illustrated by unpacking the content analyses reported earlier. Even if one is generous in classifying articles as empirical rather than theoretical, only 11 percent of the IO articles based on game theory that were published in the leading economic journals over twenty years can be called empirical, compared to 43 percent of the IO articles not based on game theory (refer,

once again, to appendix A). A chi-square analysis of the six
hundred-plus IO articles that constituted the sample indicates
that the probability that this difference was the result of pure
sampling error is 1.8×10^{-20}! The sample of game-theoretic articles published in management journals is too small to permit a
similar test, but there again only three of the fourteen articles
have empirical content beyond an abbreviated (alleged) example
or two.

While this dearth of empirical work motivated by game-
theoretic IO might, in principle, reflect a convergence of tastes
across a community of like-minded researchers, the extent to
which it is bemoaned, even by economists, indicates that it reflects technology rather than tastes: that it is a response to some
ineluctable constraints on the testing of game-theoretic models.
These constraints are several but can be grouped into two broad
categories. First, the reach of most noncooperative game-
theoretic models is very narrow. Matching models to empirical
situations is therefore a nontrivial task. Second, even if one can
settle on a particular model, its parameters tend to be hard to
measure because they include not only the old-fashioned conduct variables recognized but generally black-boxed by "old" IO
but also some of the new ones uncovered by "new" IO—order
of moves, information sets, communication possibilities, and
the like—with intertemporal effects further complicating the
picture.[4]

Both of these broad constraints hint at the optimality of narrowing of the scope of empirical work so as to increase its depth
or power. In this vein a number of prominent economists—including Camerer (1991), Spulber (1993), and Caves (1994)—have
recently called for additional use of the case method to investi-

---

4. Caves (1994) supplies some additional discussion.

gate the predictions of game-theoretic models. It is worth adding that the case method also seems responsive to the concerns about game theory raised by business strategists such as Rumelt, Schendel, and Teece (1991): Detailed analyses of individual cases can help identify phenomena worth studying, supply a direct take on the practical importance of game-theoretic thinking in general and the concept of equilibrium in particular, mitigate the curse of dimensionality by facilitating customized modeling that captures main effects while managing to be spare, and generate the kind of in-depth information that seems essential to any analysis of the extent to which observed outcomes are influenced by internal structure and efficiency rather than external interactions.[5]

Such considerations encourage the expectation that the case method can be an attractive way of confronting game theory with reality. But it would be indelicate to assume that an all-clear has been sounded: There are presumably reasons why case research has, despite a long tradition in both IO and business strategy, recently fallen into disuse and even disrepute. I therefore proceed with caution. The next section presents a miniature case study, on diamond pricing, that typifies in some respects the cases covered at greater length later on in this book. The section that follows uses this minicase as a basis for discussing some of the issues that crop up in the course of case research and the principles and procedures with which I have tried to address them. Such a discussion seems essential to convincing the skeptical reader that the detailed case studies that follow are not simply, in Caporaso's (1995, p. 457) words, "solo performances with nonreproducible insight and *Fingerspitzengefühl.*"

---

5. Some of these points are more obvious than others. They will all be reviewed in the last chapter of this book.

1.3   A Minicase: Diamond Pricing

Economists generally attribute their professional interest in diamonds—as in many other subjects—to Adam Smith ([1776] 1937, p. 28), who observed that while water has much more value in use, diamonds have much more value in exchange.[6] This contrast is underpinned of course by differences in scarcity. But modern microeconomists have ventured well beyond this basic point in their disquisitions on diamond pricing.

By way of empirical background, diamond prices are largely dictated by De Beers, which through its distribution arm, the Central Selling Organization (CSO), controls 70 to 80 percent of the worldwide sales of rough diamonds. The CSO functions as a common marketing agency, buying its roughs from "outside" suppliers as well as obtaining them from De Beers' own mines. This arrangement, along with the belief that diamonds are forever, has led many economists to think of the diamond industry as a durable goods monopoly *par excellence*.

Contemporary models of durable good monopoly can mostly be traced back to Coase (1972), who pointed out that due to durability such a monopolist would create its own future competition, and conjectured that unless it could credibly precommit to restrict such competition, its price would collapse to its marginal cost "in the twinkling of an eye" (p. 143). Subsequent work—Tirole (1988) alone lists a dozen contributions, and the Social Sciences Citation Index another dozen since the publication of Tirole's book—has largely focused on formal analysis of the Coase conjecture within Coase's basic framework but with some variation in detailed specifications. Stokey (1981) is a good example:

---

6. They could go back even farther, to John Law (1705, p. 4), who appears to have been the first to contrast water and diamonds in these terms.

She treats the length of time for which the monopolist can pre-commit to maintaining prices as given and shows that its ability to sustain prices above marginal cost varies directly with this parameter. The point of correspondence with the diamond case, counted as compelling by many of the game theorists who cite it (e.g., Tirole 1988, p. 85), is that the CSO/De Beers has long had a policy of never cutting the (nominal) list prices for its rough diamonds.

This story seems plausible—until it is scrutinized more closely. First, interviews with retailers indicate that buyers of diamond jewelry for engagements, weddings, anniversaries, *et cetera*, are somewhat timebound in their purchasing decisions and that their resale possibilities—another key plank of buyer power in models of durable goods monopoly—are restricted by sentiment as well as by transaction costs capable of exceeding 50 percent of transaction values. This divergence between reality and the assumptions that typically underlie models of durable goods monopoly should bother all but strict instrumentalists (à la Friedman 1953). Second, since even *nonstrategic* models of optimal natural resource extraction suggest that margins should increase at the interest rate, the maintenance of nominal prices is arguably a test for *strategic* behavior that is too prone to false positives (Hotelling 1931). Third, in the second half of 1995 De Beers "rebalanced" its price book by actually cutting its nominal list prices for smaller, cheaper categories of diamonds.

In *real* as opposed to nominal terms, the CSO has reduced its prices in roughly half of the years since the recession of the mid-1970s. Predicting the occurrence of a reduction rather than an increase in prices is more challenging than simply noting general downward rigidity in nominal prices. It also requires a motivation distinct from the Coase conjecture. Interviews at De Beers, the CSO, and brokerage houses as well as a reading of the trade press suggested one: that the CSO/De Beers increases prices if and only if the CSO's stock-to-sales ratio is sufficiently low.

I tested this hypothesis with yearly data obtained from a South African brokerage house, J. D. Anderson, on the CSO's stock-to-sales ratios and price changes between 1978 and 1993. It turned out that real prices increased whenever the average stock-to-sales ratio was less than or equal to 75 percent (eight years) and decreased otherwise (eight years). Even allowing for the "fitted" trigger level, the probability that purely random effects would give rise to such a pattern is $1/(^{16}_{8})$, or less than 1 in 10,000. In addition, when price changes were treated as a continuous rather than binary dependent variable, a simple regression on the stock-to-sales ratio yielded an adjusted R-squared of 54 percent and a coefficient on the independent variable that was significant at better than the 0.1 percent level.[7] Autocorrelation was tested for as well but turned out to be insignificant.

I read these results as supporting the hypothesis that the CSO/De Beers functions as a "regulator valve"—raising prices when its inventories of diamonds are low and refraining from raising them when its inventories are high. This is rather different in emphasis from the stylized assertion that the CSO behaves like a durable goods monopolist preoccupied by the gravitational pull of the Coase conjecture.

1.4   The Case Method

Considering cases does not, by itself, address all the difficulties that have held up the empirical testing of game-theoretic models.

---

7. With nominal rather than real price changes as the dependent variable, the adjusted R-squared went up to 63 percent and the significance of the coefficient on the independent variable approached 0.01 percent.

Many of the difficulties that remain are implicit in the previous section's minicase. Fortunately they can be minimized via appropriate case research design. I find it efficient to organize my discussion of these difficulties, and of countervailing design strategies, in terms of four canonical components of research design—the research question, model formulation, data generation, and data interpretation—even though they often overlap.

The Research Question

The casual citation of the diamond industry as illustrating the importance of the line of analysis pioneered by Coase highlights the way in which game-theoretic IO often presses cases into service: While causal mechanisms are handled with care, modelers often hearken to the business press, or to hearsay, to dredge up an apparent example or two. Even when such a slipshod procedure does produce a match, it fails to face up to the question that should be of central interest to researchers: Is the causal mechanism that is being invoked necessary as well as sufficient to explain what has been observed? This research question, while pertinent to all theoretical endeavors, is particularly pressing in regard to game-theoretic IO because of what one partisan characterizes as IO's *fundamental theorem:* "The degree of modeling discretion is so significant that a model can be devised to explain almost any fact."[8]

The way to address this research question is to probe cases not only for game-theoretic interactive effects but also in light of alternate hypotheses. While there will be many such alternatives in any given situation, the one explored most frequently in this book is the hypothesis that patterns of business interaction are

---

8. See Saloner (1991, p. 129).

primarily driven by differences in efficiency—possibly to an extent that swamps interactive effects, as argued by Williamson (1991). This differential efficiency (DE) hypothesis is of particular interest not only because of its purported generality but also because of the controversy that has long swirled around it in IO (e.g., section 4 of Goldschmid, Mann, and Weston 1974), and recent suggestions that IO, game-theoretic or otherwise, has little to contribute to business strategy for precisely this reason (e.g., Peteraf 1993). In addition DE-based predictions do not require much theoretical elaboration, permitting the modeling effort to focus on deducing the implications of game-theoretic considerations.

Model Formulation

Another striking aspect of the diamond minicase is that none of the dozens of published models of durable goods monopoly of which I am aware captures two key features of that industry— on the supply side, the CSO's lack of control over the production of rough diamonds (with the exception of those from De Beers' own mines) and, on the demand side, the tremendous cyclicality to which it is subject—that are jointly responsible for the most difficult decision that the CSO/De Beers (periodically) faces: whether or not to continue stockpiling in times of excess supply. The diamond industry is far from unique in this respect: Noncooperative game theory turns out not to offer entirely satisfactory off-the-shelf models for most of the other cases considered in this book either.

This predicament is related, obviously, to the narrow reach of most noncooperative game-theoretic models: to the fact that what we have in place are fragments of a mosaic rather than an architectonic theory. In response some authors have recently argued, in effect, for abandoning the standard noncooperative approach and turning, instead, to other angles of attack that promise more generality. Unfortunately, even the best work of this sort seems, so far, to have been able to achieve generality only at a significant cost in terms of specificity (see exhibit 1.3). Given that reading, I prefer to hew to the standard noncooperative approach, building on the extensive prior work within that branch of game theory whenever possible.

I should add that within the noncooperative branch, I typically focus on models with complete information and turn to ones with incomplete (private) information and signaling only as a last resort. The reasons include the difficulty of observing information asymmetries and the fundamental role that they play in the *fundamental theorem* cited above: Fudenberg and Maskin (1986) have shown that one can get a noncooperative model to predict just about any outcome one wants by injecting the "right" kind of incomplete information into it.[9] The usefulness of signaling models will be revisited in chapter 8 of this book.

In terms of formulating specific models, I first pick a particular case and then cast around for game-theoretic models developed by others that can be extended or adapted to apply to it; if none turns up, I devise my own. This is the exact opposite of the orthodox procedure of first picking a model and then casting around for data to test it on, and is likely to provoke sneers about *ad hockery*. I think that my approach is defensible, however, if one grants the scarcity of cases about which enough data are available to probe the sorts of hypotheses that are of interest, for the orthodox procedure is then tantamount to throwing darts into the air and hoping against hope that they land close to some

---

9. Postrel (1991) provides an amusing example by setting up a model in which rational bank managers set their pants on fire in public to signal high service quality.

Exhibit 1.3
Generalizing Game Theory

Game theorists, dissatisfied with the sensitive dependence of their predictions on the detailed protocols of games, are trying to develop predictions that hold more generally. Unfortunately, it has proved impossible, so far, to satisfy this craving for generality without sacrificing specificity. Consider two of the best efforts of this sort.

Sutton (1991) sticks with noncooperative game theory but succeeds in establishing a general-purpose lower bound on seller concentration as a function of market size and finds that it need not approach zero as market size increases if sunk costs are endogenous: "If it is possible to enhance customers' willingness-to-pay for a given product to some minimal degree by way of a proportionate increase in *fixed* cost" (p. 47). This formulation brackets the possibilities—concentration levels may fall anywhere between the lower bound and monopoly—but it does not pin down the outcome within this range. Nor does it directly speak to the question of central interest to business strategists: How do firms that are differently situated in the same market compete over the strategic opportunities that are open to them?

Brandenburger and Stuart (1996) and, in a recent book for managers, Brandenburger and Nalebuff (1996), turn to cooperative rather than noncooperative game theory for succor, and they stress that with freewheeling interactions a player cannot hope to capture more than its added value (defined as the value created by all players minus the value created by all the players except the one in question). Like Sutton, however, they run up against the problem of nonspecificity. For one thing, even with their maintained assumptions, a player's actual payoff can fall anywhere between a lower bound (often zero) and its added value. Second, added value may not even supply a valid upper bound when there are "frictions"—which have come to be a central concern (under rather different labels such as isolating mechanisms, sources of sustainability, etc.) of business strategy. Third, the diamond example suggests that the concept of added value may not always be operational, especially in situations with very small numbers of players. Thus, even if the actual division of value among diamond suppliers were clear cut (which it is not, because of the secrecy of the contracts between outside suppliers and the CSO, and allegations of fudging on the latter's part), it would be difficult to say whether the CSO/De Beers earns more or less than its added value because it would be difficult to imagine what the diamond market would look like without it. This is presumably why Brandenburger and Nalebuff (1996), despite discussing the diamond example at some length in

Exhibit 1.3
Continued

the chapter on added value in their recent book for managers, do not attempt to calculate that value for the CSO/De Beers. Instead they point out that the CSO restricts supply and advertises to boost demand. These are accurate observations, to be sure, but not very startling ones.

While cooperative game theory is likely to have more to offer as more work is done in this vein, it is worth adding the coda that it has proved only modestly successful in at least one other subfield where it *has* been tried out extensively. Green and Shapiro (1994, p. 143) report that the mathematical theory of legislative behavior began by focusing on cooperative game theory as a theoretical shortcut but is now turning to noncooperative formulations to take account of "the role played by the sequence in which actors move, the information that their moves reveal, their expectations of future interaction, and their ability to sanction one another." Back to the detailed protocol of the game!

data. This and other data-related issues will be elaborated on next.

Data Generation

The diamond minicase focused on (short-run) commitment decisions in a concentrated industry and drew on quantitative and qualitative information from a variety of sources, including interviews. The minicase is representative of the longer cases in this book in all these respects, although the role that the availability of information played in their selection deserves additional emphasis.

The focus on concentrated industries is warranted by the fact that even the proponents of game theory do not claim that it has much to offer in the way of useful insights for very fragmented industries. Consequently the average four-firm concentration

Exhibit 1.4
Detailed Case Studies

Companies	Industries	Types of commitment
General Electric	Large turbine generators	Price-setting
Du Pont	Titanium dioxide	Capacity addition
Ethyl	Lead-based antiknock additives	Capacity reduction
Allied Chemical	Synthetic soda ash	
Intecom	Private branch exchanges	Product innovation
Nucor	Steel	Process innovation
British Satellite Broadcasting	Satellite broadcasting	Entry/entry-deterrence

ratio in the sample of industries studied in this book is about 80 percent, or roughly twice the level of the average manufacturing industry (as reported by Kwoka 1982).

The focus on commitment decisions as the unit of analysis is only slightly less obvious. As noted in the first section of this chapter, game-theoretic IO might reasonably be expected to have the most to contribute to business strategy in regard to such decisions. Additionally this microanalytic unit of analysis maps well into extant theory, which is usually organized in terms of families of models focused on specific types of commitment decisions (cf. Tirole's 1988 textbook). What might be more of an issue is that instead of focusing on a particular type of commitment decision, this book runs the gamut, from relatively short-run commitments concerning variables such as price levels (as in the diamond minicase and the case on large turbine generators discussed in the next chapter) to major, one-of-a-kind commitments that occur only infrequently (see exhibit 1.4). If pressed to explain this choice, I would cite the higher-order objective of figuring out how much game theory can contribute to business strategy in general.

Subject to these broad criteria, the cases studied in this book were selected primarily with an eye to the availability of information detailed enough to permit the testing of game-theoretic versus non-game-theoretic hypotheses, particularly the hypothesis of differential efficiency. Antitrust/regulatory efforts helped flush out firm-specific information in most of the cases considered; most of them also draw, however, on direct interviews of industry participants and observers as well as indirect sources. I highlight the direct interviews because they are generally eschewed by economists.[10] My sense is that while business decision-makers may be prone, like many of the rest of us, to selective reporting, self-justification, embellishment, and even lies, there is surely something to be learned from talking to them if they are even half as smart as game-theoretic models assume them to be—or if they are not.

Data Interpretation

The statistical analysis of changes in diamond prices was based on sixteen datapoints. This illustrates the point that the number of observations tends to be greater than the number of cases studied. Still, staying with the minicase for a moment, sixteen datapoints can only be described as a very thin dataset by conventional standards. The thin dataset problem turns out, once again, to be endemic to the case method, even if one sets out to look for relatively data-rich cases. Interpreting such data is a major challenge.

There are no simple solutions to the problems of small n

---

10. For an exception, see Blinder (1993) who discusses the use of interviews to elicit information about otherwise unobservable factors.

research. Instead, imagination in the choice of inferential methods is imperative. Running regressions is only the most obvious possibility, and one whose applicability is largely restricted in the context of this book's concerns, to commitment decisions that are repeated a respectable number of times. For relatively infrequent, idiosyncratic commitments, other empirical approaches must be pressed into service. The quantitative alternatives touched on in this book include combinatorial analyses of probabilities, actual calculations by firms, simulations, and comparative static analyses. Qualitative approaches such as paired case analyses, comparison of the perspectives of multiple competitors confronted with the same commitment opportunity, process tracing, and the like, can be of significant value as well, as long as one respects the basic logic of scientific inference.[11]

There are also several broader considerations that should be kept in mind in evaluating the case research presented in this book. The very process of "soaking and poking" in the specifics of the cases helps build confidence in one's interpretation of them: I am more comfortable concluding that the CSO/De Beers' price changes depend on its stock-to-sales ratio, for example, than I would be if I had not spent several months studying that industry. Highly motivated readers can presumably do the same. The (meta)analysis of six cases, rather than just one, should also boost confidence levels in any general conclusions that emerge. And since this work is exploratory, it would seem to warrant more than the usual amount of tolerance for the uncertainty that accompanies all research but looms particularly large when the number of observations is small.

The foregoing discussion focused, implicitly, on the use of the case method for theory evaluation. I should add that theory de-

---

11. Consult King, Keohane, and Verba (1994) for a unified discussion of the logic of quantitative and qualitative studies in the social sciences.

velopment is another, integral purpose of the present exercise. The cases studied in this book help develop theory by suggesting new variables to study, new parametric assumptions to make, or relationships between strategic variables to emphasize. This is but a preview: I will review the developmental contributions, in the last chapter of this book, after the cases themselves have been presented. What I wish to note for now is that I see the cases as part of a broader research program, which should strengthen their claim to some attention. That is why most of the case studies conclude with recommendations for future work, even though these are the most speculative sections of the book.

In presenting the cases themselves, I have had to summarize: We can never tell "all we know" about any set of events. Tastes in regard to the optimal amount of summarization vary: Some colleagues regard the descriptions in this book as overly long; another, trained in the Harvard tradition of book-length industry studies, commented at a symposium that she found my material "lightly done." While only one of the situations discussed here has been written up in full-length book form, the fact that they *have* all been written up as teaching cases (see appendix B) should help assuage cravings for thicker description and more thorough documentation.

Relatedly I have also made an attempt to keep the technical level of the discussion manageable. I will presume some degree of understanding of game theory (as a consumer, at least) and some interest in its potential applicability to business. Having said that, I will try to avoid swamping the reader with unnecessary jargon, calculus, and nuances. What helps in this regard is that earlier versions of most of the research cases in this book have been or are being published in refereed journals. These sources, which are cited as appropriate, should be consulted for detailed (or more general) proofs of various theoretical propositions that are invoked in this book.

1.5   The Cases

Six chapters containing detailed analyses of specific cases follow. I found it convenient to organize them into two triplets. The first three of these chapters focus on competition in settings with fixed product characteristics and production technologies: Prices and capacities are allowed to vary, but the sets of possible products and production technologies are not. The three chapters that follow look at competition in settings that are more fluid: They examine, in turn, episodes of product innovation, process innovation, and competition to monopolize a new product market made possible by an innovation in process technology. Consider all these chapters one by one.

The analysis of the case on General Electric in large turbine generators, coauthored with Anita McGahan, identifies a competitive variable, order backlogs, that had not previously been analyzed game-theoretically and points out that game-theoretic thinking leads to a different prediction about the relationship between relative prices and backlog levels than does a pure focus on relative efficiency. Empirical analysis of the large turbine generator industry is consistent with the game-theoretic prediction. In addition the case highlights some of the informational and structural conditions that make game-theoretic equilibrium particularly likely to be a useful reference point.

The case on Du Pont in titanium dioxide looks at short-run competition in prices and long-run competition to add capacity. It focuses on a period of competitive interaction in which the market leader, Du Pont, appeared, in light of several indicators, to have expanded capacity preemptively, namely for game-theoretic reasons. The case permits a comparison of statistical and nonstatistical modes of analysis of preemption in a particular market, suggests a new model of preemption and highlights some of the structural conditions that are likely to lead to preemption. It also assays the role that Du Pont's efficiency played in preemption and uses historical information on how Du Pont developed its competitive advantage to shed additional light on the "resources/capabilities" school of business strategy.

A pair of cases on declining chemical processing industries come next. Both look at long-run competition to unwind capacity commitments during industry decline on the basis of (separate) work with Barry Nalebuff and Michael Whinston. The counterintuitive game-theoretic hypothesis that size hurts survivability during industry decline receives some support from the capacity adjustment patterns observed in lead additives and synthetic soda ash. The case studies can usefully be supplemented with larger sample analysis in this instance. The analysis also underscores the importance of testing general insights as well as particular models.

The case on InteCom in private branch exchanges (PBXs) looks at the conditions under which entrants have greater incentives to commit resources to product innovations than do incumbents. A model based on the successful introduction of a voice-and-data PBX by an entrant, InteCom, suggests, previous assertions to the contrary notwithstanding, that simple game-theoretic considerations *can* explain such outcomes. However, large differences in the productivity of PBX competitors' product innovation efforts suggest that optimal organization played an important part in InteCom's success. They do so in a way that emphasizes the need for additional organization-theoretic work on differences in innovative efficiency to complement what is arguably a better-developed line of game-theoretic work on differences in incentives to innovate.

The case on Nucor in the steel industry looks at process rather than product innovation. The game-theoretic question is otherwise the same as in the previous case: Under what conditions are entrants likely to have incentives to commit to innovations before incumbents? But in this case the game-theoretic analysis is accompanied by even more extensive documentation and analysis of efficiency differences as well as consideration of a common commitment opportunity from the perspective of multiple competitors. While both game theory and organization theory seem to help explain what happened in this case, the case analysis also reminds us of the need for game theorists to attend to multiple dimensions in modeling commitment decisions and for organizational theorists to pay attention to organizational rigidities—specifically, strategic, resource, and contractual precommitments—as well as capabilities. In addition, this case provides an opportunity for reviewing recent discussions about how complementarities underpin sustained competitive advantages.

The final detailed case in this book, on British Satellite Broadcasting (BSB) in satellite television, was coauthored with Adam Brandenburger, and concentrates on the ultimately unsuccessful war of attrition that BSB waged against an unexpected entrant, Sky Television. Outcomes to wars of attrition such as this one are often hard to interpret as game-theoretic Nash equilibria, raising foundational concerns. In addition some of BSB's moves seem not to have been individually rational (let alone consistent with Sky's) for reasons due to its internal structure. This case therefore reinforces the importance of analyzing the internal structures of organizations in detail rather than simply collapsing them into relative efficiency levels. It also helps sort through different degrees of uncertainty in terms of their game-theoretic implications.

The tenor of the cases obviously shifts as one proceeds through the next six chapters: The first three of these chapters emphasize the payoffs to game-theoretic thinking; the three chapters that follow conjoin game-theoretic thinking with more detailed organizational analysis. The last chapter of the book attempts to sum up the implications—descriptive, analytical, and prescriptive—of these detailed cases and an additional minicase that focuses on the widely discussed auctions of the electromagnetic spectrum in the United States.

1.6 Summary

Game theory has taken over industrial organization economics but has barely had an effect on the applied field of business strategy. The gap that has opened up between game theory's formidable analytical advances and its lackluster empirical applications appears to be a large part of the reason. The case method, sensitively handled, seems responsive to many of the problems that have held up empirical work in this area. It also seems to have the potential to contribute to theory development. It therefore merits exploration.

<table>
<tr><td>**2**</td><td>**Relative Prices and Backlogs in the Large Turbine Generator Industry**</td></tr>
</table>

It is natural to start the chain of cases in this book by looking at short-run interactions. Game theory suggests that even when the primary focus of the analysis is on long-run competition, games must be solved backward, beginning with a characterization of short-run payoffs. The analysis in this chapter will focus on short-run competition given capacity constraints; the next chapter will analyze the effects of (similar) expectations about short-run interactions on long-run competition to add capacity. As in most of the other chapters of this book, game-theoretic hypotheses about business interactions will be compared with hypotheses that emphasize differences in efficiency instead of "strategizing."

The specific case of short-run competition analyzed in this chapter, that of the large turbine generator industry, shapes the theoretical analysis by focusing it on backlog levels, a mode of adjustment to demand fluctuations that was particularly important in that industry. To understand the need for further theoretical analysis of competition along this dimension, it is useful

---

This chapter is a substantially rewritten version of Ghemawat and McGahan (1996), with the changes being my responsibility alone.

to go back to Zarnowitz's (1962) descriptive cross-industry analysis of changes in backlogs over the business cycle. Zarnowitz identified three qualitatively distinct variables that capacity-constrained firms might adjust in response to demand fluctuations: prices, inventories, and order backlogs. Zarnowitz also noted that price adjustments were accorded pride of place in economics, that inventory adjustments came second, and that backlog adjustments were largely ignored.

From a game-theoretic perspective, this bias persists. Explicitly game-theoretic analyses of adjustments to demand fluctuations remain focused on prices, although inventories have also been the subject of some study (e.g., Arvan 1985; Ware 1985; Rotemberg and Saloner 1989). The few microeconomic analyses of backlog levels that have been published in the leading economics journals all appear to pertain to the nonstrategic cases of monopoly or perfect competition (e.g., De Vany 1976 and De Vany and Frey 1982, respectively).

From an empirical perspective this bias is extremely unfortunate. Backlogs loom larger than finished good inventories in many industries. Zarnowitz (1962), for example, calculated backlog values to be four times as large as inventory values in his sample of U.S. manufacturing industries, and eight times as large in the subsample that manufactured durable goods. Given the subsequent emphasis on just-in-time management and inventory reductions, average backlog-to-inventory ratios are likely to have increased since his study.

The reason backlogs have attracted so little attention is probably related to the common tendency to treat firms as planning their output in anticipation of demand.[1] But in a wide range of manufacturing industries, most production is to order instead of

---

1. Backlog measures can be important even in such industries. In the semiconductor industry, for example, considerable attention is paid to book-to-bill ratios.

to stock: It responds to demand instead of anticipating it. In such settings backlogs are apt to be large and inventories small (or zero). The importance of backlogs has, however, been discounted by the focus of much of the research on "lean manufacturing" (e.g., Womack, Jones, and Roos 1990) on industries such as automobiles, which produce to stock rather than to order and therefore have large inventories and virtually zero backlogs. To appreciate the general importance of backlogs, look at any other category of large transportation equipment, or as Anita McGahan and I did, at the large turbine generator industry.

2.1   Case Background

McGahan and I delved into the U.S. large turbine generator industry not because we already appreciated the importance of backlogs but because of a sense that antitrust investigations of that industry had generated a particularly rich data set that had escaped the attention of analysts attuned to game-theoretic considerations. To elaborate, while the large turbine generator industry has become a staple example of game theorists eager to cite business applications (e.g., Saloner 1991), such citations focus on the institution of an imaginative pricing policy by the industry leader General Electric, in 1963, *after* the period covered by the antitrust investigations. While we will briefly discuss this new pricing policy, our major focus in this chapter will be on confronting the data on turbine generator competitors' interactions up to that point with theoretical models.

Our analysis of the U.S. large turbine generator industry therefore spans the period between 1951 and 1963 and is based, in large part, on information assembled by Sultan (1974, 1975). Sultan, in turn, drew heavily on data disclosed in the context of suits filed by the U.S. Department of Justice charging the manufacturers of large turbine generators and their senior executives with conspiring to fix prices in violation of antitrust laws. The issue of how effectively the manufacturers managed to collude instead of compete will be revisited toward the end of this section, after some background information on the industry is provided.

Large turbine generators are partially customized units used to convert steam into electrical power. Between 1951 and 1963 they were manufactured in the United States by three companies: General Electric, Westinghouse, and Allis-Chalmers, whose market shares averaged 61 percent, 32 percent, and 6 percent, respectively. Sporadic imports accounted for the remaining 1 percent of the U.S. market.

Large turbine generators were produced to order in job shops. Short-run marginal costs were roughly constant up to the point at which capacity constraints—estimated by Sultan to occur at 85 percent capacity utilization—began to pinch and then increased sharply. Other cost drivers included the physical size of the generator and its manufacturer's cumulated production experience: Both tended to reduce the cost per kilowatt of generating capacity. General Electric was well positioned along both these dimensions, which gave it a significant cost advantage: Its direct costs per kilowatt were less than $15 over the period studied, compared to more than $17 for Westinghouse and nearly $25 for Allis-Chalmers.

It took about two years, from the inception of production, to manufacture a large turbine generator. If the manufacturer that won an order was capacity constrained, it deferred its delivery and added the order to its backlog. Between 1951 and 1963 deliveries were occasionally deferred for up to four years, which was roughly the maximum lead time in adding capacity. Significantly longer backlogs were experienced only by Westinghouse during a strike in 1956. Backlogs of one to three years were the norm.

Domestic utilities accounted for more than nine-tenths of the demand for large turbine generators manufactured in the United States, and exports and industrial customers for the remainder. There were well over a thousand utilities in the United States. They purchased turbine generators when they forecasted that their current capacity would be insufficient to meet consumer demand for electricity in forthcoming years. Because the costs of underprovision of electricity were high, orders tended to fluctuate with changes in forecasts of demand, which were often correlated across utilities because of their common dependence on the national economy. Nonetheless, because of the size of individual orders and the purchasing processes they involved, contracts between turbine manufacturers and their customers were struck sequentially rather than simultaneously. Sultan (1975, pp. 55, 62) estimated the price elasticity of aggregate demand to be virtually zero in the short run and -0.11 in the long run.[2]

The process of purchasing a large turbine generator began when a utility set specifications and invited bids. Government-owned utilities, which accounted for a quarter of the domestic market, purchased from the lowest bidder and posted all bids after the award. Investor-owned utilities, in contrast, negotiated their orders in strict privacy and kept bids secret even after the award. While they weighed several factors in making their decisions, including product performance and postpurchase service, relative price usually proved decisive, since large turbine generators cost more than any other electrical equipment in a power plant. A turbine manufacturer scheduled production only after being awarded an order.

The pricing of large turbine generators was further complicated by clandestine meetings among representatives of the

---

2. Note that efforts by U.S. manufacturers to take advantage of this price inelasticity by increasing their prices may have been limited by the availability of imports as well as by domestic competition.

three U.S. manufacturers to negotiate the terms of forthcoming bids. This chapter does not, however, attempt to model or test the effects of such preplay communication on the toughness of price competition. One broad set of reasons is related to indications that the effectiveness of the clandestine meetings was limited.

First of all, the meetings did not cover many transactions. Even when meetings aimed at fixing prices were most frequent (between 1955 and 1959), competitors discussed fewer than a quarter of all transactions, and only a fraction of the discussions led to agreements on who should underbid whom. And of the agreements that *were* reached, only a fraction were honored. Scherer (1980, p. 170) noted that in 1953, for example, "One General Electric executive explained his group's decision to go its own independent way . . . [in the following terms]: 'No one was living up to the agreements and we . . . were being made suckers. On every job someone would cut our throat; we lost confidence in the group.'"

Second, multiple regression analyses suggest that with suitable control variables, prices were not significantly higher during the period when meetings to discuss them were the most frequent. Sultan (1975, p. 111) conducted the most direct test and explicitly came to that conclusion.[3] Lean, Ogur, and Rogers (1982, p. 60) also obtained negative results, although they noted that this may have reflected a misspecified model.

Third, it should be noted that 88 percent of transactions were consummated at prices lower than the list prices implied by the formulas in turbine manufacturers' price books and that figure rose to 98 percent for large transactions worth over $3 million apiece. To the extent that aggregate demand was price-inelastic

---

3. See, however, appendix 18 in Sultan (1975).

and individual customers lacked significant market power, such discounts directly imply that the attempts to fix prices were of limited effectiveness.

A different and even more compelling reason for not testing for collusion among the turbine generator manufacturers is the dearth of detailed data on absolute prices, which are required to distinguish collusive from noncollusive regimes. What *are* available are quarterly data on General Electric's average prices relative to average prices in the market as a whole. The obvious research strategy is to develop and test theoretical predictions about the dependence of the market leader's relative price on backlog levels. Given the limitations of the data, we do not attempt to develop and estimate a fully structural model of relative prices. Instead, our intent is exploratory. We identify a game-theoretic effect, buffering, that might affect relative prices and assemble some evidence that it actually manifested itself in large turbine generators.

2.2 Theoretical Analysis

This section specifies two rather different hypotheses—based on efficiency effects and game-theoretic interactions—about the links between relative prices and backlogs. Finished good inventories, the third mechanism for adjusting to changes in demand that was identified by Zarnowitz (1962), are omitted from the analysis because no manufacturer of large turbine generators held significant levels of them.

The efficiency-based hypothesis is both simple to specify and a useful benchmark. A focus on differential efficiency leads one to predict that efficiency levels will affect relative prices when there is excess supply but not when there is excess demand (because in the latter case, prices are expected to reflect willingness to pay rather than costs). In the context of the large turbine generator industry, a pure differential-efficiency perspective implies that General Electric should be expected to price lower than its competitors when backlogs are low (because its costs are lower) but to price at the same level when backlogs are sufficiently long.

Game theory, in contrast, does not offer a simple prediction of this sort because it provides a mosaic of models, not an architectonic theory of business strategy. Fortunately one can select from diverse game-theoretic predictions about relative pricing strategies on the basis of the particulars of the case being studied. Three aspects of the case are particularly helpful in narrowing the game-theoretic possibilities. First, additional entry appeared not to be a major concern for General Electric or the other competitors in large turbine generators, steering us away from limit-pricing models in which incumbents, particularly large ones, price low for purposes of entry deterrence.[4] Second, although the third largest domestic player, Allis-Chalmers, exited toward the end of the period being studied, inducing exit does not appear to have ranked high among General Electric's objectives: Even when Allis-Chalmers was active, it was marginalized by its small share and very high costs; a second source (if not a third one) was apparently dictated by buyer requirements and antitrust policies; and General Electric and Westinghouse appeared to have achieved a *modus vivendi* as the largest and second-largest players, respectively, in a range of electrical equipment markets. These considerations steer us away from models of wars of attrition, which are highlighted, in the context of rather different

---

4. Expansion into the U.S. market by foreign producers *was* more of a concern but should not be overemphasized: Over the period studied, their share of the U.S. market was limited to 1 percent by domestic producers' engagement in nonprice competition (e.g., lobbying that invoked national security concerns) as well as some price competition.

cases, in chapters 4 and 7. Finally capacity appears to have been a limiting or (in Barnard's 1938 terminology) strategic factor in the large turbine generator industry, steering us toward models of capacity-constrained pricing by incumbents who recognize that they are dependent on one another and will continue to be so.

Consider therefore a class of models that are couched in the operational short run, as a period that is too short to add production capacity or even to complete a production cycle but long enough to write contracts and thereby alter backlog levels. In other words, the time series of observations on the U.S. large turbine generator industry will be treated as a sequence of short-run outcomes given initial backlogs and capacity levels. No attempt will be made to endogenize firms' capacity strategies, although the pattern of capacity expansion in the turbine generator industry will be discussed briefly in section 2.3.

The class of models considered will focus additionally on two competitors with different initial capacities but identical marginal costs. The focus on duopoly is forced by technical complications that arise in solving pricing subgames among more than two asymmetric players that act strategically.[5] While the number of domestic competitors in the U.S. large turbine generator industry was three rather than two, the two largest competitors, General Electric and Westinghouse, accounted for more than 90 percent of industry capacity and shipments over the period 1951 to 1963. The third competitor, Allis-Chalmers, appears to have been a marginal player for the reasons mentioned above.

The duopolists' initial capacities are denoted by $x_i (i = 1, 2)$, and they are, without loss of generality, numbered so that

---

5. The upper and lower supports of the pricing strategies need not coincide in games with more than two asymmetric competitors.

$x_1 \geq x_2$. Firm i's total cost of producing an amount q_i of output is given by cq_i if $q_i \leq x_i$, and is infinite (indicating infeasibility) otherwise. For convenience this common marginal cost is normalized to zero.

The assumption of a fixed-proportions technology appears to be a good approximation to the production possibilities in large turbine generators that were described above. The assumption of identical efficiency levels is less plausible: General Electric held a significant cost advantage, even vis-à-vis Westinghouse. It can, however, be rationalized in the following terms: Label the efficiency-based hypothesis about the dependence of relative prices on backlog levels as the null hypothesis, and suppose (as will turn out to be the case) that game-theoretic reasoning which ignores differences in efficiency levels leads to a very different hypothesis. Testing these competing hypotheses on a data set drawn from an industry characterized by significant efficiency differences stacks the deck in favor of the null hypothesis. More formally, it reduces the size of type I errors (improper rejection of the null hypothesis) but increases the size of type II errors (improper acceptance of the null hypothesis). If the null hypothesis were rejected anyway, that result would constitute very strong evidence that game-theoretic effects loomed large in the case studied.

Finally the class of models considered in this chapter assume demand to be price-inelastic in the sense that there are Q customers in total, each of whom purchases one unit if it is available at a price less than or equal to u. At a theoretical level, this assumption obviates the need to postulate a specific rule for rationing customers between manufacturers when their products are available on different terms. At an empirical level, it fits with the very low price-elasticities of (aggregate) demand reported for the large turbine generator industry. Furthermore the discussion in the next chapter indicates that this particular assumption can be relaxed without qualitatively altering the conclusions from (at least) the model presented next.

A One-Period Model

Begin by considering a one-period model in which the Q customers arrive all at once, or equivalently, in which the duopolists must simultaneously precommit to their pricing levels for the period *before* the customers start arriving. This assumption is extreme but not entirely implausible: The price books of the competitors in large turbine generators over this period have been described as being as thick as Sears, Roebuck catalogs, suggesting that it was nontrivially costly and complex to communicate price changes to customers. In any case this assumption will be relaxed in the other models presented in this section.

Such capacity-constrained duopoly pricing games have been studied by many authors, beginning with Edgeworth (1897). The equilibrium pricing strategies for the inelastic demand structure assumed here were first characterized by Ghemawat (1986) in an analysis motivated by the large turbine generator industry; his proof is reproduced in appendix A of Ghemawat and McGahan (1996). There turn out to be four different regimes.

Proposition 2.1 Given $x_1 \geq x_2$, and letting the subscript j denote *not i*

a. If $Q \leq x_2$, the only equilibrium of the subgame is $p_1 = p_2 = 0$. Firm i's revenue is zero as well.

b. If $x_2 < Q < x_1$, the only equilibrium involves the use of properly mixed strategies. The probability distribution of firm i's price has the support $(u(Q - x_2)/Q, u]$ and is given by

$$\psi_i(p) = \left[1 - \frac{u(Q - x_2)}{pQ}\right] \cdot \max\left(\frac{Q}{x_i}, 1\right).$$

Firm i's expected revenue is

$$R_i = u(Q - x_2) \cdot \min\left(\frac{x_i}{Q}, 1\right).$$

c. If $x_1 \leq Q < x_1 + x_2$, the only equilibrium involves the use of properly mixed strategies. The probability distribution of firm i's price has the support $(u(Q - x_2)/x_1, u]$ and is given by

$$\psi_i(p) = \frac{[u(Q - x_2) - px_1]}{p(Q - x_2 - x_1)} \cdot \frac{x_j}{x_1}$$

Firm i's expected revenue is

$$R_i = u(Q - x_2) \cdot \min\left(\frac{x_i}{x_j}, 1\right).$$

d. If $Q \geq x_1 + x_2$, the only equilibrium of the subgame is $p_1 = p_2 = u$. Firm i's revenue is equal to ux_i.

In regime a, demand is less than *either* firm's capacity and both price at their (common) marginal cost. In regime d, demand is greater than *both* firms' total capacity and both price at their customers' (common) reservation price u. Regimes b and c are less obvious and more interesting. Both involve the larger firm (firm 1) buffering its smaller competitor by pricing higher than it in an expectational sense. The larger firm's expected operating profits equal its minmax level, and the smaller firm's the same absolute amount multiplied by its relative "effective" capacity $(x_2/\min(x_1, Q))$. It is as if the larger firm could *count* on being undercut by its rival.

Why should the larger firm be less aggressive in pricing terms than its rival despite its potential to produce more? Exhibit 2.1 indicates that in both regimes, b and c, the smaller firm (firm 2) sells less when undercut than the larger firm (firm 1) would if *it* were undercut, but stands to gain the same amount of additional volume from undercutting as the larger firm would. This makes

Exhibit 2.1
Consequences of Undercutting versus Being Undercut

Regime b
$x_1 \geq Q$ (and $x_1 + x_2 > Q$ and $x_2 \leq Q$)

	Minmax volume if undercut	Incremental volume from undercutting
Firm 1	$Q - x_2$	x_2
Firm 2	0	x_2

Regime c
$x_1 \leq Q$ (and $x_1 + x_2 > Q$ and $x_2 < Q$)

	Minmax volume if undercut	Incremental volume from undercutting
Firm 1	$Q - x_2$	$x_1 + x_2 - Q$
Firm 2	$Q - x_1$	$x_1 + x_2 - Q$

the smaller firm the more aggressive of the two. The larger firm ends up holding a price umbrella over the smaller one, as illustrated for a particular parametrization in exhibit 2.2.[6] That is the basic reason why the larger firm's expected operating profits are held to its security level.

These results suggest that when demand is low—but not so much so that it could entirely be satisfied by the smaller firm—the larger firm should be expected to price higher than ("buffer")

6. The price umbrella is, to be sure, a stochastic one: regimes b and c correspond to the classic Bertrand-Edgeworth game, which has no Nash equilibria in pure strategies, and in which firms must therefore use mixed strategies. While such mixing might be problematic as far as some readers are concerned, it does have several things to recommend it. First, it is consistent with reports from real world markets of phenomena such as price dispersion, "list" prices (u in the model) that serve as ceilings rather than floors or average tendencies, and price leadership. Second, the mixing can be thought of as building on the traditional IO notion that the outcomes of oligopolistic interaction are a priori indeterminate (Fellner 1949). The characterization of the Nash equilibrium in regimes b and c is useful in this regard because, instead of allowing all conceivable kinds of indeterminacy, it imposes some reasonable bounds on possible outcomes: neither firm should ask a price lower than $u(Q - x_2)/\min(x_1, Q)$ or higher than u.

Exhibit 2.2
Price Distributions

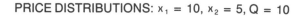

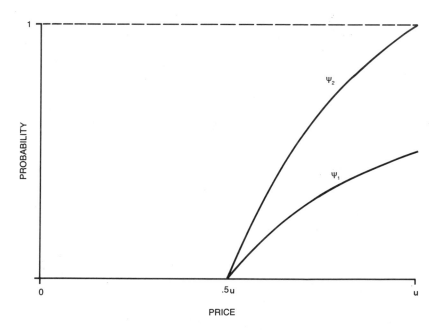

PRICE DISTRIBUTIONS: $x_1 = 10$, $x_2 = 5$, $Q = 10$

its rival. This is the opposite of the efficiency-based prediction, based on relative cost levels in the large turbine generator industry, that the larger firm should be expected to price lower when demand is low. These two predictions can and will be pitted against each other. But in view of the structural sensitivity of game-theoretic predictions, it is useful to establish first that the prediction of buffering is not predicated on the one-shot nature of the interactions presumed in this model.

A Two-Period Model

The one-period model of capacity-constrained pricing that was developed in the last section misses out on an intertemporal linkage that is important when production takes time: namely that a competitor that wins many customers today affects its ability to serve tomorrow's customers. Consider therefore a two-period variant in which $Q/2$ customers arrive in the first period and $Q/2$ customers in the second period. Posit that production takes (at least) one period, so that capacity committed to serving customers in the first period is unavailable in the second one. And to simplify the analysis, also assume that $x_1 = 2x_2 \equiv 2x$—an assumption that approximates structural conditions in the U.S. large turbine generator industry, as elaborated toward the end of section 2.3. Let $\Delta = Q/x$ parametrize the relationship between total demand (Q) and total capacity ($3x$).

The characterization of the subgame-perfect Nash equilibrium of this two-period game works back from the equilibrium in the second-period subgame, which was fully specified by the analysis in the previous subsection. The possibilities may, once again, be partitioned into four different regimes based on the value of the parameter Δ (see the appendix of Ghemawat and McGahan 1996 for a sketch of the proof).

If $\Delta \leq 1$ (regime a), demand is so small in relation to capacity that either firm could supply total demand (in both periods) by itself. Since capacity constraints are not binding for either firm, the outcome, as under unconstrained price competition, coincides with perfect competition. Both firms price at marginal cost.

If $1 < \Delta \leq 2$ (regime b), an extreme version of buffering emerges as the subgame-perfect Nash equilibrium. The larger firm (firm 1) makes sure that the smaller firm (firm 2) is the lower-priced firm in period 1. If, instead, the larger firm were lower-priced in period 1, second-period prices would collapse to marginal costs because each firm would have sufficient residual capacity ($2x - Q/2$ and x, respectively) to satisfy second-period demand all by itself. Allowing the smaller firm to sell out with probability one in period 1 avoids this dire outcome in period 2.

In other words, firm 1 buffers firm 2 in the first period to tie up its capacity in the second.

Regime c in which $2 < \Delta < 3$ is more complicated in that it involves both firms using mixed strategies. It is straightforward to check, however, that the larger firm's prices stochastically dominate the smaller firm's in a first-order sense. More often than not, the effect is to exhaust entirely the smaller firm's capacity in the first period. In other words, the larger firm is expected to buffer the smaller firm by letting the latter build up a disproportionate backlog (in period 1) before the large firm wins a greater share of orders (in period 2).

Finally, there is regime d, in which $\Delta \geq 3$. Here total demand exceeds total capacity, so both firms sell out at the price of u. As in the case of very low demand ($\Delta \leq 1$), there is no buffering. So the results for the two-period model are qualitatively similar to those for the one-period model: Buffering of the smaller competitor by the larger one is evident at intermediate levels of capacity utilization but not at the extremes.

Multiperiod Models

Do the strategic buffering effects identified in the two-period model hold up in multiperiod models, that is, models in which competitors have more than two opportunities to set prices? While a general answer to this question is beyond the scope of this chapter, affirmative answers can be given for two special kinds of multiperiod models.

Consider, first of all, a model similar to the one in the previous subsection except that the Q customers arrive one by one instead of in two batches. The duopolists bid for the business of each customer as it arrives. This sort of customer-per-period model has been analyzed by Griesmer and Shubik (1963) and Dudey

(1992). The state-space equilibria (the equilibria that arise when firms condition their strategies on state variables, e.g., backlogs or available capacity regardless of the histories that give rise to them) involve an extreme version of buffering when total demand is larger than the small firm's capacity but smaller than total capacity: The larger firm lets its smaller rival sell out first by winning the first x orders and contents itself with the $Q - x$ that remain.

The state-space restriction on equilibria may not be reasonable when interactions are repeated. In infinitely repeated games, in particular, firms can use rewards and punishments to bootstrap their way to almost any feasible and individually rational set of payoffs—especially if discount rates are low. Such "supergames" introduce so many additional equilibria that their analysis tends to focus on stationary structural conditions and strategies. We will adopt this focus as well. Consider a supergame in which $\Delta = 1$ (a particularly interesting parametric possibility, since it demarcates the two qualitatively distinct subcases of buffering, regimes b and c, identified in the prior subsection). Normalize x so that it equals one as well. Then per-period demand is one unit, and the two firms' total capacities are, respectively, two units and one unit.

With production taking one period, the larger firm will be able to employ at least one unit of capacity over any two successive periods. The question of interest is whether it should try to keep both units employed. Under the usual assumption of stationarity, the answer is negative because a strategy by the larger firm of consistently employing both units induces the smaller firm to price at its marginal cost. In contrast, a strategy of allowing the smaller firm to win whenever it has capacity available allows the larger firm to keep a unit of capacity employed at a price of u. In terms of backlogs, the larger firm optimally prices to lose whenever the smaller firm's order backlog is zero, and to win whenever the smaller firm's order backlog is one period long.

Summarizing the game-theoretic analyses in this section, the one-period model and, under auxiliary assumptions, the two-period model, the customer-per-period model, and the infinitely repeated model all suggest that with strategic behavior (behavior that accounts for mutual dependence and anticipates subsequent interactions) the larger firm should buffer its smaller rival when supply exceeds demand—unless the smaller firm can satisfy total demand all by itself. Buffering is designed to keep the smaller firm's backlog level high enough to avert a price war.

2.3 Empirical Analysis

In the context of the large turbine generator industry, efficiency-based reasoning that ignores game-theoretic effects and game-theoretic reasoning that ignores efficiency effects offer opposed predictions about relative pricing patterns: The former suggests that the (efficient) market leader should price relatively low when backlogs are low, and the latter that it should price relatively high. It is time to confront these predictions with data.

The data on relative prices and backlog levels in the large turbine generator industry between 1951 and (the third quarter of) 1963 that are employed to test these hypotheses are drawn from Sultan (1974, 1975), who synthesized them from more detailed data disclosed in the course of antitrust proceedings against the industry incumbents. Thus, Sultan aggregated across the prices bid by all domestic competitors on all orders assigned to a particular quarter to calculate General Electric's average price relative to the industry (including General Electric) for that quarter (chart number 13.2 from Sultan 1975, p. 232). The other charts of interest are those tracing backlogs and capacities in millions of kilowatts (chart numbers 2.7 from Sultan 1974 and 11.1 from Sultan 1975, respectively): The first series can be divided by the second to yield a temporal measure of industry backlog levels.

We sought to obtain the raw data on which these charts were based from Sultan, but he had discarded them. Our attempts to track down the data in General Electric's archives and through court records were unsuccessful as well. We therefore had to engage in the unorthodox procedure of manually deplotting them ourselves. Independent deplots by a research assistant supplied some reassurance that the additional errors introduced by this procedure were relatively small: The correlation coefficient between our estimates of relative prices and the research assistant's, for example, was 0.988.[7]

Given these data, the relationship between backlog levels and relative prices takes the form that is depicted in exhibit 2.3. Simple inspection suggests that General Electric tended to price relatively high when backlogs were low and relatively low when backlogs were high, favoring the hypothesis based on game theory over the null hypothesis based on efficiency differences. A simple linear regression supports this inference by yielding the following estimate of the relationship between the variables in exhibit 2.3 (with standard errors reported in parentheses):

GEPREM = 1.5437 − 0.7114 × backlogs.
            (0.3078)   (0.1248)

It should be added that there are 51 observations, that the adjusted R-squared equals 38.6 percent, and that the F-statistic is 32.5.

A variety of other specifications were considered as well, including treating individual firms' backlogs rather than

---

7. We also ran the regressions described below with the values deplotted by our research assistant. This made no material difference to the results.

Exhibit 2.3
General Electric's Pricing Strategy, 1951–1963

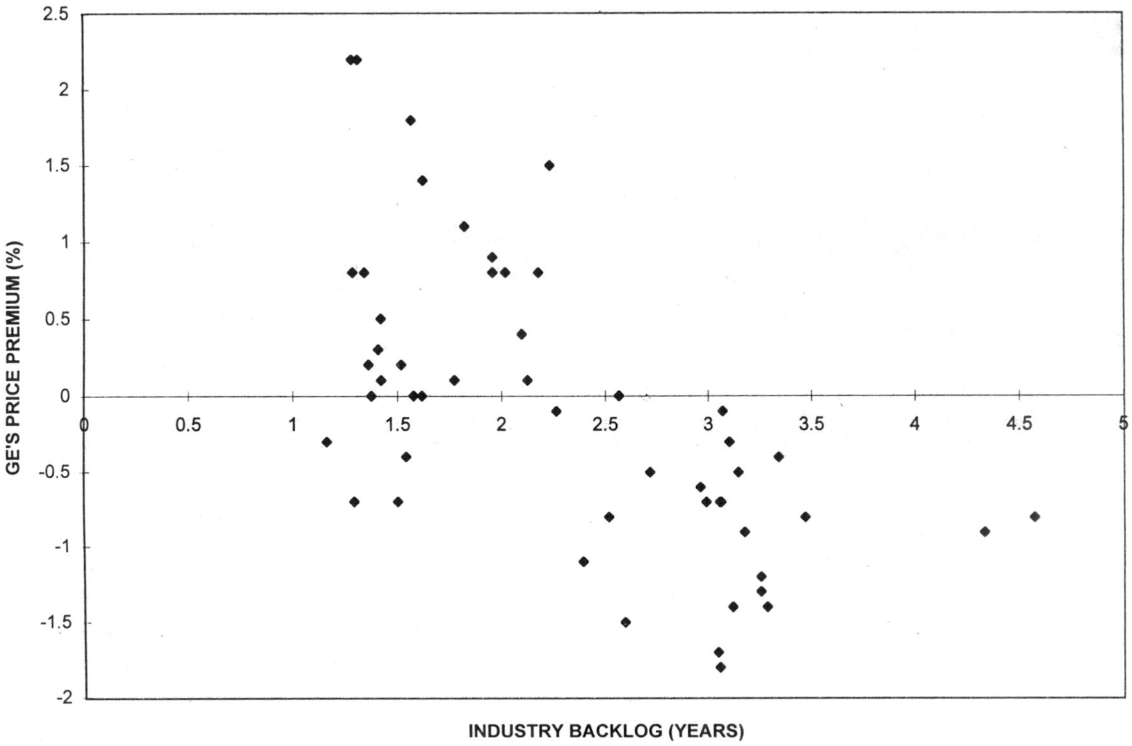

GE'S PRICE PREMIUM (%)

INDUSTRY BACKLOG (YEARS)

industry-level ones as the independent variables, coding General Electric's relative price as a binary variable (higher/lower) rather than a continuous one to minimize the effects of small errors in deplotting its values, and correcting for serial correlation. Some of the results are reported in Ghemawat and McGahan (1996). All of them supported the basic game-theoretic hypothesis of buffering, but none of them added much (if anything) to the overall explanatory power of the simple linear regression model estimated above.

It is useful therefore to look more closely at the residuals associated with the linear regression model. The largest differences, in absolute terms, between the relative prices predicted by the regression and their actual values turn out to be associated with relatively low backlog levels. In the terminology of the one- and two-period models discussed above, it is tempting to conjecture that this reflects the diminution and ultimate disappearance of buffering as one moves toward regime a.

Such changes in regime could, in principle, be estimated with a switching regression setup. That option is not pursued here because of the difficulty, due to important lags, of assigning observations to different regimes. For example, given a certain level of orders in a particular period, the extent of excess capacity would depend not only on currently available capacity but also on old capacity that would be freed up as a result of order fulfillment and new capacity that would soon be added. The latter, in particular, was clearly endogenous to the game being played by turbine generator manufacturers.

Endogenization of the capacity expansion paths in an industry like large turbine generators is beyond the scope of this chapter. It *is* worth remarking, however, that General Electric and Westinghouse began the 1950s with a 2-to-1 capacity ratio, which

they roughly maintained through 1963 by expanding in tandem.[8]
Consider, in particular, the three largest year-to-year expansions
by General Electric: the only ones that involved absolute increases in capacity of at least 1.5 million kilowatts apiece or
percentage increases of more than 15 percent. Each of these
increases was closely matched by Westinghouse, in percentage
terms, within a year. In 1950 General Electric increased capacity
by 57 percent (2 million kilowatts); Westinghouse followed with
a 56 percent increase (1 million kilowatts) in 1951. In 1957, in
the aftermath of a strike at Westinghouse that had reduced that
company's available capacity by as much as 60 percent, General
Electric expanded capacity by 31 percent (another 2 million kilowatts); Westinghouse followed in 1958 with a 34 percent increase
(1.4 million kilowatts). And in 1960 General Electric increased
capacity by 16 percent (1.5 million kilowatts); Westinghouse increased its own capacity that year by 12 percent (0.7 million kilowatts). Note that these three episodes of capacity expansion
accounted for more than 60 percent of the total capacity added
by each of these two leading competitors between 1950 and
1963—a period over which they more than tripled their total
capacity.[9]

Such close (percentage) matching of capacity additions hints
that General Electric and Westinghouse managed to accommodate each other on capacities (based on perpetuation of their historical shares) as well as prices. Both verbal analyses (e.g., Fellner
1949) and formally game-theoretic ones (e.g., Fudenberg and
Tirole 1986b) indicate that oligopolistic "quasi-agreements"
about capacity (restraint) are most likely to prove sustainable

---

8. Between 1951 and 1963 the ratio of General Electric's capacity to Westinghouse's
capacity had a mean of 1.95 and a standard deviation of 0.66.
9. Given the exit of the third domestic competitor, Allis-Chalmers, at the end of 1962,
its net contribution to capacity increases between the late 1940s and 1963 was
negative.

when capacity additions are relatively nonlumpy, as in the case considered in this chapter. The effects of very lumpy capacity additions are probed formally in the next chapter.

2.4 Reflections

Relative prices in large turbine generators between 1951 and 1963 seem to have varied with relative backlogs in a way that contradicted purely efficiency-based predictions but fit fairly well with customized game-theoretic predictions. Relative capacity addition patterns also cast doubt on the null (efficiency-based) hypothesis: While General Electric apparently tried to maintain a 2-to-1 capacity ratio relative to Westinghouse, it should have tried to seize all the capacity expansion opportunities in large turbine generators for itself, on the basis of its superior efficiency, if efficiency were all that mattered.

While contradiction of purely efficiency-based reasoning clearly counts for something, it does not, by itself, clinch the value of formal game-theoretic analysis. In particular, the idea that a market leader may find it advantageous to buffer smaller competitors—or, in more managerial terms, to pay attention to the structure of its industry as well as to its competitive position within that structure—is neither new nor especially counterintuitive. Indeed, one of my colleagues at Harvard Business School, Richard Meyer, points out that this is how he used to teach the General Electric–Westinghouse case to MBA students more than fifteen years ago—well before the game-theoretic revolution in IO.

The best reply to such criticisms, I think, is that even when game theory yields predictions that are not particularly counterintuitive, it contributes a useful *stability* criterion to the study of business interactions. Specifically it lets one examine whether a hypothesized strategy (in this case, buffering by the market leader) will still make sense after allowing self-interested behavior by other players (in this case, the follower). Such stability is valuable for the reason articulated so well by von Neumann and Morgenstern (1944) in their pathbreaking book on game theory: It is hard to be satisfied with the generality of principles whose success depends on their not being widely grasped.

When is the sort of stability criterion embedded in game-theoretic analysis of equilibrium points most likely to provide a useful reference point? Note that the large turbine generator case was selected nonrandomly to exemplify some of the attributes that are most likely to increase the payoff to self-consciously interactive reasoning and strategy selection. In other words, students of other cases may be able to improve their assessments of how much game-theoretic analysis is likely to contribute to their case studies by comparing them with large turbine generators along the following indicators which affect one or both of the two possible routes to equilibrium, introspection and learning.

1. *Concentrated competition.* The two largest manufacturers of large turbine generators controlled more than 90 percent of the U.S. market, with a third competitor (which seems to have been strait-jacketed since it exited in 1963 after years of operating losses) accounting for nearly all the remainder. Such concentration is likely to amplify the marginal effects of one rival's choices on another's payoffs, increasing the importance of careful competitive analysis. It is no accident that the other cases discussed in detail in this book also involve, as noted in chapter 1, concentration levels significantly higher than the cross-industry averages. Additional significance might be attached to the inference that there were only two competitors in the large turbine generator industry with significant strategic discretion. There is a sense in which the conditions required for the realization of an equilibrium via player-by-player introspection are weaker in two-player games than in general n-player games (e.g., Aumann and Brandenburger 1995).

2. *Mutual familiarity.* The competitors in large turbine generators, particularly General Electric and Westinghouse, were familiar with each other in the sense that they had decades of experience competing with each other in the turbine market and in several other electrical product markets. While this description of mutual familiarity is loose, it has affinities with the more stringent restriction of mutual knowledge of strategies, which is required to ensure equilibrium through introspection (Aumann and Brandenburger 1995). Note that the gap between mutual familiarity and mutual knowledge of strategies was likely to have been narrowed in this particular case by preplay communication, the public posting of bids on government-owned utilities' orders, and the distinct but consistent strategic roles selected by General Electric and Westinghouse (see below). In addition it is plausibe to think that mutual familiarity increases the likelihood and speed of the convergence of adaptive, dynamic learning processes to an equilibrium point.

3. *Repeated interaction.* There were at least two distinct senses in which the pricing interactions among the competitors in large turbine generators were repeated. First, short-run pricing decisions recurred more frequently than most other types of commitment decisions (which had the useful side effect, in this case, of facilitating statistical testing). Second, the multimarket contact between General Electric and Westinghouse can be seen as further increasing the number of interactions between them. Such repetition coupled with structural stability increases the likelihood that competitors will learn to achieve a particular equilibrium as a result of an adaptive, dynamic learning process—even if they start without mutual knowledge of each other's strategies. Put differently, equilibrium may be a more plausible outcome in repeated instead of one-shot interactions.

4. *Consistent strategic roles.* The two largest competitors in large turbine generators seemed to pursue distinct strategic roles which were, nevertheless, consistent with each other: General Electric could clearly be characterized as the leader and Westinghouse as the follower. In fact these strategic roles seem to have extended beyond turbine generators to the corporate level. General Electric also held leading market shares in a number of other electrical

equipment industries in which Westinghouse was its largest rival. Such mutual consistency of strategic roles increases, relative to the benchmark of inconsistency, the likelihood and speed of convergence to an equilibrium. Thus equilibrium proves to be a more useful reference point in this case than in the final detailed case considered in this book, in which both British Satellite Broadcasting and Sky Television strove for a number of years to be *the* leader in the British market for satellite TV.

5. *Strategic complementarity.* Interaction among the manufacturers of large turbine generators was subject to local "strategic complementarity": A competitor's optimal response to price increases by its rivals was typically to increase its price as well. Theorists have demonstrated that strategic complementarity, along with single-peaked payoff functions, ensures convergence to an equilibrium if players repeatedly play the same game (Milgrom and Roberts 1990a; Krishna 1992). While these theoretical results assume global strategic complementarity as well as stationarity, even local strategic complementarity should increase the likelihood of convergence relative to the benchmark of strategic substitutability, which increases the likelihood of cycling around the equilibrium point.

Having cited these five general influences on the likelihood and speed of convergence to equilibrium, I should add the caveat that the outcomes of actual market games may be heavily influenced by idiosyncratic, case-specific circumstances. In large turbine generators, for instance, much of the decline in pricing discipline that accompanied declining capacity utilization in the late 1950s and early 1960s seems attributable to informational imperfections: uncontrollable errors—due to customized, complex product specifications—in calculating book prices (and their discounted levels) and imperfect information about the prices negotiated by rivals with investor-owned utilities.

The importance of informational considerations is corroborated by developments subsequent to the period considered in this chapter. In 1963 General Electric changed its pricing policy to adhere strictly to the levels published in a simplified price

Exhibit 2.4
General Electric and Westinghouse's Multipliers, 1963–1968

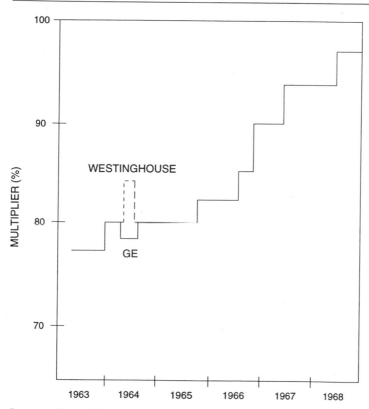

Source: Allen 1976

book adjusted by a prespecified multiplier. After a period of learning that lasted about one year, the book prices and multipliers for both General Electric and Westinghouse (Allis Chalmers had exited) came to coincide, and remained the same until the early 1970s, when the two companies were confronted with another antitrust challenge (see exhibit 2.4). In the context of the models developed in this chapter, it is tantalizing to conjecture that the new pricing policy permitted the large turbine generator manufacturers to exploit more effectively the possibility of tacit collusion via "noncooperative" strategies that was identified by the customer-per-period model.

Finally, other recent discussions of General Electric's pricing policies have emphasized that major changes in price levels were linked to major organizational changes. Thus the emergence of large discounts from book prices in the late 1950s has been attributed, in part, to General Electric's switch to a decentralized organizational structure. According to a General Electric employee quoted in Mullin (1995, p. 15),

Before decentralization, when all types of turbine generators . . . were under one man, he could decide to let sales of 10,000-kilowatt units go and concentrate on sales of 100,000-kilowatt units. But when you are decentralized, one man is being measured on sales of 10,000-kilowatt units and a different man is being measured on sales of bigger units. So you lose some flexibility.

Similarly Cyert, Kumar, and Williams (1995) have emphasized that after 1963, strict adherence to a simplified price book implied a significant recentralization of pricing decisions into a single multiplier determined at the level of each competitor's turbine business.

Both informational and organizational considerations will recur in all the cases discussed in detail in this book. They will shed additional light on what game theory can do for business strategy, and what it cannot.

2.5 Summary

The theoretical and empirical analysis in this chapter has made a number of contributions. First, it has highlighted the role that backlogs can play in affecting competitive behavior. It has done so in a way that illustrates the potential payoffs to combining theoretical and empirical analysis: Looking at the real world can suggest additional variables that are worth analyzing theoretically. Nevertheless, the analysis of backlogs that McGahan and I undertook can only be billed as exploratory. One promising avenue for further research involves additional modeling (under a wider range of assumptions) of the effects of backlogs on incentives to compete as well as additional studies of industries in which backlogs are important. Another involves endogenization of firms' capacity expansion strategies in light of their anticipations about consequent product-market interactions. The second avenue is pursued, in the context of a rather different kind of industry, in the next chapter of this book.

Second, the analysis has emphasized the fact that even pricing decisions, which are often treated as being easily reversible, can have significant short-run commitment value (for contractual reasons). This is consistent with, and a contribution to, recent empirical work in industrial organization that highlights price-related rigidities (e.g., Carlton 1989). It also reinforces an emerging theme in strategic management: that it is important to attend to the commitment or irreversibility that is integral to most competitively significant moves (Caves 1984; Ghemawat 1991a).

Finally this case study has illustrated the payoffs of allowing for strategic (i.e., self-consciously interactive) behavior and, in particular, of focusing on equilibrium. While such analysis entails significant complexity and costs, it can also deliver significant benefits. The benefits of equilibrium analysis are particularly likely to exceed the costs in cases that share some of the features of the large turbine generator industry: concentrated competition, mutual familiarity, repeated interaction, consistent strategic roles, and strategic complementarity.

3

Preemptive Capacity Expansion in the Titanium Dioxide Industry

Moving from the short run toward the long run, the second case in this book considers competition to expand capacity. More specifically it looks at an apparent episode of preemptive capacity expansion in the U.S. titanium dioxide industry in the 1970s.

The rationale for applying game-theoretic thinking to a case of capacity expansion is rather different from its previous application, to backlogs. Competition to add physical capacity has been one of the longest running attractions in game-theoretic IO, for reasons that include tangibility of this resource, the simple scalar way in which it affects product market opportunities, and the common (if sometimes incorrect) presumption that capacity-driven industries tend to produce commodities, finessing the difficulties of dealing with product differentiation. Many of the numerous theoretical analyses of long-run competition over physical capacities, including some of the earliest game-theoretic modeling in IO (e.g., Spence 1977, 1979; Dixit 1980) focus precisely on the conditions under which first-movers (incumbents) will build up "excess" capacity to deter entry, namely preempt.

While game-theoretic analyses of capacity preemption are abundant, apparent examples are not. The U.S. titanium dioxide industry in the 1970s is a rare exception to that rule. It is also a

case about which there is a rich body of publicly-available information, largely due to an antitrust case brought by the Federal
Trade Commission (FTC) in 1978 against the alleged preemptor,
Du Pont. It is therefore a natural case to study, not just to shed
some light on whether preemption took place in titanium dioxide but to extend and probe established lines of theoretical
research.

   This chapter begins, like the previous one, with some background information on the case being studied. But given the
plethora of game-theoretic models of preemptive capacity
expansion and the problems of selecting among them, it reverses
the order of the analytical sections in the previous chapter. The
empirical analysis of the titanium dioxide industry comes first
and suggests that Du Pont *did* preempt, namely that it seemed
to be motivated by considerations of market power as well as
differential efficiency, and that customized theoretical modeling
is necessary to check whether this outcome made game-theoretic
sense. The theoretical analysis follows and confirms that the
sorts of price-raising considerations that appear to have motivated Du Pont's move do manifest themselves in a simple game-
theoretic model of duopolistic competition to add lumpy capacity. The analysis suggests both opportunities for additional
game-theoretic research and implications for the "resource-
based" view of the firm that has become fashionable in strategic
management.

3.1 Case Background

This description of the U.S. titanium dioxide industry focuses
mostly on the 1970s and is based largely on the information in
FTC Docket No. 9108. I documented this case extensively in an
early research paper (Ghemawat 1984) and provided additional
analysis in Ghemawat (1990), on which this chapter is based.

Titanium dioxide is a whitener that is used in paints, paper, and plastics. Apart from differences in the whiteness of its two product grades, it is effectively a commodity that is sold on price. Demand for titanium dioxide is thought to be relatively price-inelastic because of its small share of total costs in its applications and its importance for their quality. Du Pont, for instance, estimated titanium dioxide's price elasticity at around −0.3 in the early 1970s.

In 1972 there were seven manufacturers of titanium dioxide in the United States: Du Pont, which accounted for 34 percent of total industry capacity of about 770,000 tons, the traditional industry leader, National Lead, which had seen its domestic share drop to 23 percent, American Cyanamid with 14 percent, SCM with 10 percent, Gulf & Western with 9 percent, Kerr McGee with 6 percent, and Sherwin-Williams with 4 percent. These manufacturers produced titanium dioxide *via* the sulfate batch process, which used low-grade ilmenite ore and the newer chloride continuous process, which could be configured to handle either higher-grade rutile ore or lower-grade ilmenite. Du Pont was the only competitor that had mastered the challenges of operating ilmenite-based chloride technology, which used lower-grade ore and accounted for more than two-thirds of its total capacity. National Lead reverted to total dependence on the sulfate process in 1972, when it shut down a rutile chloride unit that had not been operating satisfactorily. The next three largest producers in the U.S. market were each dependent on the ilmenite-based sulfate technology for about two-thirds of their capacity and on rutile chloride for the remainder. The two smallest competitors relied solely on rutile chloride technology.

These technological differences mattered because in 1970 and 1971 environmental shocks significantly altered the relative cost positions of the three production technologies. Australian restrictions on mining rutile from beach sands forced rutile prices up by more than 70 percent; ilmenite prices went up as well, but by a much smaller fraction. And in the United States much more stringent emissions standards were mandated, hitting the sulfate process particularly hard because it was the dirtiest of the three. Based on Du Pont's estimates, the standard costs of a 50,000 ton-per-year ilmenite chloride plant appeared to increase by about 10 percent, for a comparable rutile chloride plant (which was close to parity with the ilmenite chloride plant prior to the ore price increases) by about 20 percent and those for a comparable sulfate plant (which was significantly less efficient to begin with) by about 20 percent as well. Industry observers expected much of the sulfate capacity to shut down as a result.

These environmental shocks precipitated a change of strategy at Du Pont. In 1972 it decided to add an ilmenite chloride plant with capacity of about 200,000 tons per year, at a capital cost of about $1,000 per ton. Site selection, regulatory clearance, and construction would take more than four years, ensuring that the first of the two planned 100,000 ton lines could not be started up before 1977, with construction of the second line slated to begin a year or two later. In the meantime incremental ilmenite chloride capacity was to be obtained by expanding existing facilities to their practical limits. Along with the incremental expansions the new plant was supposed to give Du Pont the additional capacity to absorb the bulk of the 300,000 to 400,000 tons of growth expected in U.S. demand through 1985, to an annual level of about 1 million tons. Du Pont's share of industry capacity was supposed, as a result, to increase to 65 percent.

Within two months of formally adopting this growth strategy, Du Pont refused to follow a price increase led by Kerr McGee, even though it lacked the excess capacity to force other producers to rescind their increases. But as shortages developed and costs soared in 1973 and 1974, Du Pont found itself powerless to resist further price increases. It did, however, announce in November 1973 that it had begun to study the possibility of adding a major new ilmenite chloride plant at De Lisle, Mississippi. And in July 1974, in the aftermath of Kerr McGee's announcement that it would add a 50,000 ton-per-year rutile chloride plant, Du Pont publicly announced—and overstated—its commitment to building the De Lisle plant. Throughout this period, Du Pont also refused to entertain requests from its domestic competitors to license its ilmenite chloride technology.

In January 1975, against a backdrop of softening market conditions and significant excess capacity, Du Pont succeeded at forcing the rollback of another significant price increase led by Kerr McGee. But it also began to scale back its capacity expansion plans, for several reasons. First, the industry was suffering a severe downturn in demand, which was now expected to lag the forecasts made in 1972 at least through 1980. Second, unexpected leniency in the enforcement of pollution controls had let competitors' sulfate units continue to operate. Third, low capacity utilization and sharp increases in construction and chlorine costs meant that Du Pont's cumulative cash flow from the titanium dioxide business would be significantly negative for some years to come, rather than positive—a significant concern, since limits were being imposed on capital spending at the corporate level in order to preserve Du Pont's AAA bond rating.

As a result, in February 1975, plans for the second line at De Lisle were postponed indefinitely, and expansions of existing plants that were to have been completed by 1975 were staggered until 1977. The major question that Du Pont continued to wrestle with concerned the timing of the first line at De Lisle. Key managers of Du Pont's Pigments Department analyzed the financial implications of two alternate strategies in great detail. A new "maintain" strategy targeted a 1985 market share of 43 percent and, at least initially, required just expansion of existing facilities rather than completion of the first line at De Lisle. A modified "growth" strategy targeted a 1985 market share of 55 percent and specified that De Lisle be started up in either late 1978 or early 1979. The calculations of the payoffs to these strategies assumed that delaying De Lisle would let competitors raise prices in the short run, increasing the amount of capacity they would add and depressing long-run prices. They suggested that startup in the third quarter of 1978 would be the most profitable option if demand recovered as expected.

Demand continued to trail forecasts, however. By October 1977 it was clear that Kerr McGee had deferred its expansion plans indefinitely so that no major competitive expansion would occur before 1982. The need for capacity no longer dictated the immediate startup of the first line at De Lisle. But precommitment of much of the project cost as well as apprehensions about cost escalation, the ability to renew environmental permits and future credibility meant that further delay was seen as disadvantageous. The De Lisle plant was started up in 1979.

3.2   Empirical Analysis

Can it be determined whether Du Pont engaged in preemptive capacity expansion in the titanium dioxide industry? While Du Pont did seem to build up capacity ahead of demand, some of the gap appears to have been inadvertent, namely based on overly optimistic demand forecasts. And Du Pont's plans to increase its share of industry capacity from 34 to 65 percent, subsequently scaled back to 55 percent, can be rationalized in terms of the large cost advantage that the environmental shocks of the early 1970s conferred on it, followed by diminution of both the

Exhibit 3.1
Average Costs of Titanium Dioxide Production (¢/lb)

	1972	1975
Du Pont	17	38
National Lead	20	44
Kerr McGee	21	42
American Cyanamid	22	42
Gulf & Western	22	44
SCM	23	47

estimated advantage (in percentage terms) as well as the perceived need for new capacity after 1975 (see exhibit 3.1). The
interesting issue is whether efficiency-based effects are sufficient
to explain the pattern of capacity expansion in titanium dioxide
or whether it is also necessary to appeal to interactive effects of
the sort that are prominent in game-theoretic analyses of competition to expand capacity.

The September 1990 issue of the *International Journal of Industrial Organization* (IJIO) contains not one but two attempts to sort
through this issue that use the data disclosed by the antitrust
case in very different ways: one by Hall (1990) and another by
Ghemawat (1990). As the author of one of these papers, I cannot
credibly claim to be evenhanded. I nevertheless discuss Hall's
paper as well as my own in some detail because her analysis is,
in some respects, representative of a research thrust that is referred to as the New Empirical Industrial Organization (NEIO).
NEIO emphasizes specification of the behavioral equations by
which firms set prices or quantities and estimation of their
parameters, unlike the older statistical tradition in IO, which
tended to examine the reduced-form relationship between

industry structure and market performance. NEIO has been celebrated by its practitioners in near-hegemonic terms, so much so
that the chapter in the *Handbook of Industrial Organization* devoted
to the empirical analysis of market power in individual/related
markets (Bresnahan 1989) focuses exclusively on studies in this
vein. The titanium dioxide case will provide a useful perspective
on this mode of empirical analysis.

Hall (1990)

Hall began by positing a two-stage model in which Du Pont set
capacity in the first stage and quantity in the second stage and
its competitors reacted to its capacity choice and to their conjectures about its quantity in the second stage by setting their own
quantities. With this structure, she effectively assumed that Du
Pont's competitors always held the cost-minimizing level of capacity and focused on whether Du Pont did as well. And instead
of testing directly for whether Du Pont's incremental capacity
expansions crowded out competitors, she looked at whether Du
Pont's expansions between 1972 and 1977 appeared to dampen
competitors' quantity choices above and beyond the implied reductions in Du Pont's marginal costs.

It should be noted at the very outset that Hall's approach devi-
ated from standard NEIO in two respects that seem, at least to
me, to be very sensible. First, she employed the rich cost data
disclosed by the antitrust case and summarized in exhibit 3.1,
even though NEIO typically eschews the use of accounting data
on costs and profitability—an approach that Caves (1994, p. 14)
has labeled as "Look ma, no hands!" Second, instead of focusing
on just short-run quantity (or price) decisions, she attempted to
incorporate capacity, the primary focus of long-run competition
in the titanium dioxide industry, into her analysis.

The aspects of Hall's analysis that *do* fit well into the standard NEIO frame are more problematic. First of all, there is her reliance on conjectural variations. This empirical construct has been the subject of considerable game-theoretic skepticism (cf. Tirole 1988, pp. 244–45). In particular, a skeptic might regard it as well specified only when conjectural variations are zero.

Second, even if one finds the conjectural-variations approach adequate, issue must be taken with Hall's assumption that capacities were optimized year by year. Her procedure ignored the demand fluctuations in the titanium dioxide market, particularly the downward shock in the middle of the period studied, namely in 1975. Before the shock, Du Pont was unable to add capacity as rapidly as it would have liked; after the shock, it staggered incremental expansion efforts to which it had already committed some resources. Neither subperiod sits well with the assumption of intertemporally unconstrained year-by-year optimization of capacity levels. This is typical of another problem with NEIO: In looking closely at short-run choices, it tends to lose sight of the long-run effects of resource irreversibility or commitment.

Finally perhaps the most striking omission from Hall's analysis is that by focusing on the period from 1972 to 1977 (for which a relatively complete set of data was disclosed by the antitrust case), it omitted Du Pont's startup of the large new plant at De Lisle in 1979. So while it afforded some (equivocal) insights into patterns of incremental capacity expansion, it ignored the single biggest capacity-related move—the one that arguably *was* preemptive—in the titanium dioxide industry in 1970s! Once again there is a generic source of difficulty: Major one-of-a-kind commitments often do not lend themselves to the running of regressions, NEIO-sanctioned or not. Yet surely such events should not be submerged from consideration simply because of a fixation with large-sample analysis.

Ghemawat (1990)

In another article in the same issue of the IJIO, I took a second, more direct look at whether preemptive considerations influenced Du Pont's capacity expansion decisions. My approach was based on the availability of considerable public information on Du Pont's deliberations about the first line at De Lisle—deliberations that were apparently meant to be private. The record of what Du Pont thought it was doing when it decided in 1975 to start up the first line at De Lisle in 1978 or 1979, instead of postponing startup indefinitely, seemed to be worth referring to.

Recall that in 1975 Du Pont was evaluating two alternative strategies: a maintain strategy (M) under which it would maintain its share of total industry capacity at 43 percent by expanding two existing plants, and a growth strategy (G) under which it would increase its capacity share to 55 percent by adding an efficiently scaled new plant. Du Pont reckoned that titanium dioxide prices would be lower in the short run if it followed G because it would have to add capacity ahead of demand in order to preempt incremental expansions by competitors. What is even interesting, though, is that Du Pont also expected the two strategies to lead to different price levels in the long run. The reason, according to Du Pont's internal memoranda, was that if it did not increase its share of the expanding market, "Competitive expansion and the resulting scramble for sales will affect price," and "Du Pont would then no longer be an industry leader and would be facing the prospect of competing on a 'me-too' basis." Du Pont calculated that after 1981, G would lead to prices about 3 percent higher than strategy M, factored this difference into its financial analysis of the two alternatives, and decided on G.

The skeptical reader may wonder whether the pursuit of market power—3 percent higher prices seven years into the future—

played a big role in Du Pont's selection of G. After all, Du Pont also enjoyed a cost advantage, which sometimes suffices to ensure market dominance. In other words, a skeptic might hypothesize that the net present value of a growth strategy without elevated prices H would come close to matching the net present value of G. Fortunately the available data allow us to discount this hypothesis. Let V_I denote the expected net present value of an arbitrary strategy I, and define

$$\Delta \equiv V_G - V_H.$$

Then the hypothesis that Du Pont's choice of G was largely attributable to its greater efficiency amounts to the assertion that Δ was, in some sense, small.

The magnitude of Δ cannot be assessed directly because we do not know V_H. But we can construct a proxy for V_H by simulating the financial consequences of a hybrid strategy H' that combines the capacity and output sequences implied by G with the long-run prices implied by M. Define

$$\Delta' \equiv V_G - V_{H'}.$$

Note that Δ' is a conservative measure of Δ in the sense that if Du Pont *did not* gain any market power by increasing its share of industry capacity from 43 to 55 percent, H would lead to long-run prices no higher, and almost certainly lower, than the ones plugged into H' (from M). That is because under H, the most efficient competitor, Du Pont, would no longer be restricting its expansion so as to keep its capacity share constant. And although the output levels plugged into H' (from G) might not exactly mirror the output sequence implied by H, that should not create strong biases toward the rejection of the null hypothesis: If H involved compensating *decreases* in output, that would increase Δ without changing Δ' because prices were expected to substantially exceed marginal costs over the entire forecast period; H could not involve large compensating *increases* in output because under G, Du Pont, as the most efficient producer, already expected to exceed 99 percent capacity utilization over the period of higher long-run prices.

Exhibit 3.2 uses data from Du Pont's own analysis of strategies G and M to trace V_G, V_H, and V_M as functions of its percentage cost of capital for this business, r. Note that Δ' is a strictly decreasing function of r: $\Delta'(10) = \$106$ million; $\Delta'(25) = \$27$ million. Since we do not know Du Pont's estimate of r, how can we assess whether it thought Δ' was significantly greater than zero? One approach is to note that Du Pont picked G instead of M, implying that its estimate of r was less than 19.6 percent. Therefore, Du Pont must have thought that the power to push up prices was worth more than $\Delta'(19.6) = \$42$ million, which is a nontrivial amount. The second approach combines the 19.6 percent ceiling on estimates of r with the following inequality:

$$V_G(r) - \Delta'(r) < V_M(r) \qquad \forall r \geq 13.2.$$

So if our prior assumption about Du Pont's estimate of r is given by the density function $g(r)$ over the support $[0, 19.6]$, we can attach a probability $\int_{13.2}^{19.6} g(r)dr$ to the belief that Du Pont picked G instead of M only because it thought that G would help to push up prices. In light of the fact that yields on 10-year Treasuries and AAA-rated corporate bonds were running at 7.3 and 8.8 percent, respectively, in mid-1975, I would guess the value of that integral to be close to one.

In summary, neither of the two approaches is congenial to the hypothesis that Du Pont's choice of G instead of M was almost entirely attributable to its greater efficiency. Instead, the price-raising possibilities associated with market power appear to have affected both firm strategy and industry evolution!

Exhibit 3.2
The Financial Consequences of Different Strategies

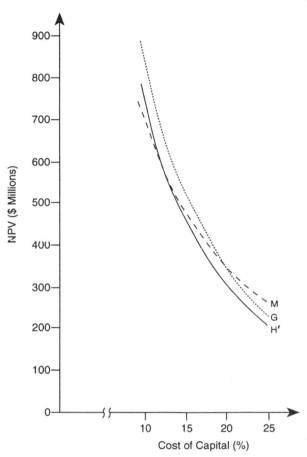

Source: FTC Docket 9108

3.3   Theoretical Analysis

The conclusions from the empirical analysis focus theoretical attention on the sorts of price-raising effects that apparently swayed Du Pont's commitment decision. Purely efficiency-based considerations seem incapable of explaining why industry prices should be expected to go up as the most efficient producer's share of industry capacity increases. The issue of interest, then, is whether game-theoretic analysis provides more explanatory power.

To pursue this issue, consider a game-theoretic model of interactions between two competitors with different initial capacities (numbered so that $k_1 > k_2$). The assumption of duopoly, while less literal than in the turbine generator case analyzed in the previous chapter, can be rationalized in terms of the prevalent theoretical stratagem of specifying strong cases that highlight the operation of certain effects—in this context, interactive ones (Blaug 1980). In the long run (stage 1) these two competitors vie to add an efficiently scaled plant, and in the short run (stage 2) they compete on price—assumptions that approximate basic conditions in the titanium dioxide industry in the early 1970s. As usual, this game will be solved by working backward, from stage 2 to stage 1.

In stage 2 (the pricing subgame) it seems efficient, because of the relative inelasticity of demand for titanium dioxide, to invoke the same structure (and notation) as in the one-period model developed in the previous chapter.[1] As a result proposition 2.1 continues to apply. If total demand is less than the capacity of the smaller firm, prices collapse to the duopolists' common marginal

1. Ghemawat (1990) demonstrates that concave but differentiable demand curves imply pricing strategies and capacity expansion patterns that are qualitatively similar to the ones derived here under the assumption of inelastic demand.

cost, which is normalized for convenience to zero. If total demand is greater than total capacity, prices equal customers' common reservation level, u. At intermediate levels of capacity utilization, the duopolists employ mixed strategies that involve the larger firm holding a stochastic price umbrella over the smaller one. The larger firm then expects to earn its security level, and the smaller firm the same absolute amount scaled by its relative effective capacity, as discussed in the previous chapter. The sum of these two terms can be used to identify the relationship between the industry's expected operating profits and its concentration level at intermediate levels of capacity utilization.

Proposition 3.1   If $x_2 < Q < x_1 + x_2 + 1$, the industry's expected operating profits are higher the greater is the share of aggregate capacity accounted for by the larger firm, firm i.

Proof   Define X as the aggregate capacity with which the duopolists enter stage 2 $(= k_1 + k_2 + 1 \equiv x_1 + x_2)$, and hold X constant. Write x_j as $X - x_i$ so that the comparative statics analysis can be conducted in terms of x_i alone. Over the assumed levels of capacity utilization, the larger firm's expected operating profits are given by

$$R_i = u(Q - X + x_i).$$

Differentiating this expression,

$$\frac{dR_i}{dx_i} = u.$$

In tracing the effects of x_i on R_j, two subcases (labeled in terms of the regimes laid out in proposition 2.1) must be considered.

For the eventuality $Q \leq x_i$, the smaller firm's expected operating profits are given by

$$R_j = u(Q - X + x_i)\frac{X - x_i}{Q}.$$

Differentiating,

$$\frac{dR_j}{dx_i} = u\left[\frac{2X - 2x_i - Q}{Q}\right].$$

The expression in square brackets is equal to -1 only in the limit where the capacity of the smaller firm is vanishingly small; otherwise, it is greater than -1.

For the eventuality $Q \geq x_i$, the smaller firm's expected operating profits are given by

$$R_j = u(Q - X + x_i)\frac{X - x_i}{x_i}.$$

Differentiating,

$$\frac{dR_j}{dx_i} = u\left[\frac{X^2 - QX}{x_i^2} - 1\right].$$

The expression in square brackets is always greater than -1 given the assumption that $X > Q$. As a result both subcases imply that

$$\frac{d(R_i + R_j)}{dx_i} \geq 0,$$

with the inequality holding strictly except when Q is less than x_i and x_j (i.e., $X - x_i$) equals zero.   □

The comparative static result in proposition 3.1 identifies a positive relationship between an industry's concentration (defined as the larger firm's share of total capacity) and its (expected) operating profits that does not depend on either of the usual assumptions (discussed at length by Schmalensee 1987) of differential efficiency or collusion. It reflects, instead, the tendency deduced in proposition 2.1 for the smaller firm to price more aggressively than the larger one. Thus it is the smaller firm that acts as the "spoiler" in the stage 2 subgame. The greater its capacity, the more weight it has to throw around. So holding the industry's total capacity constant, the greater the share of it controlled by the larger firm, the better that will be for the total operating profits the industry expects to earn at intermediate levels of capacity utilization.

This characterization of payoffs in the stage 2 subgame can be used to pin down the outcome of stage 1 competition to add an efficiently scaled new plant, a process that must now be specified in more detail. Stage 1 competition is modeled as an auction in which the competitor that bids more for the right to add a lump of capacity is the one that gets to expand. While rights to add capacity were not actually auctioned off in the titanium dioxide industry, this bidding mechanism (which was first proposed by Barzel 1968 in the context of innovative rivalry and adapted to capacity competition by Gilbert and Harris 1984) serves as a static approximation to dynamic competition over opportunities to make lumpy investments. To move first to add a lump of capacity, a competitor must "outbid" its rival in the sense of shouldering the extra costs of accelerating plant construction or holding excess capacity for a longer period. Both types of extra costs were evident in the new plant that Du Pont added at De Lisle.

Proposition 3.2 If $x_2 < Q < x_1 + x_2 + 1$ and competitors are risk-neutral, firm 1, which is initially larger, is willing to bid strictly more for the additional unit of capacity.

Proof The maximum price firm i is willing to bid for the additional unit of capacity is given by

$$V_i(x_i, x_j) = R_i(x_i + 1, x_j) - R_i(x_i, x_j + 1).$$

But by proposition 3.1,

$$R_1(x_1 + 1, x_2) + R_2(x_2, x_1 + 1) > R_1(x_1, x_2 + 1) + R_2(x_2 + 1, x_1)$$

because the expression on the left-hand side corresponds to the more concentrated industry structure. Rearranging terms,

$$R_1(x_1 + 1, x_2) - R_1(x_1, x_2 + 1) > R_2(x_2 + 1, x_1) - R_2(x_2, x_1 + 1),$$
$$\Leftrightarrow V_1(x_1, x_2) > V_2(x_2, x_1). \qquad \square$$

To aid visualization of this result, an example with $x_1 = 3$ and $x_2 = 1$ is graphed in exhibit 3.3a. Part b of that exhibit also traces the maximum prices that the duopolists are willing to bid, with the same initial capacities, for the additional unit of capacity if they behave "nonstrategically" (i.e., ignore the threat that if they do not build, their rival will). These nonstrategic bids are given by

$$D_i(x_i, x_j) = R_i(x_i + 1, x_j) - R_i(x_i, x_j).$$

The example in exhibit 3.3 suggests, and more general analysis confirms, that the addition of capacity by the larger firm is predicated on strategic behavior: With nonstrategic behavior the smaller of two equally efficient firms would be the one that would add the new unit of capacity. So game-theoretic considerations *are* necessary, in the present context, to explain why the larger firm might add capacity first even if does not have an efficiency advantage.

To summarize, if $x_2 < Q < x_1 + x_2 + 1$, strategic behavior implies that the initially larger firm will outbid its rival for the new unit of capacity; that is, differences in initial size will snowball. The parametric restriction that underpins this prediction seems to be quite mild. Hall's work (1986, 1988), for instance, suggests that most U.S. industries are stuck with some excess capacity most of the time (corresponding to $Q < x_1 + x_2 + 1$ in the context of the model) but not with so much as to force them

Exhibit 3.3
An Example with $x_1 = 3$ and $x_2 = 1$

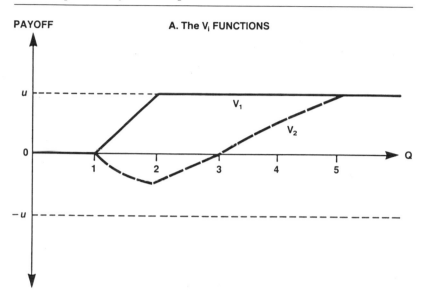

PAYOFF

A. The V_i FUNCTIONS

V_1

V_2

u

0

$-u$

Q

1 2 3 4 5

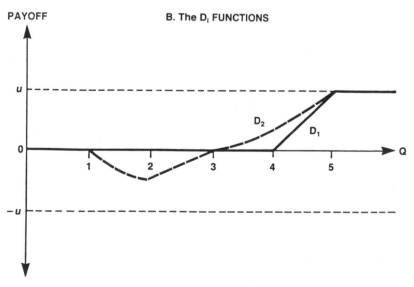

PAYOFF

B. The D_i FUNCTIONS

D_2

D_1

u

0

$-u$

Q

1 2 3 4 5

to price at marginal cost (corresponding to $Q > x_2$). And in any event this parametric restriction can be weakened substantially by building demand uncertainty into the basic model. The next section of this chapter will, among other things, discuss such an extension.

3.4 Reflections

The theoretical analysis in this chapter has some broader implications for the ways in which game theorists think about modeling capacity expansion in particular and strategic behavior in general, and the empirical analysis for the "resource-based view" of the firm that has become fashionable in strategic management. Both sets of implications deserve some additional discussion.

Models of Capacity Expansion

The reason for presenting a new theoretical model (based on Ghemawat 1990) in this chapter is the unavailability, despite more than a decade of prior game-theoretic work focused on capacity expansion, of an off-the-shelf model that fit the circumstances of the titanium dioxide case reasonably well. Kreps and Scheinkman's (1983) seminal model of capacity-constrained price competition came closest: Their analysis of the stage 2 pricing subgame given elastic demand is qualitatively similar to (and served as the basis of) the characterization, given inelastic demand, of pricing strategies in the previous chapter as well as in this one. Their stage 1 setup, however, differs from the present one in a subtle but important way: They assumed that the firms simultaneously and independently set their capacities instead of competing for an expansion slot. This assumption, the significance of which they did not spell out, is entirely responsible for their conclusion that the shares of duopolists with identical costs will tend to converge rather than diverge.

This difference between Kreps and Scheinkman's model and the one presented in this chapter illustrates, once again, the narrow reach of most noncooperative game-theoretic models and the consequent importance of matching models to the circumstances of particular cases. Thus I would argue that the model developed in this chapter fits the circumstances of the titanium dioxide case better than Kreps and Scheinkman's in light of the large scale of the expansion that was contemplated at De Lisle and the likelihood, given the low industry growth rate and elasticity of demand, that it would crowd out greenfield additions of capacity by competitors. Of course, Kreps and Scheinkman's model might fit better in other cases.[2] The point is that this is one of the attractions of the case method that was advertised in chapter 1: The specifics of the case can help steer one toward a particular theoretical model.

The specifics of the titanium dioxide case also suggest the usefulness of enriching models of capacity expansion in particular and strategic behavior in general with uncertainty. Although Du Pont's preemptive strategy ultimately proved very profitable—it is still the only operator of the ilmenite chloride technology and has become the global leader in titanium dioxide—it was nearly derailed by the unexpected drop-off in demand in the second half of the 1970s. Other case studies as well as interviews confirm that uncertainty, particularly about demand, is one of the factors that most complicates managerial decision-making about capacities.

Fortunately, the model developed in this chapter can easily

---

2. For instance, there is evidence that the ascendance of the less lumpy rutile chloride technology in the 1960s prompted the titanium dioxide competitors to take turns adding new plants over that decade.

be extended to incorporate imperfect information (common uncertainty) about demand by multiplying demand by a shift parameter whose value is unknown when firms make their stage 1 capacity-related decisions but is revealed before prices are set in stage 2. Ghemawat (1990) analyzes such a setup with price-elastic demand and finds that uncertainty of this sort does not, contrary to conventional wisdom (e.g., Porter and Spence 1982), shrivel the incentive to preempt that is identified by the model in this chapter.[3] In fact, because of the implied "smearing" of demand across regimes in which preemption pays and those in which it does not, such uncertainty can even be said to *increase* the likelihood of preemption! This contradiction suggests that the likelihood of preemptive behavior is reduced not by demand uncertainty per se but by private information about demand (instead of an uncertain but common prior). In another paper (Ghemawat 1987), I analyze how private information about demand can lead to a "winner's curse," dampening preemptive propensities, but much more work remains to be done in this area.

It is hard to mention private information in this context without also saying something about an aspect of it that *has* been subject to considerable analysis: the theoretical possibility of "limit pricing," in which an incumbent deliberately holds prices low in order to signal to its competitors that it has a lower cost structure than they might otherwise expect, and thereby tries to discourage them from entering or expanding. While there is direct evidence from the internal documents subpoenaed in the titanium dioxide case that Du Pont did try to hold down prices over much of the period studied to deter capacity expansion by its competitors, it seemed to have been counting on behavioral

---

3. The risk-aversion arguments that Porter and Spence (1982) rely on are overturned, in the present context, by the fact that the larger firm's expected payoffs from expansion stochastically dominate the smaller firm's.

responses—involving capital constraints and, in the case of at least two competitors, mechanistic capacity expansion strategies triggered by profitability—that were rather different from the behavioral mechanism stressed in game-theoretic models of limit pricing. Unless one can uncover cases in which a more prominent role is played by the sort of sophisticated inferential calculus that is a staple of signaling models, questions are in order about the usefulness of what has become a very large *corpus* of theoretical work. I return to this issue in chapter 8.

Finally it is worth emphasizing that although game theory permits rigorous analysis of strategic interactions and the way they feed back into industry structure, it has not entirely superseded the older, structural approach to IO in its usefulness. The titanium dioxide case exhibits many of the structural/basic conditions that old IO identified as conducive to preemption: On the supply side, factors such as large minimal efficient scales, experience curves, and high capital-intensity, and on the demand side, factors such as low price-elasticity, convergent expectations, and modest (expected) growth rates. See, for example, the discussion in chapter 15 of Porter (1980).

The Resource-Based View of the Firm

In addition to suggesting ways in which game-theoretic analysis of capacity expansion might usefully be redirected, the case considered in this chapter provides some perspective on the "resource-based" view of the firm (Wernerfelt 1984) that has become fashionable in strategic management. Du Pont's (unique) mastery of ilmenite chloride technology can readily be identified as a resource (or competence, or capability) that helped sustain its superior performance. The case helps suggest answers to half a dozen questions about such resources that are frequently

fumbled by proponents of the resource-based view or answered
without recourse to empirical evidence, especially evidence of a
"micro" sort that might address the issues of firm heterogeneity
in which they are so interested.[4]

First, what are the preconditions that a resource must fulfill in
order to be a potential source of sustainable competitive advantage? Resource-based theorists often manage to tie themselves
into tautological knots on this subject. For example, a recent textbook treatment by Barney (1997) focuses on whether resources
are valuable and rare, but fails to address the question of the
resource characteristics that lead to those outcomes. The Du Pont
case, in contrast, hints at two conditions that are generally necessary (but not sufficient) for resources to be sources of sustainable
advantage in the face of competitive threats: durability and
specialization.

Second, how do firms manage to accumulate bundles of competitively valuable resources? Some authors in the resource-
based tradition (e.g., Barney 1986) have insisted that ultimately,
luck is all. In the present case they might assert that the environmental shocks of 1970 and 1971 constituted such a windfall for
Du Pont: that Du Pont did not anticipate them in the 1940s when
it began to develop the process for chlorinating titaniferous ores
and that it focused, fatefully, on low-grade ilmenite ore solely
because that is what its captive mines supplied at the time. While
that is true as far as it goes, it is hard to maintain that purely
random processes were what led Du Pont to develop a new production process. According to archival information, Du Pont's
attempt to develop a new production process was a deliberate
effort to create a competitive advantage in titanium dioxide by
using superior corporate technical capabilities to tap potential

---

4. For additional elaboration of these ideas, see Ghemawat (1991b).

economies of scale (Hounshell and Smith 1988). Many would argue that deliberate efforts of this sort should be treated as the essence of strategic management instead of being reduced, by chronological backwardation, to the luck of the draw.

Third, how do superior resources evolve over time? The resource-based view has tended to focus on the initial heterogeneity of resources and has therefore recently been supplemented with a more dynamic view of the firm that stresses the possibility of improving capabilities (or more prosaically, opportunity sets) over time by performing activities or processes in appropriate ways (Teece and Pisano 1994). Such feedback effects, from activities to capabilities, are evident in the titanium dioxide case: Learning-by-doing clearly reduced Du Pont's production costs over time. But the titanium dioxide case also supplies a reminder that capabilities and competitive positions are affected not only by the cumulative effect of many small decisions but also by a few large decisions, such as the commitment to start up the first line of De Lisle. That particular decision cemented Du Pont's leadership of the U.S. market and has probably helped to sustain its status as the sole operator of ilmenite chloride technology through the mid-1990s. Big decisions can be individually important.

Fourth, how are such big, relatively irreversible decisions to be analyzed? The resource- and capability-based views are largely silent on this issue, beyond asserting that the most useful insights are likely to be derived from an internally oriented analysis of firms' resources rather than from an externally oriented analysis of their product market positions. Once again the titanium dioxide case contradicts such assertions. The evidence from the antitrust case indicates that Du Pont identified, evaluated, and elected to persist with the strategy of starting up De Lisle on the basis of detailed comparisons of its own costs of

producing titanium dioxide with its competitors'. Or, in game-
theoretic terms, it analyzed long-run resource commitments by
anticipating their implications for product market interactions.

Fifth, why aren't superior resources imitated more quickly? A
number of resource-based theorists have answered this question
in terms of *intrinsic inimitability:* inimitability stemming from factors such as unique historical circumstances, causal ambiguity,
and the social complexity of organizational phenomena that may
make it impossible for firms to systematically manage or influence them (e.g., Barney 1997). These are, to varying extents, useful constructs, but in stressing the strict infeasibility of imitation,
they exclude consideration of the important possibility that imitation may be feasible but uneconomical. The titanium dioxide
case provides an example: While Du Pont regarded its competitors as being technically able to imitate its ilmenite chloride technology, it counted on the fact that the U.S. market would be able
to accommodate only one efficiently scaled new plant over the
next decade to deter them from doing so. Another example that
highlights the economic barriers to imitation in the context of
somewhat less lumpy capacity decisions will be considered in
chapter 6.

Finally, what are the implications of resource-based competition for social welfare? According to some of its proponents, the
resource-based view of the firm is a theory of efficient production, so that taking resources seriously implies that "Strategic
management research can be perfectly consistent with traditional social welfare concerns of economists" (Barney 1991, p.
116). Alas, shifting the basis of market power from product positions to resource positions is an insufficient basis for such opti-
mism. The purely pecuniary persistence-of-dominance result in
this chapter was meant to make the point that it is rash to assume
that whatever happens in freely functioning markets is always

for the best. Note that this theoretical conclusion is not confined to the case of the titanium dioxide industry.

3.5 Summary

The theoretical and empirical analysis in this chapter has made a number of contributions. First of all, it has supplied another illustration of the power of game-theoretic thinking. Du Pont apparently expanded capacity preemptively in titanium dioxide in order to raise long-run prices. Explicitly strategic (interactive) thinking is required to rationalize such preemption-induced price rises: Nonstrategic thinking would under the same circumstances rule out preemption.

Second, since the titanium dioxide case has been analyzed both statistically and nonstatistically, that permits a comparison of these two fundamentally different modes of empirical analysis. The comparison turns out not to be to the advantage of sophisticated statistical analysis in this case, but I hasten to add that that is not intended as a general conclusion. The previous chapter contained some useful statistical analysis; the next chapter will further illustrate its potential utility. The only point about empirical methodology that this chapter aims to make is that nonstatistical analysis can supplement, and sometimes even surpass, statistical analysis in its usefulness.

Third, this chapter aims to make a theoretical point about methodology as well. Given the profusion of game-theoretic models, it is hard, in the abstract, to figure out which one(s) to focus on. A focus on individual cases helps alleviate this problem by helping direct (and redirect) modeling efforts.

Fourth, the case also shed light on the "resource-based" view of the firm in strategic management. Du Pont's superior resources or capabilities were durable and specialized to the titanium dioxide market, stemmed from a deliberate effort to build up competitive advantage, and were profoundly influenced by lumpy capacity decisions. These decisions had to be evaluated in terms of their implications for product market interactions, and were motivated by pecuniary economies that helped deter imitation as well as by efficiency effects. Lurking behind all these points is the broad implication, noted in chapter 1, that game-theoretic IO would appear to complement rather than be compromised by the resource-based view of the firm.

4 Capacity Reduction in
Declining Chemical
Processing Industries

This chapter, like the previous one, focuses on long-run competition in capacities. But it shifts attention from capacity expansion in growing markets to capacity reduction in declining ones. The original rationale for applying game-theoretic analysis to such settings was that they had been ignored, until then, by the new (game-theoretic) IO. The problem was not that IO economists had overlooked the influence of capacity commitments on long-run competition. Rather their analyses of capacity-driven industry evolution had been shaped by a specific—and specializing—parametric assumption: that the rate of growth of demand was positive rather than negative.

My own interest in negative rates of growth, namely industry decline, was motivated by my experience working for McKinsey & Company, a management consulting firm, in London in the early 1980s. My work was concentrated in the chemical processing sector, and much of it involved plant closures in response to the capacity glut that had developed after the second oil shock. I remember being particularly struck by my colleagues' suggestion that in such settings, efficient plants sometimes got closed before inefficient ones.

This empirical motivation resulted, after I returned to the Harvard Business School, in a stream of game-theoretic research

with Barry Nalebuff on equilibrium patterns of capacity reduction in declining industries. Our modeling efforts predicted that
size should hurt survivability during industry decline in a way
that might sometimes lead to the closure of efficient plants operated by large firms before less-efficient plants operated by small
firms. This broad prediction and the follow-on theoretical work
that it has inspired will be reviewed in the first section of this
chapter. The second section will review the two case studies on
capacity reduction in declining industries that have been most
prominently cited in the game-theoretic literature, as well as the
available cross-industry statistical analyses and explain why I regard this body of evidence as supportive of a specific version of
the size-hurts-survivability prediction. The third section of this
chapter will offer some broad strictures about methodology as
well as touch on some of the specific implications of this line of
research for strategic management.

4.1   Theoretical Review

This section will briefly describe Ghemawat and Nalebuff's
(henceforth, G-N) 1985 model of capacity reduction during industry decline and various extensions, including G-N (1990).
Most of the papers referred to have already been published in
scholarly journals. This review will therefore focus on the development of a particular theme in this literature: that other things
being equal, size should hurt survivability during industry decline. The two G-N models can be thought of as establishing this
proposition in the context of two limit points to the set of possible assumptions about (downward) capacity flexibility: the setting in which capacity reduction is all or nothing (G-N 1985) and
the setting in which capacity can be reduced continuously
(G-N 1990).

I should add that this focus on G-N (1985), and extensions thereof, precludes detailed discussion of an alternate line of theoretical research on exit, involving incomplete information, that was proposed by Fudenberg and Tirole (1986a) in another early paper on the subject. This tilt can be justified on the grounds that Fudenberg and Tirole's proposal has led to little in the way of follow-on research, theoretical or empirical. It can be argued that informational asymmetries of the sort invoked by Fudenberg and Tirole are a sideshow in most declining industries (see G-N 1990, pp. 169–70): Competitors are more likely to be familiar with one another, and the production technologies embodied in extant investments are more likely to be common knowledge. That, at any rate, is what is assumed in this chapter, in the interest of generating testable predictions. Chapter 7 reconsiders the Fudenberg and Tirole (1986a) model in a context in which it is more likely to be appropriate—that of an emerging market.

Ghemawat and Nalebuff (1985)

Barry Nalebuff and I first established the size-hurts-survivability proposition in the context of a model constructed to highlight the exit decision (G-N 1985). Consider an undifferentiated market in which demand is declining smoothly toward zero for exogenous reasons. As demand declines, capacity must be reduced to maintain profitability. At each instant active firms make a single, dichotomous decision about whether to continue to operate at their initial capacity levels or to exit the market in toto. For simplicity it is useful to begin by focusing on the case in which there are just two firms of different sizes but identical efficiency levels.

This duopolistic exit game, like many other wars of attrition, has more than one Nash equilibrium. If each firm takes the other's strategy as given, the large firm can threaten to remain active and thereby force its smaller rival to leave first; the reverse is equally possible. But the outcome in which the larger efficient firm leaves before the smaller one emerges as the sole equilibrium if the requirement of subgame perfection (Selten 1975) is imposed. Subgame perfection requires not only that each player's strategy be an optimal response to other players' strategies but also that this optimality be reevaluated continually as the game proceeds. Using this requirement, it is possible to work backward in time to show that a small firm, because of its longer tenure as a profitable monopolist, can credibly promise to produce over a longer period than its larger rival, inducing earlier exit by the latter. The unique outcome is due to the fact that most (sometimes all) Nash equilibria disappear when a war of attrition is truncated at some finite time (Wilson 1983): As demand declines toward zero, all profitability is eventually exhausted.

To be more specific, let p denote price, q stand for industry output, and t index time, and assume that $\partial p(q, t)q/\partial q > 0$. This assumption of positive marginal revenue is not really necessary (see the discussion of Hunsaker and Kovenock 1995 below), but it does keep the analysis from getting bogged down in the mechanics of short-run output adjustment.

At time 0 two firms, indexed by $i = 1, 2$, serve this market. Firm i's capacity is k_i: k_1 is greater than k_2. The two firms' cost flows per unit of capacity are assumed to be common knowledge and, provisionally, to be identical and equal to c. Neither firm incurs any other operating costs, so by our assumption of positive marginal revenue, available capacity is always fully used. The capacity cost, ck_i, can be avoided only by exit. Note that ck_i is *not* a sunk cost. Firms can either pay at the rate of ck_i and operate or not pay and shut down. This cost structure best approximates settings in which the marginal cost of producing up to historic capacity levels is low: Fixed costs dominate, resulting in tremendous pressure to fill up capacity. At the beginning of the planning horizon ($t = 0$), both firms are just breaking even: $p(k_1 + k_2, 0) = c$. Over time, as demand shrinks, pressure will build up to eliminate this capacity. At each instant a firm that is still active in the market chooses between continuing to operate at its initial capacity level and exiting costlessly and completely from the market. Entry by other firms is precluded by setup costs, and reentry is not allowed.

To identify equilibria, it is useful to be more explicit about the strategy space for the two firms. Firms' strategies are simply a probability distribution of exit times, conditional on the other firm's participation. Let $D_i(t, i + j)$ be firm i's action at time t, conditional on the presence of both firm i and firm j. $D_i(t, i + j) = 0$ denotes continuing to produce k_i at time t, and $D_i(t, i + j) = 1$ denotes the decision to exit at that time.

Given this framework, what are the Nash equilibrium exit dates for each firm? Define the dates t_1^* and t_2^* such that $p(k_i, t_i^*) \equiv c, i = 1, 2$. From the first-order conditions for profit maximization, firm i, if alone in the market, would choose to continue to operate until t_i^*. Left alone, the smaller firm would operate longer: t_2^* is greater than t_1^*.

Let z be the last date such that *both* firms are serving the market. $C_i(z, t_0)$ denotes firm i's nonpositive profits (losses), discounted back to an arbitrary date, t_0 from operating over the period $[t_0, z)$. $V_i(z, t_0)$ represents firm i's discounted profits from operations after its rival exits at z. If z is less than t_i^* and the discount rate is constant at r, we have

$$C_i(z, t_0) = \int_{t_0}^{z} [p(k_1 + k_2, t) - c] \, k_i e^{-r(t - t_0)} dt$$

and

$$V_i(z, t_0) = \int_z^{t_i} [p(k_i, t) - c] \, k_i e^{-r(t-t_0)} dt.$$

When z is greater than or equal to t_i^*, $V_i(z, t_0)$ equals zero.

If firm i outlasts firm j, then their respective profits over the time horizon are

$$P_i(z, 0) \equiv V_i(z, 0) + C_i(z, 0)$$

and

$$P_j(z, 0) \equiv V_j(z, 0) < 0.$$

The fact that only one firm can make money after time 0, combined with firm i's desire to exit by time t_i^* at the very latest, leads to only two possible Nash equilibria. They result from the following pure strategies:

$$D_i(t, 1 + 2) = \begin{cases} 0 & \forall t < t_i^*, \\ 1 & \forall t \geq t_i^*, \, i = 1, 2, \end{cases}$$

$$D_j(t, 1 + 2) = 1 \quad \forall t \geq 0, \, j \neq i.$$

In words, either firm 1 exits at time 0 and firm 2 at time t_2^*, or firm 2 exits at time 0 and firm 1 at time t_1^*. The second solution is a Nash equilibrium only if $P_2(t_1^*, 0)$ is less than or equal to 0. Otherwise, firm 2 finds it profitable to suffer losses up to time t_1^* in order to garner monopoly profits from t_1^* to t^*_2. This qualification does not apply to the first solution because the larger firm (firm 1) can only expect to lose money if it outlasts firm 2 past time t_1^*. G-N (1985) discuss in more detail why no other Nash equilibria exist for firms using either pure or mixed strategies.

The two Nash equilibria are not equally appealing. Firm 2 is the "stronger" firm in that if it is left alone, it remains profitable longer than firm 1. As a result the Nash equilibrium which has firm 2 exiting immediately is not a subgame-perfect equilibrium. If firm 2 "trembles" and somehow fails to leave immediately, firm 1's plan to stay in until t_1^* is no longer optimal.

Exhibit 4.1
Dupolist's Profits

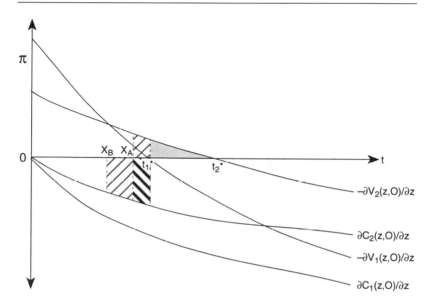

Proposition 4.1 The only perfect equilibrium is the one in which firm 1 exits immediately and firm 2 stays in until t_2^*:

$$D_1(t, 1 + 2) = 1 \qquad \forall t > 0,$$

$$D_2(t, 1 + 2) = 0 \qquad \forall t \in [0, t_2^*).$$

Proof The argument is illustrated in exhibit 4.1, where the ordinate measures instantaneous profits and the pattern of shading and overlay follows the first two steps in the proof. Define the time x_A as the first date such that firm 2 is willing to sustain losses over the period $[x_A, t_1^*)$ in order to reap monopoly profits over $[t_1^*, t_2^*)$:

$$P_2(t_1^*, x_A) = V_2(t_1^*, x_A) + C_2(t_1^*, x_A) \equiv 0.$$

Firm 1 must exit by time t_1^*: That is the date after which its operating profits will be negative, even under the optimistic assumption that it manages to monopolize the market. Therefore the most pessimistic assumption that firm 2 can make is that firm 1 remains active until time t_1^*. Even with this pessimistic belief, firm 2, upon surviving until time x_A, will then choose to remain active up to time t_2^*. Hence, if firm 2 somehow manages to stay in the market until time x_A, firm 1 can make no credible threat to prevent firm 2 from surviving and staying on until t_2^*. Since the continued operation of both firms implies losses for firm 1 over $[x_A, t_1^*)$, firm 1's optimal decision on reaching time x_A is to exit immediately:

$$D_1(t, 1 + 2) = 1 \qquad \forall t \in [x_A, \infty).$$

The argument proceeds by recursion. Firm 2 is assured of monopoly profits after time x_A. Calculate the earliest date x_B such that firm 2 is willing to sustain losses over the period (x_B, x_A) in order to garner monopoly profits over $[x_A, t_2^*)$:

$$P_2(x_A, x_B) = V_2(x_A, x_B) + C_2(x_A, x_B) \equiv 0.$$

Since firm 2 finds it optimal to stay in the market until t_2^* if it remains active at time x_B, firm 1 will find it optimal to exit immediately once it reaches time x_B. Now calculate x_C using the fact that firm 1 must exit by time x_B at the very latest. Note that x_C is a *larger* step back from x_B than x_B was from x_A; the steps are moving toward the origin at an increasing rate because with each successive step backward the total remaining monopoly profits are greater, and because the offsetting duopoly losses are occurring earlier and are therefore smaller.[1] Hence this process of backward induction continues until $P_2(x_N, 0)$ is greater than or equal to zero. When this inequality is satisfied, firm 2 can credibly commit to staying in over $[0, t_2^*)$, and firm 1 finds it optimal to exit at time 0.

---

1. Ghemawat and Nalebuff (1985) show that this dominance argument is independent of the discount rate.

Note that a similar argument eliminates all mixed-strategy Nash equilibria. Over $[x_A, t_1^*)$, firm 1 will not randomize its exit decision; firm 2 will stay in with probability 1. Thus firm 1 will choose to exit with probability 1 by the time x_A. One can use this argument to work backward to time x_B, and eventually, to time 0.   □

G-N (1985) go on to apply similar arguments to solve for the exit decisions of duopolists (and oligopolists) with different cost levels. Purely efficiency-based arguments predict that the high-cost firms will exit first. But game theory predicts that the last firm to exit is the one with the longest profitable tenure as a monopolist. If the smaller firm's unit cost (c_2) is lower than the larger firm's (c_1), the two predictions coincide. If, however, the larger firm benefits from scale or absolute cost advantages, c_1 will be less than c_2. To analyze this possibility, begin the planning horizon so that at $t = 0$ both firms are profitable:

$$p(k_1 + k_2, 0) > c_i, \qquad i = 1, 2.$$

And define t_i' to be the date after which firm i incurs losses as a duopolist:

$$p(k_1 + k_2, t_i') \equiv c_i, \qquad i = 1, 2.$$

Given the assumption that $c_1 < c_2$, it follows that $t_1' > t_2'$: As a duopolist, the smaller, less-efficient firm begins to lose money before its larger rival. Thus, even if the smaller firm would last longer as a monopolist $(t_2^* > t_1^*)$, its initial duopoly losses may induce it to withdraw first.

If firm 1 has a cost advantage so great that $t_1^* > t_2^*$, then firm 1 will outlast firm 2. The reasoning exactly parallels that used in the proof of proposition 4.1 with the roles of firm 1 and 2 reversed. One cannot make an equally unequivocal prediction about the outcome in the case in which firm 2 can last longer as a monopolist but is the first to lose money as a duopolist. Recursion shows that once firm 2 reaches t'_1, it will stay in until t^*_2. But is it worthwhile for firm 2 to shoulder losses over (t'_2, t'_1) to earn profits over $[t'_1, t^*_2)$ later on?[2] The answer will depend on the specific parameterization. But, in general, game theory suggests that if firm 2's cost disadvantage is sufficiently small, it will outlast its larger rival.

Extensions

G-N (1985) have inspired a number of theoretical extensions in which, overall, the size-hurts-survivability prediction proves reasonably robust. Some of them add a decline stage onto the immature/mature industry taxonomy proposed in Kreps and Spence's (1987) classic survey article and proceed to analyze capacity competition over all the stages of the product life cycle. Londregan (1990), for instance, allows for the possibility of reentry after entry and exit and shows that with positive reentry costs, there will continue to be a unique subgame-perfect equilibrium in the all-or-nothing exit (sub)game with complete information in which smallness is an advantage during decline and, by backward induction, also during the growth stage. Fishman (1990) also works backward from our characterization of the exit subgame during decline to show that it can influence entry conditions in the growth stage even if decline is scheduled to occur in the arbitrarily distant future.

A second set of extensions deals with the impact of probabilistic decline (uncertainty about demand) on exit patterns. Fine and

---

2. Here the assumption of no reentry is important. If reentry were allowed, firm 2 would temporarily exit at t'_2 and reenter at t'_1 to avoid all duopoly losses. Firm 2's longer tenure as a monopolist ($t^*_2 > t^*_1$) would then force firm 1 to exit permanently at t'_1.

Li (1989) argue that probabilistic decline allows the possibility of multiple Nash equilibria in the exit game. This multiplicity turns out, however, to be an artifact of the long time periods they assume between decisions. If the intervals between decisions are sufficiently short, an equilibrium in which the smaller firm outlasts its larger competitor emerges, once again, as the only subgame-perfect one. And Huang and Li (1986) study exit decisions in a model with random drifts in demand (rather than probabilistically worsening realizations). Because demand might not decline, there is no end game to work backward from in their specification. Even so, if the state space is continuous so that demand changes smoothly, a unique subgame-perfect equilibrium in which the smaller firm is never forced out by its larger rival reemerges.

A third, more recent extension by Hunsaker and Kovenock (1995) relaxes the assumption of capacity-clearing prices for the special case of linear demand. The authors claim that the smaller firm may as a result exit a declining market first even if its cost disadvantage is arbitrarily small. Their analysis rests, however, on the imposition of an additional source of lumpiness—a fixed cost that each firm must pay to remain active irrespective of its scale—which, as one might expect, helps the larger firm (on a per unit basis). If this fixed cost is dispensed with, the small firm continues to outlast its larger rival with identical efficiency levels—and by continuity, with a small cost disadvantage—even if production is subject to excess capacity.

Nalebuff and I have focused on a rather different extension in our subsequent work, for empirical reasons. In actual episodes of capacity reduction during decline, one nearly always encounters multiplant operation. Is it possible to extend the size-hurts-survivability proposition from the all-or-nothing decisions considered in G-N (1985) to separable decisions about multiple lumps of capacity (plants)? Intuition suggests that this extension should be feasible and even facile. If two firms operate significantly different numbers of otherwise identical plants, the larger firm has an incentive to be the first to shut one down because the price increase associated with a one-plant reduction in capacity will be worth more to the larger firm, given its greater inframarginal volume, than to its smaller rival.

Proving as much, however, turns out to be difficult. The difficulties are several, and they are nicely illustrated in a modeling effort by Whinston (1988). Whinston considers multiplant firms capable of adjusting capacity in lumps equal to plant size and shows that it is difficult to reach any general conclusions about the pattern of plant closures in such a framework. When each firm operates several plants of different sizes, there is no clear theoretical prediction about the order of exit, for more than one reason. A firm that withdraws a small plant might be at a strategic disadvantage later on if its remaining plants were large. Or a firm with many small plants might find this flexibility disadvantageous against a larger firm with one big plant. Thus it is hard to separate out the effect of flexibility versus size. To focus on size alone, Whinston considers a special case in which all plants are of equal size. There is still a complication: Who will move first to break a tie between the two largest firms? The size-hurts-survivability pattern reemerges when the equilibrium play is independent of the tie-breaking rule (a quasi-Markov equilibrium): Only the largest firms reduce capacity.

In G-N (1990), originally issued in working paper format in 1988, we take a different, more radical approach to incorporating flexibility (or what Tirole 1988 refers to as the ability to go on a diet) into capacity endgames in declining industries. We focus on the limiting case of zero lumpiness by allowing firms to adjust capacity continuously. This lets us sidestep the integer constraints that required Whinston to rule out the dependence of tie-breaking rules on earlier play in order to prove that size hurts survivability even in the simple case plants of equal sizes (see G-N 1990 for additional discussion). We can dispense with tie-breaking rules because with continuous capacity adjustment, unlike lumps of any size, there is no tension between two firms of equal size as to who moves first: They smoothly reduce capacity together.

The motivation behind this result is that marginal revenue is inversely proportional to firm size. In the absence of economies of scale, bigger firms therefore have a greater incentive to reduce capacity. Although the proof is technical, the intuition for it is simple. Imagine that all firms act "myopically"; namely each firm seeks to maximize only its current-period profits. This behavior leads to a sequence of period-by-period Cournot-Nash equilibria. Since marginal costs are equal, the firms with the smallest outputs have the greatest marginal revenue. This implies that the smallest firms never act first to reduce capacity.

This sequence of period-by-period equilibrium strategies turns out to be the unique subgame-perfect equilibrium. When each firm acts myopically, any deviation in output must lower current-period profits. The only reason to deviate therefore would be to raise future profits. But maintaining capacity in excess of the myopic equilibrium has no effect on future outcomes. Since demand is declining, the firm will already have some excess capacity; extra units of excess capacity do not convince competitors to further reduce their output. And a reduction of capacity below the myopic solution also fails to increase future profits. It may even decrease profits by encouraging competitors to increase their future outputs (temper their reductions).

To illustrate what is novel about these results, consider a duopoly in which firm 1 operates four machines and firm 2 operates two machines, all of which are of equal size and efficiency. If the firms must make a dichotomous choice between operating at full capacity or exiting in toto, G-N (1985) demonstrate that as demand declines, the capacity vector evolves from (4, 2) to (0, 2) to (0, 0). In contrast, if firms may withdraw machines continuously, G-N (1990) show that the only subgame-perfect equilibrium for the industry capacity vector is from (4, 2) to (X, 2) to (2, 2) to (Y, Y) to (0, 0), where X falls smoothly from 4 to 2 and Y falls smoothly from 2 to 0. In other words, the larger firm reduces capacity until its size equals that of its smaller competitor. Once parity is reached, the two firms shrink together.

4.2   Empirical Analysis

The most striking similarity between the two G-N models is that both predict that size will hurt survivability in declining industries. Both empirical predictions are also subject to caveats about efficiency differences (the effects of which could be characterized analytically in the first model but not in the second one). Thus direct tests of whether size hurts survivability are testing not just the models themselves but the auxiliary hypotheses that the effects of efficiency differences and of other omitted variables (e.g., lumpiness in the second model) are sufficiently small for purely size-based effects to have a discernible impact on the actual pattern of capacity reduction.

It is also important to recognize the differences between the two models. These can best be illustrated by separating industry decline into a shrinkage stage, in which plant closures involve no exit, and an exit stage, which starts with the first plant closure that involves exit. Shrinkage may of course continue during the exit stage, but the two models are most clearly distinguished in terms of their focus when shrinkage and exit do not overlap thus:

that is, when all competitors shrink down to one plant apiece before any exit occurs. In such a context the G-N (1985) model can be thought of as a size-hurts-survivability prediction about the exit stage—that the largest plants will be the first to leave—and the G-N (1990) model as a similar prediction about the prior shrinkage stage—that firms with more plants are more likely (than purely random processes would imply) to start shutting them down before firms with fewer plants do. These predictions will be looked at directly in the case studies on antiknock lead additives and synthetic soda ash, both of which turn out to exhibit a clear separation between the shrinkage and exit stages.[3]

A second important difference between the two models is that while the first model predicts only the order of plant closures, the second offers predictions about the concentration of capacity or output among surviving firms. More specifically, G-N (1990) predict that concentration—or more precisely, the coefficient of variation of survivors' sizes—should decrease during industry decline. This prediction exploits information about cutbacks in plant scale as well as plant closures, and it has permitted cross-sectional statistical analysis of shrinkage patterns, some of which is discussed after the two case studies.

Antiknock Lead Additives

The case of antiknock lead additives represented an early empirical effort by Michael Whinston and me to understand the dynamics of plant closure in a declining industry with multiplant as well as single-plant firms. It benefited from access to the market leader, the Ethyl Corporation, and from information

---

3. Note that this clear separation in the two cases is in the spirit of the game-theoretic prediction that size will hurt survivability.

Exhibit 4.2
Plant Closures in Lead-Based Antiknock Additives

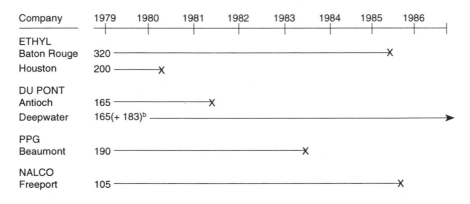

Company	1979	1980	1981	1982	1983	1984	1985	1986
ETHYL								
Baton Rouge	320 ——————————————————————X							
Houston	200 ——X							
DU PONT								
Antioch	165 ——————————X							
Deepwater	165(+ 183)[b] ——————————————————————————————→							
PPG								
Beaumont	190 ——————————————————X							
NALCO								
Freeport	105 ——————————————————————————X							

[a] Plant capacities are in millions of pounds.
[b] Du Pont closed the 183 million pound batch process plant at Deepwater, but kept the 165 million pound continuous process plant there running.

disclosed in a roughly contemporaneous antitrust suit against the competitors in this industry.

U.S. shipments of lead-based antiknock additives peaked in 1972 and then began to decline because of regulations enacted by the Environmental Protection Agency (EPA) pursuant to the 1970 amendments to the Clean Air Act. The EPA mandated reductions in motor vehicles' hydrocarbon emissions—reductions that manufacturers began to achieve by fitting new vehicles with catalytic converters that required lead-free gasoline. More directly, the EPA also required refiners to phase down the average lead content of their gasoline so as to limit atmospheric emissions.

By 1979 U.S. demand for lead-based antiknock additives had declined by more than one-third and was expected to decrease even more rapidly in the next few years. Capacity utilization had already dropped to 54 percent, although the four competitors (listed in exhibit 4.2) continued to enjoy operating margins of 30 to 40 percent on sales. At this point they began to shut plants.

By 1986 U.S. demand had declined to one-quarter of 1972 levels and only one plant, out of the original six, remained open, rendering the order of plant closures determinate. That order is summarized in exhibit 4.2 and separates neatly into a shrinkage stage that lasted through 1982 and an exit stage that began in 1983. About 32 percent of initial industry capacity was eliminated in the shrinkage stage and 53 percent in the exit stage (through 1986).

Working backward, the most striking feature of the exit stage, in light of G-N (1985), is that there was no direct or even simple relationship between plant scale and order of closure. Since Whinston and I were unable to obtain good cost estimates for all four of the plants that survived until the exit stage, it is hard to say whether the observed pattern could be reconciled with the G-N (1985) analysis of equilibration between scale, or absolute cost, economies on the one hand, and pure size-based effects, unrelated to efficiency, on the other. We did, however, use our access to Ethyl to get some perspective on its choice about which of its two plants to close first. This choice will be discussed in the next section.

The shrinkage stage fits a bit better with the size-hurts-survivability prediction from G-N (1990). Each of the two-plant operators, Ethyl and Du Pont, went down to one plant before any of the four competitors exited. The odds that this order of closure of the first two plants was the outcome of a purely random process are 4/15—less than 50: 50 but not overwhelmingly so.[4] This is one of the reasons that G-N (1990) focused on a different case example to illustrate their model.

---

4. In addition the coefficient of variation of firms' sizes declined over the shrinkage stage, from 0.65 in 1979 to 0.46 in 1983.

The second reason for looking for another case is related to evidence of tacit collusion by competitors in lead-based anti-knock additives (the basis of the antitrust suit): Through the early 1980s, product prices and operating margins increased, despite capacity utilization rates that fell as low as 35 percent, to an extent that largely offset the effect of declining volume on total operating income. A closer look at the competitors reveals pricing policies that are well-known facilitators of tacit collusion, particularly most-favored-nation clauses and advance notification of price changes. If tacit collusion is perfect, the industry's total profits will be invariant—up to efficiency differences—to the distribution of a given amount of capacity across competitors. Yet strategic models such as the ones discussed in the preceding section rely on precisely such profit differences to pin down subgame-perfect capacity-reduction strategies. By implication it is awkward to look to such models to explain capacity reduction in industries characterized by successful price collusion.

Synthetic Soda Ash

In looking for another example of the size-hurts-survivability result, G-N (1990) focused on Harrigan (1980) because of the richness of her industry descriptions and settled on synthetic soda ash because it was the only one of the seven industries described in her book that produced a commodity product and was concentrated and capacity-driven.

U.S. shipments of synthetic soda ash peaked in 1967 when almost three-quarters of the soda ash consumed was synthesized from limestone and salt. The five firms listed in exhibit 4.3 accounted for virtually all domestic synthetic soda-ash capacity. All five employed the mature and very capital-intensive Solvay

Exhibit 4.3
Plant Closures in Synthetic Soda Ash

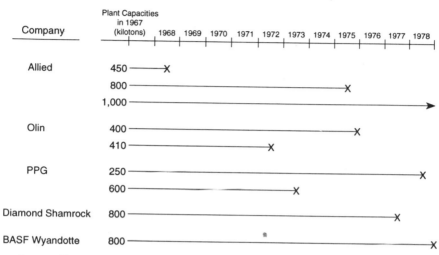

Company	Plant Capacities in 1967 (kilotons)	1968	1969	1970	1971	1972	1973	1974	1975	1976	1977	1978
Allied	450											
	800											
	1,000											
Olin	400											
	410											
PPG	250											
	600											
Diamond Shamrock	800											
BASF Wyandotte	800											

Source: Harrigan 1980

process. The remainder of the U.S. soda-ash market was supplied by natural deposits in Wyoming that began to be mined in the 1950s. Though natural soda ash cost significantly less to "produce" than synthetic soda ash, the costs of transporting it were higher because most soda-ash customers were located east of the Mississippi, closer to synthetic soda-ash capacity. Under pressure from natural soda ash, synthetic soda-ash producers operated at 89 percent of their combined capacity in 1967—a level probably just below break-even. Over the next decade the tide continued to turn against synthetic producers. Wyoming relaxed its regulations governing the mining of natural soda ash. Higher energy costs and stricter environmental regulations undercut the Solvay process as well because it was more energy- and emission-intensive. Since the Solvay capacity required substantial reinvestment to be kept operational, the stage was set for plant closures.

By 1979 the output of synthetic soda ash had fallen by two-thirds, and only one Solvay plant out of the original nine remained operational, rendering the order of plant closures determinate. The pattern of plant closures is summarized in exhibit 4.3. As in the previous case it separates neatly into a shrinkage stage, which lasted part way through 1975, and a subsequent exit stage. About 41 percent of initial industry capacity was eliminated in the shrinkage stage and another 41 percent in the exit stage (through 1979).

Once again, the exit stage does not exhibit the direct relationship between plant size and order of exit that was proposed, other things being equal, by G-N (1985). In particular, Allied's Syracuse plant, which lasted the longest, was the largest in the industry. Harrigan does report, however, that the Syracuse plant benefited from its eastern location and access to cost-effective waste disposal.

As in the preceding case the shrinkage stage is more consistent with the prediction in G-N (1990). Shrinkage involved a reduction of plants from nine to five, with the first shutdown undertaken by the only three-plant competitor, Allied, and the next three shutdowns distributed evenly among the (residual) two-plant competitors. The odds of purely random processes generating this order of closure of the first four plants are only 1/168.

Finally it should be added that the pattern of capacity shrinkage in synthetic soda ash also conforms to G-N's (1990) prediction of declining size dispersion: The coefficient of variation of the size of synthetic soda-ash competitors decreased from 0.59 at the beginning of the shrinkage stage to 0.48 by its end. It is difficult, however, to know how much significance to attach to such a change. Fortunately some cross-industry statistical analyses are available.

Cross-Industry Analyses

To ascertain whether the size-hurts-survivability effect holds up more broadly, I used Harvard University's PICA data base to analyze the determinants of changes in four-firm concentration ratios between 1967 and 1977 in 294 four-digit U.S. manufacturing industries (Ghemawat 1985). Since it is difficult to control for intraindustry differences in efficiency based on publicly available data, my basic specification did not attempt to do so. To the extent that one believes that size is positively related to efficiency, this omission is likely to bias the results toward the null hypothesis that size-related effects do not matter.

I found that even in the absence of controls for cost differences, a dummy variable indicating declines in real industry output over the sampled period was positively associated, at the 5 to 10 percent level of statistical significance, with decreases in industry concentration. When the rate of decline was introduced as a continuous independent variable, I again found a significant correlation: The higher the rate of decline, the greater was the observed rate of decrease of concentration.

Lieberman (1990) offered more precise but narrower-gauge cross-industry tests of the predictions implied by the theoretical models of exit and shrinkage. He focused on a sample of thirty chemical products, each of which experienced chronic declines in output lasting five years or longer, and found statistically significant evidence of convergence in the sizes of survivor firms due to more rapid divestment by the largest producers in steeply declining industries.[5] Specifically, of the 17 products in

---

5. Lieberman (1990) discusses in some detail why a focus on changes in the coefficient of variation of the sizes of survivors offers the most powerful test of the Ghemawat and Nalebuff (1990) model.

Lieberman's sample that experienced declines in capacity of 35 percent or more, 13 exhibited convergence in the sizes of the survivors. In addition Lieberman found that after controlling for plant size, the probability of plant closure increased with firms' capacity shares, consistent with the G-N (1990) model.

Meta-analysis

Looking across the cross-industry analysis and the two case studies, it appears that as far as size-hurts-survivability predictions are concerned, G-N (1990) holds up rather better than G-N (1985): During drastic industry decline the predicted share-related effects show up in shrinkage patterns but not in exit patterns. With the benefit of hindsight, the exit-related predictions can be expected to prove weaker, empirically, for several reasons. First of all, as Hunsaker and Kovenock (1995) demonstrate in their extension of G-N (1985), allowing for excess capacity (prices that do not clear all available capacity) reduces the effect of size-related disadvantages and therefore the size of the cost advantage required by large firms to force smaller rivals to exit first. This criticism of G-N (1985) does not extend to the G-N (1990) model: If continuous capacity reduction is possible, it never pays to hold excess capacity.

Second, exit activity in many industries appears to be dominated by recent entrants who appear to have failed to achieve sustainable efficiency levels and are therefore subject to shakeout effects of the sort modeled by Jovanovic (1982). The G-N models, in contrast, focus on stakeout by incumbents who are initially viable and know each other well. This divergence dilutes the applicability of G-N (1985), which focuses on exit. G-N (1990), in contrast, focuses on shrinkage and is therefore less affected by "noise entrants" who enter at small scales but quickly exit if they prove unsustainably inefficient—particularly if empirical analysis focuses on a relatively limited number of leading competitors in defining concentration levels (e.g., Ghemawat 1985). Note the theoretical opportunity to meld models of stakeout with those of shakeout.

Third, it is plausible to suppose that because of its discreteness, exit is a more difficult decision organizationally than is shrinkage. As a result the timing of exit may be more heavily influenced by factors other than relative size and efficiency.[6]

Finally, while there is no systematic evidence on this score, managers do not seem to use elaborate chains of backward induction (up-to-date game theory) when they find themselves in wars of attrition of the sort stipulated. Intuition may not necessarily lead them to adopt strategies that make game-theoretic sense but are counterintuitive. The logic of exit in G-N (1985) turns out to be harder to explain to managers than the logic of shrinkage in G-N (1990), since in the latter case the subgame-perfect Nash equilibrium coincides with the myopic Cournot-Nash equilibrium. Perhaps predictions about shrinkage are more likely to be borne out than predictions about exit for this reason as well.

4.3 Reflections

The theoretical and empirical analysis in this chapter makes a specific contribution to strategic management. It also offers some broader insights into how the contributions of game theory to strategic management might further be enhanced.

---

6. Examples of organizational influences on capacity reduction decisions are discussed in the next section of this chapter.

Implications for Strategic Management

What has analysis that is attuned to game-theoretic considerations added to preexisting knowledge in strategic management
about capacity reduction in (drastically) declining industries?
Harrigan's (1980) insightful, but pregame-theoretic, book on declining industries supplies a useful benchmark. Several specific
differences stand out.

First, game-theoretic analysis alters the set of variables
deemed to affect behavior in endgames. It indicates that size is
an important exogenous variable that creates incentives to be
statesmanlike in declining industries; Harrigan does not. It also
hints at the endogeneity of some of the variables that Harrigan
cites as being exogenous. Consider the pattern of price changes
during industry decline. The two cases described varied significantly in this regard: Prices stayed high in antiknock lead additives but quickly dropped most of the way down to marginal
costs in synthetic soda ash. The ability of the competitors in antiknock lead additives to collude tacitly on prices would appear
to have been helped by greater concentration, more modular
plants, and less price-sensitive customers in that industry.

Second, the case of Ethyl, the one-time market leader in lead-
based antiknock additives, also suggests that the firm-specific
barriers to exit on which Harrigan focused can be offset by gate-
ways to exit: that firm history can promote as well as retard exit.
Ethyl had high barriers to exit in all the senses specified by Harrigan: Lead-based antiknock additives accounted for more than
a quarter of Ethyl's sales in 1978; the company and industry were
eponymous; Ethyl was locked into long-term customer relationships, as evinced by the fact that it still resells lead-based antiknock additives in the U.S. market; and it was vertically
integrated into sodium production. But despite its potential to

be the industry wildcard, Ethyl proved statesmanlike during industry decline. This profitable outcome may have had something to do with the fact that exit from a dominant business had served the family that controlled Ethyl, the Gottwalds, quite well in the past. They had previously run a small paper company and had bought Ethyl in an early leveraged buyout in 1962 because the ballpoint pen had begun to depress the demand for their primary product at that time, blotting paper.

Third, looking at the order in which Ethyl closed its plants at Houston and Baton Rouge does reinforce the policy concern that motivated game-theoretic analysis of capacity reduction in the first place: that efficient plants may sometimes be closed before inefficient ones. Houston's capacity was 200 million pounds—arguably closer to long-run requirements than Baton Rouge's 320 million pounds. Houston also had lower variable production costs and transportation costs (for the export market) and probably afforded proportionately lower fixed-cost savings from shutdown because the site would still have to be kept running for other product lines. Nevertheless, Houston, not Baton Rouge, was the first lead-additive plant Ethyl shut down. This choice appears to have been related to the way Ethyl was organized. Its Chemicals group shared the Houston site with its Plastics group but was the sole operator of the site at Baton Rouge and seemed to have been particularly eager to preserve the latter for that reason.

For even clearer evidence of organizational effects on capacity reduction decisions, consider Sull's (1996) analysis of the closure of bias tire plants in the United States in response to the shift from bias to radial architecture. Sull found a weak positive link between the probability of closure of a particular plant and the market share of the firm that owned it. In addition unpublished data which he was kind enough to share with me indicate that the coefficient of variation of the capacities of firms that continued on in bias tires declined marginally between 1973 and 1987 (the end points of his data set). However, these relationships paled into insignificance compared to organizational factors. In particular, new CEOs from "outside" proved much more likely to disinvest than did "insider" CEOs.

To summarize this subsection, the existing game-theoretic literature on exit/shrinkage in drastically declining industries is important to strategic management but would benefit from being supplemented with considerations of internal organization. That last conclusion is reinforced by the cases studied in the following chapters.

Implications for Game Theorists

What else might researchers attuned to game theory do in order to maximize their impact on strategic management? The most obvious recommendation based on the literature reviewed in this chapter concerns the extent to which game-theoretically motivated research about industry decline has focused on developing theories as opposed to testing them. Occupational specialization by microeconomically minded researchers, into theorists and empiricists, has helped a bit with testing, but theoretical analyses continue to pile up faster than empirical analyses can sort through the theoretical possibilities. This suggests that economists cannot be counted on to allocate their talents across theoretical and empirical analysis in a way that is efficient from the more applied perspective of strategic management. Given the general dearth of counterintuitive but testable game-theoretic predictions, researchers in strategic management confronted with such a prediction (e.g., that size hurts survivability during drastic industry decline) might be expected to allot more of their attention to testing than to additional theorizing (much of which, in IO, has been negative in the sense of trying to demonstrate that size need not hurt survivability).

An empirical perspective reinforces a recommendation proffered in the preceding chapter: Incomplete information is a Pandora's box that should be opened only when strictly necessary. Compare, in this regard, G-N (1985) with another early, very different contribution to the theory of exit, Fudenberg and Tirole (1986a). The latter has, as noted above, inspired rather less in the way of follow-on research, a fact that may be connected to its focus on informational asymmetries. Fudenberg and Tirole showed that asymmetric expectations about each other's costs can permit any order of exit by duopolists with different levels of efficiency. The averral that anything can happen is a staple of game-theoretic models with incomplete information. It is also a standard empirical stumbling block given the difficulties of observing competitors' expectations.

A third area of recommendations concerns the testing rather than the modeling of game-theoretic effects. There is, as noted in the preceding chapters, a tendency among practitioners of the new empirical IO to treat regression analyses as the touchstone of meaningful empirical tests. In the context of this chapter, the proponents of such a view might point to the fact that Michael Whinston and I, relying on the same base of empirical information but without the benefit of regression analysis, reached divergent conclusions about whether the capacity-reduction patterns observed in lead-based antiknock additives were consistent with the size-hurts-survivability hypothesis.

I have already explained what I regard as the principal reason for this divergence of opinion: the difference between the G-N (1985) model, which seems to be controverted, and the G-N (1990) model, which seems to be (weakly) supported. I have also argued that because of successful tacit collusion on prices in lead-based antiknock additives, this industry may not, with the benefit of hindsight, have been the most appropriate arena for testing the game-theoretic models of interest. But these may strike the skeptical reader as immunizing stratagems. So let me address the underlying inferential issue head-on: If researchers unconstrained by the rigors of regression analysis are too prone to claim cases as their own, does that clinch the case for empirical analyses based on regressions?

I think that the answer to this question is negative because regression analyses of cases are often prone to subjectivity as well. To be concrete, let me cite two specific examples in this regard. The elaborate regression analysis of the titanium dioxide industry cited in the preceding chapter is one: Hall (1985) and Hall (1990) managed to reach divergent conclusions about whether Du Pont had actually engaged in preemptive capacity expansion. In the context of this chapter, a second example is provided by Deily, whose analysis of shrinkage/exit by integrated steelmakers in the United States focused on reinvestment levels rather than plant closure decisions. Deily (1985, p. 144) stated that "In general, the larger firms were investing less than the smaller firms . . . [giving] support to the Ghemawat [and Nalebuff] theory." Yet Deily (1988, p. 599) concluded on the basis of the same data, that "The results . . . do not support theories [Ghemawat and Nalebuff's] that predict a simple relationship between firm exit decisions and firm size."

These examples suggest that in a world of stylized theoretical models and imperfect data, researchers retain considerable discretion in the results that they report—even if they do run regressions. Given such discretion, it is absolutely critical that researchers document the data they have used and describe the ways, qualitative or quantitative, in which they have derived conclusions from those data. Subject to these caveats, the empirical analysis in this (and other) chapter(s) suggests that methodological eclecticism, rather than absolutism, is to be encouraged.

4.4 Summary

This chapter, like the two previous ones but arguably to an even greater extent, illustrates the power of game-theoretic thinking. The size-hurts-survivability hypothesis is counterintuitive but seems to pack some power in explaining capacity-reduction patterns in declining industries, at least within the chemical processing sector.

The empirical analyses reported on in this chapter also have some broader methodological implications—even for those who seek significance in solely statistical terms. In the cases of lead-based antiknock additives and synthetic soda ash, order statistics were used to test models of shrinkage and exit, reminding us that statistical analysis does not always require the running of regressions. And Lieberman's work, in particular, derived its power from its analysis of multiple chemical processing industries rather than econometric esoterica. What it suggests is that multi-industry analyses, often focused on a particularly choice sector, may be as important in helping us probe game-theoretic models statistically as the increasingly involved regression analyses of competitive processes in individual industries that have become fashionable in the new empirical IO.

Finally this chapter hints at the value, from the perspective of strategic management, of conjoining game-theoretic analyses of external (competitive) interactions with considerations of internal organization. This theme is developed further in the three chapters that follow.

5   Product Innovation in the Private Branch Exchange Industry

The first three case studies in this book were relatively simple, in the sense that they focused on models of competition with fixed product characteristics and production technologies: Prices and capacities were allowed to vary, but the sets of possible products and production technologies were not. The two case studies that follow, in this chapter and the next, permit such variation: They focus in turn on product and process innovation.

The case of product innovation discussed in this chapter is drawn from the U.S. private branch exchange (PBX) industry. After being opened up to competition in the late 1960s, it attracted a steady stream of entrants, some of whom carved out profitable niches on the basis of innovative products. Incumbents, particularly the one-time monopolist, AT&T, appeared to trail technologically. Why weren't PBX incumbents, particularly AT&T, able to leverage their multiple marketing advantages into technological leadership, or at least parity?

Further investigation seemed in order because of the light that it might shed on "incumbent failure," a phenomenon that has been discussed for decades and is supposed to be particularly common, according to a recent review of the literature, in the context of product innovations (Utterback 1994, p. 205). I therefore decided to examine in some detail the introduction in the early 1980s, of an economically significant innovation—described at the time as the first voice-and-data PBX—by an entrant, InteCom. Accordingly, in 1985 I conducted a series of interviews with the top management of InteCom as well as with managers at AT&T and two other leading PBX manufacturers.[1] This chapter begins by summarizing what I learned about the PBX industry in general, and InteCom's innovation in particular. Then, as background, it introduces some of the theoretical literature on product innovation. The chapter goes on to present a model that conforms more closely to the circumstances of the voice-and-data PBX innovation. The aim is to provide additional perspective on the "incumbent failure" doctrine.

5.1 Case Background

PBXs are switches located on customer premises that concentrate phone calls to central exchanges. Exhibit 5.1 summarizes their evolution through the early 1980s. The first automated switch of this sort was patented in 1891 by Almon Strowger, a Kansas City undertaker, who is alleged to have been convinced that when customers tried to reach him, an operator rerouted their calls to her (the operator's) husband's funeral parlor. Strowger's first-generation electromechanical design, which established a dedicated path through the switching matrix for the duration of a call, continued to be refined but dominated the PBX market until

---

1. I also relied on earlier fieldwork at InteCom by Elon Kohlberg and Jean-Francois Mertens and on industry studies from half a dozen different commercial sources. Some of these are cited in a teaching case on InteCom (Ghemawat 1985), which offers a more detailed description of the PBX industry through the early 1980s as well as the voice-and-data innovation.

Exhibit 5.1
Generations of PBX Technology

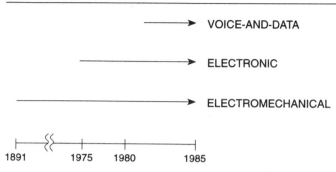

the 1970s, when second-generation electronic PBXs began to be introduced.

All PBXs classified as second-generation products used software control and solid-state time-division switching. But their ability to transmit data as well as voice continued to be constrained, in practice, by the need to transmit data in digital form, not just through the switch but also along the connecting wires to and from the switch, and by the need to add (expensive) capacity in the switching matrix, since data calls tended to last longer than voice calls. For small numbers of data lines, second-generation PBXs were generally adequate (with add-ons such as modems), but they failed to fulfill the requirements of some large buyers. Third-generation PBXs which made the transmission of voice and data totally transparent—namely free of special cards or connections—did not become available until the early 1980s.

As of 1980, the U.S. PBX industry continued to be dominated by AT&T, which had monopolized the market until it began to be deregulated in 1968. AT&T had managed to hold on to a 58 percent share of the industry's installed base and a 46 percent share of line shipments. Its two largest competitors, Rolm and Northern Telecom, had been quicker to move into electronic

Exhibit 5.2
PBX Manufacturing Costs in the Early 1980s

Company	Material costs	Labor costs	Plant/overhead costs	Overall
Fujitsu	2	2	2	2
GTE	5	4	5	5
Mitel	2	1	1	1
NEC	2	2	3	2
Northern Telecom	4	3	2	3
Rolm	5	5	2	4
Western Electric	4	4	4	4

Source: Northern Business Information, Inc., 1983
Cost ranking: 1 = low, 5 = high.

technology, and accounted for 10 and 8 percent, respectively, of total line shipments by 1980.

AT&T's ability to sustain its dominance was not due to manufacturing efficiencies: The costs of its manufacturing arm, Western Electric, were generally reckoned to be the highest in the PBX industry (see exhibit 5.2). Its product development costs were considered high as well. Furthermore Western Electric's second-generation product, Dimension, fell short of the eventual dominant design because it transmitted a finite duration pulse of the original analog (voice) signal instead of totally digitizing all signals. Instead, switching costs appear to have been the primary driver of AT&T's dominance: It was reported to have higher "win rates" for new system sales at sites that already had AT&T electromechanical installations.

A wide variety of switching costs can be discerned in AT&T's sustained dominance of customer-premise switching equipment, although it is difficult to calibrate their impact with much precision. Perhaps the most important switching cost was the risk aversion of PBX purchasers (typically voice communications managers) because of the high organizational and personal costs of a PBX failure. AT&T's reputation, familiarity with its salespeople, and its unique leasing policies mitigated the perceived risk of purchasing a dud. According to an industry cliché, "Nobody ever got fired for picking AT&T."

AT&T also controlled various complementary assets which further increased the costs to competitors of getting its customers to switch to them. First, AT&T's comprehensive customer records gave it an advantage at targeting replacement demand. Second, it owned the wiring in its PBX installations and refused to sell it to competitors. As a result a competitor who won a client away from AT&T had to rewire the premises at a cost that could account for up to 40 percent of the total price to the end-user. Finally AT&T also owned the largest distribution channel in the PBX industry, the Bell Operating Companies, and through them the largest service force, 60,000 people strong. Imitation of AT&T's service arrangements would have been costly and time-consuming for competitors; substitution (by relying on third parties) would have stoked buyers' worries that the product might not be serviced properly and therefore made sense only for small, commodity PBXs that did not require much after-sales service.

AT&T's dominance of the market for PBXs notwithstanding, by the late 1970s a few leading-edge buyers were casting around for voice-and-data PBXs that would transmit data more effectively than existing products. While this market segment was relatively small, reservation prices within it were relatively high. Venture capitalists obviously thought rents could be earned from it because they advanced several new ventures the funds required to develop voice-and-data PBXs.

Most of the rents that attracted venture capitalists appeared to hinge on a monopoly of the voice-and-data market. Through the mid-1980s, only one or two dozen large voice-and-data systems would be sold each year, at several million dollars apiece. Given past purchasing policies, each buyer would probably set stringent specifications and solicit bids from all qualified vendors. Price would be very important in the multiattribute evaluation because of the magnitude of the projected expenditure and because almost all potential buyers treated their telecommunications departments as cost centers rather than profit centers. Unless successful innovators entered voice-and-data with different competitive positions, most of the potential rents could be wiped out by competition over a few large, well-publicized purchases.

The carryover of AT&T's advantages at marketing old generations of PBXs to the voice-and-data innovation appeared to be limited, although once again it is difficult to be precise in this matter. The leading-edge buyers who were interested tended to be particularly well informed (and particularly sophisticated at using the information available to them) in making PBX purchases.[2] Given the visibility of the few potential voice-and-data buyers, AT&T's customer records did not help it much either. Potential voice-and-data buyers also had burgeoning transmission needs; inadequate documentation typically precluded expansion of their embedded AT&T wiring, forcing them to re-

2. I do not mean to imply that AT&T (or Rolm or Northern Telecom) would not have enjoyed *any* reputational advantages over entrants in marketing large voice-and-data PBXs: Buyers still needed some assurance that the vendor they selected would survive to support and service its products. But such reputational advantages should not be overstressed since would-be entrants into voice-and-data could and, in some cases, did form alliances with large, established firms from outside the PBX industry. For instance, InteCom, which pioneered the voice-and-data PBX innovation, teamed up with Exxon, which was then making a major push into office automation, to sell such PBXs.

wire regardless of the voice-and-data vendor they selected. Finally, the salespeople in AT&T's Bell Operating Companies were not versed in data transmission and were therefore unlikely to prove effective at selling voice-and-data PBXs.[3]

Competition to introduce the first voice-and-data PBX was concentrated instead among roughly a dozen entrants or fringe players (incumbents with less than 1 percent apiece of the large PBX segment). InteCom was the first to succeed. It was founded in 1978, sold its first voice-and-data PBX in 1981, and went public in late 1982. InteCom's total market capitalization at the end of 1982 exceeded $400 million, transforming its founders' initial investment of $1.5 million into stock holdings worth over $100 million. Clearly there were rewards for winning the race to innovate.

The race to develop the first voice-and-data PBX was largely a race in software development. With electronic PBXs—unlike electromechanical ones—high reliability could be achieved by using off-the-shelf components and building in redundancy. As a result software development had come to account for the largest fraction of R&D expenditures, which in the aggregate ranged from 5 to 15 percent of major competitors' revenues.

Several aspects of the process of developing software for PBXs are worth remarking because of their implications for the model developed later in this chapter. First, it did not seem cost effective to compress the development process past a certain point by simply increasing the number of programmers working on software. A detailed statistical analysis by Jones (1996) of nearly fifty major PBX development projects in the 1970s and 1980s

---

3. An attempt by the successful voice-and-data innovator, InteCom, to use the Bell Operating Companies as its second distribution channel after divestiture decoupled them from AT&T, provides confirmation. That attempt is widely judged to have failed.

confirms that large development teams led to significantly higher development costs, without significantly shortening development times. This outcome may reflect the increased complexity of coordination wrought by large development teams (although one cannot discount the hypothesis that large development teams simply increased the financial losses racked up by product development efforts that were preordained to fail for technical reasons). At any rate, the successful voice-and-data innovator, InteCom, explicitly chose to work with a two-layer development team rather than the three-layer teams favored by many of its competitors (e.g., CXC and Ztel) for coordination-related reasons.

Second, even after controlling for differences in the size of development teams, the productivity of competitors' product development expenditures seemed to vary significantly. Once again Jones's cross-project analysis supplies the best evidence in this regard: It reveals significant firm-specific differences in product development productivity after controlling for team size, product size and product features. (Exhibit 5.3 provides a scatterplot along one of these dimensions.) In particular, Jones's analysis suggests that going firms were less efficient at R&D than *de novo* entrants. For example, AT&T and IBM each spent over $100 million on their first voice-and-data PBX projects but failed. In contrast, InteCom succeeded at introducing its voice-and-data innovation, the IBX, after spending less than one-tenth as much (albeit on a less ambitious design).

Third, the process of innovation was marked by substantial spillovers of R&D across firms' boundaries. Competitors raided one another's pools of engineers to improve their information about the prospects for a particular development path. While such spillover effects tend to be difficult to identify through statistical studies like Jones's, the case of InteCom illustrates their

Exhibit 5.3
Product Development Projects in the PBX Industry

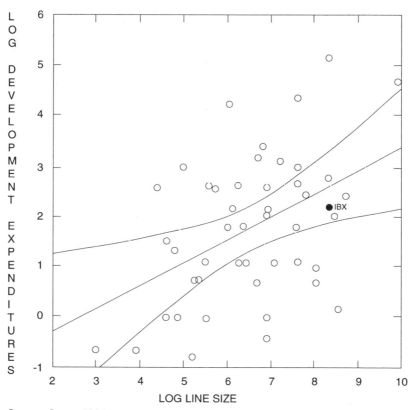

Source: Jones 1996

potential importance. InteCom's four founders had all previously worked on PBX development at another small manufacturer, Dan-Ray.[4] They quickly hired six of the thirty call-processing experts in the world whom they regarded as having relevant

4. I should add that InteCom was sued after its success in the marketplace by Northern Telecom, which had since acquired Dan-Ray. But the legal sanctions on poaching proved quite ineffective in this case. InteCom settled by paying Northern Telecom half a million dollars, or about 0.1 percent of its market value after its initial public offering in 1982.

expertise to form the core of InteCom's development team. Of course, after that team succeeded, InteCom had to deal with the downside of spillovers. According to its CEO, Mike Bowen, anybody who wanted to copy InteCom's voice-and-data design could have done so within twelve to eighteen months through similar tactics—despite InteCom's use of a low-level assembly language for its software that complicated imitation as well as upgrades.

To summarize, the voice-and-data innovation seemed to be subject to significant time incompressibilities, differences in innovative efficiency, and spillovers. These attributes seem to have had a significant impact on the development effort of the successful innovator, InteCom. The question of theoretical interest is whether these attributes of the innovation process should be expected to induce lags in innovation by incumbents.

5.2   Theoretical Background

Game-theoretic analyses of product innovations offer mixed predictions about whether incumbents should lag at innovation, for reasons that are most easily articulated in the canonical context of an incumbent monopolist facing threats of entry by innovators. Will the monopolist's incentives to innovate be greater or less than a potential entrant's? Because of two opposed effects this question cannot be answered without imposing more structure on the problem. One of those effects, identified before microeconomics embraced game theory, concerns cannibalization. The monopolist cannibalizes its own sales when it innovates, whereas a potential entrant faces the rosier prospect of going from zero sales and profits to a position that may yield profitable sales. So there is a sense in which potential innovations must cross a higher (expected) profit threshold to appeal to an incumbent monopolist than to appeal to potential entrants. The cannibalization effect was originally remarked by Arrow (1962) in the context of process innovations, which will be discussed in the next chapter. Moorthy (1984) supplied a nice illustration in the context of product innovations by showing that a monopolist serving multiple segments might maximize its profits by offering fewer products than segments—even if the fixed cost of an additional product offering were zero—out of fear of cannibalizing itself.

The other effect, grounded in interdependent (game-theoretic) as opposed to independent reasoning, turns on the fact that industry (operating) profits are likely to be greater under a monopolistic (or concentrated) structure than under a duopolistic (or fragmented) structure because increases in the number of product market competitors typically increase consumer surplus at the expense of producer surplus. Anticipated industry profit levels can affect innovative behavior because the incumbent loses more operating profits by going from a monopolistic position to a duopolistic one than the entrant can gain from establishing a foothold in the market. An incumbent may therefore have more of an incentive to innovate than entrants if it can thereby exclude them from the market. In other words, there may be a strategic incentive to innovate in order to affect market structure.

Which of the two effects will dominate the other depends on the specifics of the situation. Clear-cut results have been derived in the game-theoretic literature only by effectively assuming one of the two effects away. At one extreme, Reinganum (1983) assumed that the entrant becomes a monopolist if it manages to innovate first. Since there is no dissipation of product-market profits under this assumption, the cannibalization effect dominates, leading to the prediction that potential entrants have more of an incentive to innovate than the incumbent monopolist. At the other extreme, Gilbert and Newbery (1982) assumed that innovation can cost-effectively be accelerated by spending more money on it. Since this leads to very fast innovation, the monopolist is more concerned about entry threats than about the date at which it cannibalizes itself. By implication the incumbent monopolist has a greater incentive to innovate as long as it can exclude would-be competitors by doing so, since that maximizes industry profits and therefore its own.

Neither of these two extreme characterizations seems to apply to PBX innovations in general, or to the voice-and-data PBX in particular. There is a mismatch with Reinganum's model because of the overlap between successive generations of technology, and with Gilbert and Newbery's model because of time incompressibilities and the infeasibility of patent-based preemption. In addition the particulars of the voice-and-data innovation suggest that what is required is more than a model intermediate to the two. A more appropriate model would allow for spillovers of innovative success and differences in innovative efficiency. It would also distinguish between the technological development of an innovation and its commercial introduction (for cannibalization effects may, it turns out, induce incumbents to "warehouse" innovations they have already developed). Since none of the off-the-shelf models of which I am aware has all the desired characteristics, a customized model is in order.

5.3 Theoretical Analysis

The theoretical model presented and analyzed in this section concerns an incumbent monopolist facing the threat of entry. The monopolist initially serves the entire market with just an old ("first-generation") product. In the context of the voice-and-data PBX innovation, the first generation can be interpreted as the voice-only technology. Each of the n customers in the market purchases a quantity of x of the first-generation product if at least one variety is priced below its (common) reservation value u, and none otherwise. Normalize nx to unity.

Assume provisionally that the incumbent monopolist, firm A, faces just one potential entrant, firm B. This entrant can produce a first-generation product for the same marginal cost c_1, as the incumbent but is at a competitive disadvantage because firm A's past customers face switching costs of s if they shift their purchases to firm B. Under the assumption that $c_1 < u < c_1 + s$, entry into the first-generation product is blockaded in the sense originally specified by Bain (1956): The incumbent covers the entire (first-generation) market and can price without having to worry about competitive threats.

The new product technology is superimposed on these initial conditions. Either firm A or firm B can, if it succeeds at innovation, produce a second-generation product at the marginal cost of c_2 ($>c_1$). On the demand side any substitution between the two generations is one to one in quantities. But product design differs so drastically across the two generations that customers regard second-generation products as identical irrespective of their purchasing histories. In other words, switching costs are generation-specific: Because of the radical character of innovation, the durable specific complements that customers acquired in using firm A's first-generation products cannot be applied to either A's or B's second-generation products. This assumption is meant to reflect the sense that the voice-and-data innovation largely severed the link between customers' voice-only purchasing histories and their choice among voice-and-data products.

I also assume that customers attach varying values to the new generation over the old: The voice-and-data innovation, for instance, mattered more to some customers than to others. More specifically, I assume that a fraction $h(p_2 - p_1)$ of all customers prefers a second-generation product priced at p_2 by either firm A or B to a first generation product priced at p_1 by firm A. Some boundary and regularity conditions are imposed on h:

$$h(c_2 - c_1) = \theta > 0; h(p) = 0 \ \forall \ p \geq \bar{p}; h' < 0; h'' < 0.$$

Competition to supply the second-generation product unfolds in three stages. In the first "innovative" stage, firms decide whether to attempt innovation. In the second or "entry" stage, attempts at innovation and their success are common knowledge; each successful innovator chooses between entering the second-generation market and staying out of it. In the third or "pricing" stage, entry decisions are common knowledge; firms set prices for each generation they have entered and meet the demand that results.

This game, like many with multiple moves, has several Nash equilibria. Once again, Selten's (1975) criterion of perfection will be used to select among them. Hence it makes sense to work backward in time, starting with the productive phase. Price competition, an important attribute of competition in voice-and-data PBXs, simplifies the payoffs in the third and last phase. If both firms stay out of the second generation (O, O), firm A continues to monopolize the first generation at a price of u. If only firm A has entered the second generation (E, O), it does even better, while firm B continues to post zero sales. If only firm B has entered the second generation (O, E), it makes positive profits on positive sales; firm A does worse in that subcase than under (E, O) but better than under the final subcase, in which both firms enter the second generation (E, E) and unbridled competition drives second-generation prices down to c_2.

The difference between the (O, E) and (E, E) subcases is critical to pinning down what happens in the earlier stages of this game. If both firms have succeeded at innovation in stage 1 (i.e., actually face a decision in stage 2 about whether to enter the second-generation market), firm B's strategy of entering no matter what carries the day. Given firm B's (weakly) dominant strategy, firm A must compare its payoffs from (O, E), in which it stays out of the second generation and $p_2 > c_2$, and from (E, E), in which firm A enters and $p_2 = c_2$. Firm A makes more money (from the first generation, which is cannibalized less) under (O, E). Therefore firm B will enter the second generation if it has innovated, and firm A will elect to stay out, namely shelve its innovation.

Working back to the innovative phase, consider the (truncated) game tree in exhibit 5.4. Uncertainty has been introduced by allotting moves to nature (denoted by C for chance) as well as to the two firms. Firms A and B simultaneously decide whether to incur fixed costs F_A and F_B respectively—in an attempt to innovate (I), or to pay nothing and refrain from innovation (N).[5] Firm A succeeds at attempts to innovate with probability y. Firm B succeeds with probability z_1 if firm A chooses I and succeeds; with probability z_2 if firm A chooses I and fails; and with probability z_3 if firm A chooses N.

The payoff vectors at the ends of the tree in exhibit 5.4 can be derived from the earlier analysis of the subsequent entry and pricing stages. If firm B innovates successfully, it monopolizes the second generation, irrespective of whether firm A also succeeds at innovation (nodes O_1, O_4, O_7). If firm B has not innovated, its profits are zero while firm A's are positive and depend

---

5. The results derived in this section continue to hold if firm A moves first as long as the exit costs it would incur in withdrawing from the second generation *after* entering it are sufficiently small. In other words, the incumbent's vulnerability is *not* predicated on its inability to precommit to innovation. Rather it is based on the fact that given the payoff structure, the incumbent cannot credibly precommit to marketing the second-generation product: If the entrant also succeeds at innovation, the incumbent's best response is to withdraw from that segment. See Judd (1985) for an elaboration of this logic.

Exhibit 5.4
Competition in the Innovative Stage

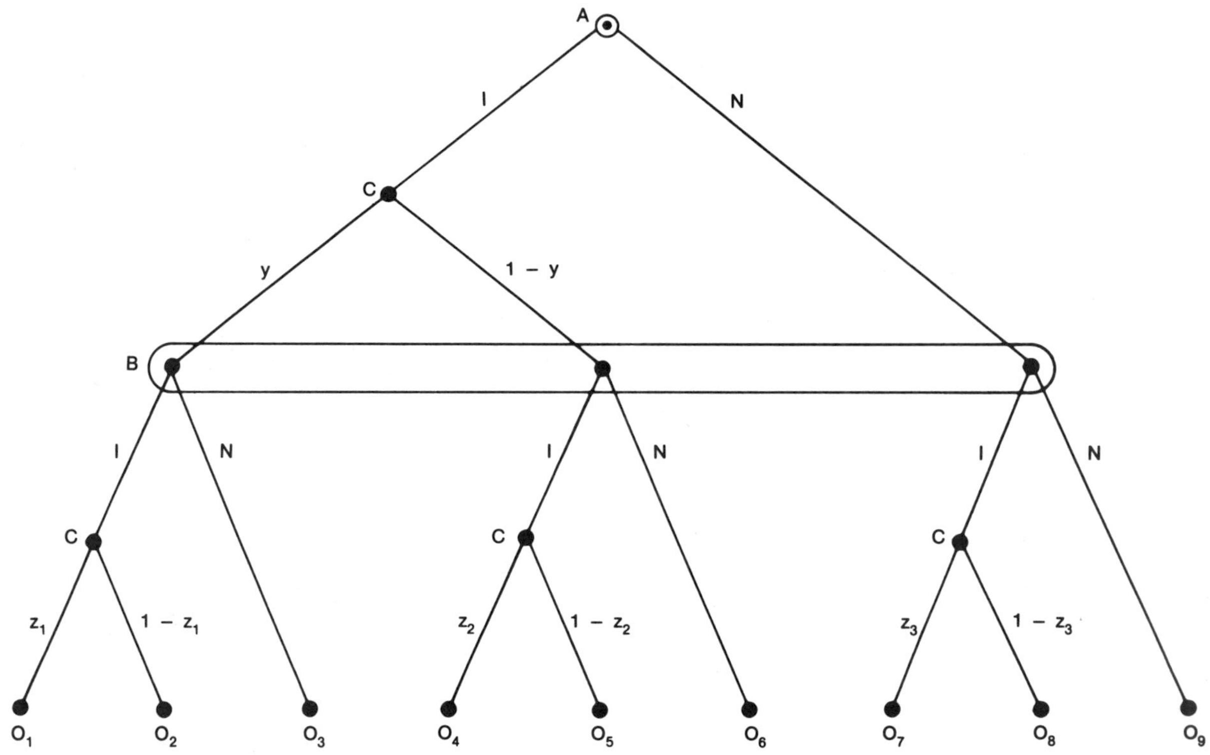

on whether it has successfully innovated (nodes O_2, O_3) or not (nodes O_5, O_6, O_8, O_9).

To advance the analysis, I provisionally assume that given the probabilities of success at innovation, either firm would incur the costs of innovation if success assured it a monopoly of the second-generation:

$$\Pi_A(E, O) - \Pi_A(O, O) > \frac{F_A}{y},$$

$$\Pi_B(O, E) > \frac{F_B}{\min(z_1, z_2, z_3)},$$

where $\Pi_i(\cdot, *)$ denotes firm i's payoff in the pricing stage given the outcome $(\cdot, *)$ in the innovative stage. In words, innovation is "viable" for both firms A and B.

Proposition 5.1 If the two firms' probabilities of succeeding at innovation do not depend on each other and are identical ($y = z_1 = z_2 = z_3$), firm B is more likely to introduce the second-generation product.

Proof Given the viability condition, firm B always attempts innovation and successfully enters the second generation product with probability y. In contrast, firm A sometimes does not attempt innovation; even when it does, its probability of entering the second generation is only $y(1 - y)$, for it must succeed at innovation and B must fail. Firm B is therefore more likely to introduce the second-generation product than is firm A: Fears of cannibalization stack the odds against introduction by the incumbent. Furthermore the result is somewhat robust to the differences in innovative efficiency (which, according to Jones's 1996 analysis, were evident in the PBX industry). If firm A is less efficient than firm B ($F_A/y > F_B/\min(z_1, z_2, z_3)$), that further tips the odds against attempts at innovation by firm A, the incumbent.

Less obviously, even if the entrant, firm B, is less efficient, it continues to be more likely to introduce the second-generation product than firm A provided that the efficiency differences are sufficiently small. So there *was* some reason to expect the voice-and-data innovation to be developed by an entrant rather than an incumbent.   □

Next consider what happens when innovation is subject to spillover effects, as it seemed to have been in the PBX industry:

Proposition 5.2 Sufficiently high interim spillovers of success at innovation further reduce the likelihood that firm A will attempt to innovate.

Proof Positive correlation of firms' probabilities of success implies that in the game being analyzed, $z_1 \geq z_2 \geq z_3$, with at least one of the two inequalities holding strictly. The fact that firm B is certain to attempt innovation simplifies the analysis, which can be conducted in terms of a nonnegative spillover parameter, δ such that $z_1 \equiv z + \delta \leq 1$, $z_2 \equiv z$, and $y \equiv y + \delta \leq 1$. Now firm A's expected profit from *not* attempting innovation, $E_A(N)$, is invariant to δ. Its expected profit from attempting innovation, however, is

$$E_A(I) = (y + \delta)(1 - z - \delta)\Pi_A(E, O) + \{(y + \delta)(z + \delta) \\ + (1 - y - \delta)z \} \Pi_A(O, E) \\ + (1 - y - \delta)(1 - z)\Pi_A(O, O) - F_A.$$

Differentiating this equation with respect to the degree of spillovers,

$$\frac{\partial E_A(I)}{\partial \delta} = (1 - z)\{\Pi_A(E, O) - \Pi_A(O, O)\} \\ - (y + 2\delta)\{\Pi_A(E, O) - \Pi_A(O, E)\}.$$

Since $\Pi_A(E, O) > \Pi_A(O, O) > \Pi_A(O, E)$, the condition $y + z + 2\delta \geq 1$ is sufficient to ensure that the derivative in the previous equation is negative. Therefore, for arbitrary fixed costs F_A, sufficiently high interfirm spillovers (δ) reduce the likelihood that firm A will attempt to innovate. In the limiting case in which the correlation is perfect ($z_1 = 1$), the incumbent will never attempt to innovate because it knows that it cannot profitably apply an innovation that the entrant has also mastered.   □

In summary, then, the theoretical model developed in this section implies that the characteristics of the voice-and-data innovation process noted earlier combined to stack the odds of innovation and introduction in favor of entrants rather than incumbents. While the theoretical analysis was simplified by assuming away differentiation between second-generation products, Judd's (1985) analysis of the credibility of spatial preemption suggests that the effect identified also applies to new products that are horizontally differentiated.

5.4 Reflections

The most obvious contribution of this chapter has been to rationalize why incumbents might have lagged at innovation in the PBX industry in game-theoretic terms. But the analysis also has broader implications.

To game theorists the analysis should illustrate the usefulness of trying to devise models that are somewhat responsive to empirical reality, even if only in the sense of approximating the particulars of one case. Looking at a single case may not lead to the right inferences about stylized facts, but it seems more likely to do so than not looking at all. The voice-and-data PBX innovation supplies a particularly good example. Several attributes of its development guided the model developed in the previous section: overlapping product generations, differences in efficiency, and spillovers. Research indicates that the voice-and-data innovation was representative rather than remarkable in these respects: product generations often do overlap (Norton and Bass 1987); there seem to be large differences in innovative efficiency, particularly between entrants and incumbents (Utterback 1994) and significant spillovers (and imitation) are apparently the rule rather than an exception (e.g., Mansfield et al. 1981 and Levin et al. 1987). Yet off-the-shelf models did not fit these regularities, which is why a case-based approach led me to develop a new one.

The analysis in this chapter also suggests a problem with game-theoretic modeling that, while generally troublesome, is particularly acute in the context of innovation: Many environments offer virtually open-ended possibilities for progress that are hard to accommodate within simple two- or three-stage models. Opportunities for continuing technological progress are responsible for the biggest mismatch between the model developed in this chapter—in which the threat of pure price competition prevents the incumbent from entering a new generation if the entrant already has or can—and the case setting, in which AT&T (and other incumbents) did invest in and eventually introduced new generations of products. There *has* been some rather stylized theoretical work recently on races up quality ladders. But multidimensional progress and the integration of R&D expenditures within generations and R&D expenditures intended to introduce new generations continue to be significant theoretical challenges.

Other implications of the present analysis for researchers on product innovation are even more important. First, the analysis should sound a cautionary note about assuming that game-theoretic IO offers a unified set of predictions about competition along this particular dimension. Game theory is a method for analyzing competitive interactions, the predictions from which turn out to be very sensitive to situational attributes. Yet in the context of product innovation, game-theoretic reasoning has been asserted to imply that incumbents will lag when innovation is drastic (when product generations do not overlap, as assumed by Reinganum 1983) and lead when innovation is incremental (when product generations do overlap, as implied by Gilbert and Newbery 1982). That the incremental voice-and-data innovation does not line up neatly with these predictions should in the first instance raise questions about these particular models rather than about game theory in general.

The avowal that game theory does not offer a unified set of predictions is sometimes seized upon by those who favor other analytical approaches as a particularly important limitation of the theory. Apart from noting that the empirical concreteness of case-based analysis helps ameliorate this problem, it should be added that the predictions afforded by other analytical approaches tend to be fragmentary as well. Consider the history of attempts to predict, on the basis of other, mostly organizational, approaches whether incumbents or entrants are likely to lead in the process of innovation. What we might call "first-generation" organizational predictions turned on the distinction between incremental innovations that refine an existing design and radical innovations that depart in a significant way from past practices (Mansfield 1968; Freeman 1982). Incumbents were predicted to hold a comparative advantage with respect to relatively continuous incremental innovations and entrants with respect to relatively discontinuous radical innovations. Probably the most dramatic evidence corroborative of this conjecture, from the perspective of a strategy audience, was Cooper and Schendel's

(1976) documentation of a number of episodes in which "traditional" firms were unable to respond effectively to major (relatively discontinuous) technological innovations that originated outside their industries.

"Second-generation" organizational predictions focused more directly on the effects of technological change of firms' capabilities or competencies. In particular, they recognized that even discontinuous technological changes might usefully be divided in terms of whether they were competence-enhancing or competence-destroying from an incumbent perspective, and predicted that incumbents would cope substantially better with the former than with the latter (Abernathy and Clark 1985; Tushman and Anderson 1986). This prediction is backstopped by a number of empirical studies. In particular, a recent meta-analysis of more than forty discontinuous innovations by Utterback (1994) supports this prediction at better than a 99 percent level of significance.

As in the PBX industry, the definitions of generations of organization-theoretic thinking seem to get blurred after the first two. Still there are at least two other influential conceptualizations that are worth mentioning. Henderson and Clark (1990) classify innovations (of assembled products) in terms of whether they change linkages between "core" concepts and components as well as whether they enhance or destroy those core concepts. They suggest that incumbent failure is also likely in the case of "architectural" innovations, which change those linkages rather than the core concepts themselves. This hypothesis is supported by the case of photolithography, which is analyzed in detail by Henderson (1993).

Another conceptualization, rooted in Christensen's (1992) work on the disk-drive industry, is offered by Rosenbloom and Christensen (1994), who suggest that the failure of incumbents often stems from their reluctance to make timely commitments to new capabilities and new strategies. While their diagnosis might seem to dovetail with the game-theoretic analysis of incentives to commit to innovation that was laid out in the preceding section of this chapter, Rosenbloom and Christensen (1994) have a rather different, nonoptimizing mechanism in mind. They suggest that incumbents are likely to fail to commit adequate resources to an innovation only when it entails changes in their "value networks," particularly their customer bases. Christensen and Bower (1996) elaborate the ways in which customer-driven resource allocation processes can lead to such a suboptimal outcome.

These conceptualizations of incumbent failure are obviously quite different: Henderson and Clark focus on the difficulties that incumbents confront in developing new technological capabilities and Christensen with Rosenbloom and Bower on their tendencies to make the wrong strategic choices. My reading is that subsequent work on product innovation does not clearly support either of these two perspectives—nor earlier ones. Consider two recent examples.

One such example is provided by Jones' (1996) statistical study of the U.S. PBX industry, which has already been mentioned. Looking at the history of that industry, Jones concludes that incumbents generally *were* able to develop the new technological capabilities required for radical/architectural product innovations. And while he argues that this result is consistent with Rosenbloom and Christensen (1994) because value networks were "at least partially preserved" (p. 298), one could almost as easily focus on the ways in which value networks were *not* preserved and argue that incumbent success was therefore anomalous with respect to Rosenbloom and Christensen's predictions. The uncertainty surrounding Jones' conclusions about the PBX industry hints at a broader ambiguity in the definition of value networks and what it takes to disrupt them.

A second recent example is provided by the transition from bias to radial architecture for tires for passenger cars. Rosenbloom and Christensen (1994) explicitly recognize that this innovation is a problem for conceptualizations based on value networks, since the relevant value network did not change even though U.S. incumbents (particularly the larger ones, Goodyear and Firestone) trailed in moving to radials in the 1960s, took the plunge in the 1970s, and yet ended up largely succumbing to foreign competition in the 1980s: By 1990 Goodyear was the only major U.S.-owned and managed firm left in the industry. Deeper analysis of this case by Sull, Tedlow, and Rosenbloom (1997) suggest that the observed pattern of events is better explained by the influence of managerial pre-commitments rather than incentives or competencies.

What are we to make of the proliferation of organizational theories about technological change and their apparent case-specificity? Rosenbloom and Christensen (1994, p. 657) are refreshingly candid in this regard:

Kuhn (1962) noted that in the early stages of research in a given field, the most that scholars typically can do is report the phenomena they observe, without a unifying theory or framework to help them make sense of what they see. As a result, this stage of knowledge accumulation is characterized by confusion and contradiction. Theories are put forward, but reports of anomalous phenomena accumulate. This seems to us to be a fair characterization of the present state of scholarship on radical technological innovation.

If one agrees with this characterization, it would seem to be premature to assay the relative effectiveness of game theory and organization theory in explaining observed patterns of innovation. And while both types of theorizing are sensitive to case particulars, game-theoretic analyses are linked by the logic of interactive profit maximization. Even more work therefore is needed on organization-theoretic explanations than on game-theoretic ones before the two theories can jointly be tested. In the meantime the opposition between game-theoretic incentives and organization-theoretic capabilities that is often invoked seems a bit overdrawn. In the analysis of the voice-and-data PBX innovation, at least, it proved possible to fold differences in organizational capabilities into game-theoretic models of competition. Such subsumption possibilities will be explored further in the two chapters that follow.

5.5 Summary

The theoretical and empirical analysis in this chapter has made a number of contributions. First of all, it has illustrated the role that detailed analyses of individual cases can play in helping theorists pick modeling assumptions that are empirically sensible. Modeling assumptions motivated by the voice-and-data PBX example helped to rationalize the widely noted phenomenon of incumbent failure at product innovation in game-theoretic terms.

Second, the analysis supplied additional perspective on a research strategy that is increasingly common in strategic management: looking at patterns of product innovation to compare the importance of game-theoretic (interactive) effects and organization-theoretic (efficiency) effects—or more crudely, to rank the extent to which the roots of advantage are external as opposed to internal. The analysis in this chapter raised questions about this research strategy because neither game theory nor organization theory offers a unified set of predictions about product innovation. Finer-grained theoretical and empirical mapping of the parametric possibilities and their implications seems necessary before broad dicta about incentives versus capabilities can be dispensed.

Third, the analysis in this chapter also suggested that it might be possible to fold organization-theoretic effects into models of competition instead of holding them apart as alternate explanations of observed patterns. Of course the tack taken in this chapter—treating the differences in innovative efficiency implied by the empirical analysis as exogenous—may not appeal to hardcore theorists who insist on individually optimized behavior. Endogenization of organizational structure and efficiency is an alternate approach, albeit a demanding one. A third approach is suggested by the next chapter, which focuses on an instance of incumbent failure to apply process, as opposed to product, innovations.

6   Process Innovation in the Steel Industry

This chapter, like the previous one, looks at an apparent instance of incumbent failure to lead technologically and rationalizes the observed pattern in game-theoretic terms by developing a customized model of competition to innovate. But there are also two important differences between these two chapters.

The first difference is that this chapter focuses on process innovation, which has attracted rather less empirical attention recently than product innovation, the topic of the previous chapter.[1] This imbalance is probably due to the observation that product innovations tend to be more important than process innovations in the earlier, more fluid phases of an industry's evolution (Abernathy and Utterback 1978) and the inference that product innovations therefore have more of an impact on industry structure. But there is also evidence that process innovations can have a major transformational impact, particularly in industries that produce nonassembled products (e.g., Utterback 1994, chs. 5 and 6). The case of process innovation studied in this chapter, the thin-slab casting of steel, certainly has this character. U.S. Steel, the largest steelmaker in the United States since it was

---

1. For an important recent exception, consult Pisano (1996) on process development in pharmaceuticals.

formed through merger in 1901, may soon be displaced from that position by the first adopter of thin-slab casting technology, Nucor, a minimill that makes steel from scrap. In addition thin-slab casting, along with other process innovations, is threatening the viability of most of the integrated steelmakers that, like U.S. Steel, make steel from iron ore (Schorsch 1996).

The second difference is that this chapter goes beyond the broad distinction between incumbents and entrants to discuss some of the finer-grained, firm-specific features that drove technology choices. Thus there is discussion not only of why Nucor, which used thin-slab casting to enter the half of the steel market that it had previously been locked out of, was the first to adopt the new technology but also why two other apparent candidates for adopting the new technology, Chaparral, another progressive minimill, and U.S. Steel, the leading integrated incumbent, have yet to do so. The task of connecting these outcomes to antecedent choices is simplified by the limited degree of technological uncertainty in this case.[2] The explanation of the choices themselves is illuminated by interviews with key decision makers at Chaparral and U.S. Steel as well as at Nucor. In-depth analysis from the perspective of multiple competitors deepens and broadens our understanding of the roots of sustained differences in the performance of competitors within the same industry.

This chapter begins with some background information on the thin-slab casting innovation. It then considers whether received game-theoretic models explain the pattern of adoption of thin-slab casting, concludes that they do not, and suggests the reason is that those models fail to distinguish between process innovations that reduce scale requirements—an attribute of thin-slab

---

2. Process innovations are often asserted to be subject to less uncertainty, ceteris paribus, than product innovations. Consult, for instance, Stobaugh (1988) on petrochemicals.

casting that was of particular interest to Nucor—and innovations that do not. A model that picks up on this distinction shows that there was indeed a game-theoretic reason to expect the first adopter of the scale-reducing technology to come from the ranks of minimills, which had historically been locked out of the large, lucrative flat-rolled sheet segment because of scale requirements. (The integrated steelmakers were the incumbents in flat-rolled sheet, having retreated to that segment under pressure from minimills and imports.)

The chapter then shifts from theoretical analysis to empirical analysis at the level of individual firms instead of strategic groups. It begins by elucidating the firm-specific reasons that Nucor was the first minimill "entrant" to adopt the new technology and proceeds to consider nonadoption decisions by Chaparral (another potential "entrant) and U.S. Steel (an "incumbent"). The discussion of Nucor exposes the organizational bases of its superior operating and investment capabilities; the discussions of Chaparral and U.S. Steel highlight other organizational influences on innovation decisions.

6.1 Case Background

The principal process innovations in casting molten steel can broadly be characterized as part of a thrust to cast it thinner, that is, closer to final form for most applications. Between the 1850s and the 1950s steel was batch-cast into ingots two or more feet thick, which were cooled and stored before being reheated and crushed into thinner shapes in rolling mills. Continuous casting, which began to be commercialized in the late 1950s, marked a major advance. It permitted steel to be cast into a continuous ribbon, typically 8 to 10 inches thick, that was sliced into slabs 20 to 40 feet long. These slabs were later reheated and crushed into flat sheets less than one-quarter of an inch thick (the bulk of the demand for steel).

Since reprocessing slabs that thick into flat-rolled sheet was still quite costly, steelmakers continued to hunt for ways to cast steel even thinner. More than two dozen efforts at casting steel directly into sheet—successors to an initiative of Sir Henry Bessemer's in the 1850s—were underway in the 1980s, but none was expected to yield a commercializable process until after the millennium. This anticipated lag stoked interest in the idea of casting thin slabs only one to two inches thick in order to reduce the reheating and rolling costs associated with conventional continuous casting.

In 1983 SMS, a West German company that was a leading designer of conventional casting and rolling equipment, hit upon an idea for a new mold that might facilitate thin-slab casting. It invested in a stationary test device in 1984 and a pilot plant in 1985 and, armed with the results, began to promote its thin-slab casting process to as many steelmakers as possible. More than one hundred companies reportedly sent their engineers or executives to view SMS's pilot thin-slab caster, but nothing happened until early 1987, when Nucor announced that it would pioneer the commercialization of SMS's technology.

In 1986, Nucor derived virtually all of its sales ($755 million) and net income ($46 million) from steelmaking and fabrication at ten sites around the United States. Its total market capitalization was $645 million at the end of that year. Its steelmaking capacity of 2.1 million tons, 1.6 percent of the U.S. total, made it the second largest minimill in the country. Though Nucor's sales and profits had grown very rapidly in the 1970s, they had been stagnating in the 1980s, as minimills saturated their traditional product segments.

Nucor had begun to search for a casting technology that would allow it to enter the flat-rolled sheet segment in 1983, a year after experiencing its first sales decline since Kenneth Iverson began to run it in 1965. In late 1986 it decided to pioneer SMS's thin-slab casting technology by adding a plant with close to one million tons of capacity at a total capital cost, including startup expenses and working capital, that was expected to exceed $300 million. Although Nucor incurred substantial cost overruns, primarily in startup, on its first thin-slab caster, its use of that technology as a springboard into the flat-rolled sheet segment is regarded as the key driver of the firm's subsequent success. By 1994 Nucor's sales had quadrupled from 1986 levels, its net income had increased fivefold, and its market capitalization tenfold. By the end of 1994, Nucor's total steelmaking capacity exceeded seven million tons (of which four million tons was accounted for by thin-slab casting). The company seemed on track to meet its stated objective of becoming the largest U.S. steelmaker by the millennium.

Despite SMS's eagerness to license its thin-slab casting technology to other steelmakers, competing thin-slab casters did not begin to come on stream in the United States until 1995. The lack of quick imitation, especially after Nucor had proved the technology, is puzzling. Fortunately Chaparral and U.S. Steel, two steelmakers that had been obvious candidates to adopt thin-slab casting but had chosen not to, proved willing to discuss their choices.

6.2 Theoretical Background

Several different levels of decision-making can be discerned within the sequence of events described in the last section: SMS's decision to develop a process technology that threatened to cannibalize its existing business, its decision to license that technology nonexclusively and nondiscriminatorily, and the adoption and nonadoption decisions that followed. The theoretical analysis in this chapter treats SMS's technology development and licensing decisions as given and focuses on the adoption pattern they induced. More specifically, it examines whether a minimill entrant into flat-rolled sheet might be expected to adopt the thin-slab casting innovation before the incumbents, integrated steelmakers, for game-theoretic reasons. Note that this focus on adoption as opposed to innovation reduces the importance of uncertainty and tilts the theoretical analysis toward a deterministic model (although adoption costs could easily be allowed to be stochastic without altering the analysis that follows).

The theoretical modeling focuses once again on the behavior of an incumbent monopolist facing threats of entry induced by innovation. As in the previous chapter, there is no general answer to the question of whether the incumbent's incentives to adopt a new technology first will be greater or less than a potential entrant's because of the opposed effects: the cannibalization effect (Arrow 1962) which, in the context of declining adoption costs, implies earlier adoption by an entrant and the business-stealing effect which, if dominant, induces earlier adoption by the incumbent (Fudenberg and Tirole 1986b).

Theoretical models of monopolist-entrant interaction suggest that the weight of the business-stealing effect, and consequently the likelihood that an incumbent will adopt before an entrant, depends on at least three sets of conditions. First, it matters whether an innovation is *drastic* or *nondrastic*—that is, whether the profitability of being its sole adopter would be independent of or constrained by the availability of old technology to competitors. Nondrastic innovation implies that industry profits will be lower if the entrant adopts the new technology than if the incumbent does, generating a business-stealing effect (Fudenberg and Tirole 1986b).

Second, the anticipation of tough rather than soft competition from an entrant directly heightens concerns about business stealing. Bertrand competition in prices, for example, is likely to induce the incumbent to adopt first because, under certain auxiliary assumptions, it can deter entry forever, whereas Cournot competition in quantities is more likely to induce the entrant to adopt first (Tirole 1988).

Finally, whether adoption is a stochastic process is also important. Intuition suggests that with a random as opposed to a deterministic date at which a rival will adopt if a monopolist does not, the monopolist will rationally pay more attention to the flow of profits from the old technology and will therefore be less likely to move first. (Once again, compare Gilbert and Newbery 1982 and Reinganum 1983.)

The thin-slab casting innovation seemed to satisfy all three conditions that typically increase the weight attached to the business-stealing effect. First, thin-slab casting appeared to be relatively modest and therefore was a nondrastic innovation. The operating costs of producing the basic flat-rolled sheet product, hot-rolled coil, via thin-slab casting in a minimill, were projected to be about $225 per ton, compared to $260 per ton via the conventional process (at an efficient integrated mill) and preentry price realizations of $325 per ton. However, more than half of thin-slab casting's operating cost advantage was expected to be wiped out by price penalties due to surface-quality problems with its output. There was also an initial investment of more than $300 per ton of capacity to be recovered. Finally demand for flat-rolled sheet appeared to be rather price inelastic: Adams et al. (1985, p. 98), for instance, estimated its price elasticity et al., as -0.27. Given these figures, optimal markup rules, in which the markup equals the inverse of the (absolute) price elasticity, suggest that it is very unlikely that a thin-slab monopolist would elect to set its price lower than the operating costs of competitors using older technologies if it did not have to contend with them at all.

Second, competition in the flat-rolled sheet segment had been intense even when it was the preserve of integrated steelmakers. It could be expected to intensify further in the event of successful entry by minimills. Indicators of intense competition in flat-rolled sheet prior to Nucor's entry announcement included the predominant role of price in product-market competition, domestic capacity utilization rates that hovered around 60 percent, import threats, and the fact that the market-to-book values of the half-dozen largest U.S. integrated steelmakers, who depended on flat-rolled sheet for nearly three-quarters of their shipments in 1986, averaged significantly less than one. Minimill entry into flat-rolled sheet was expected to intensify competition further because minimills had historically used low prices to penetrate new segments. Nucor itself was perceived to be a minimill that was particularly aggressive in cutting prices.

Third, adoption of thin-slab casting appeared to have been a relatively deterministic or certain process rather than an uncertain one. Nucor, U.S. Steel, and other industry participants regarded SMS's thin-slab casting process as a relatively incremental innovation: The lens-shaped mold was the only new equipment. Corroboration comes ex post from the technical success that has attended all the attempts of which I am aware to adopt this technology.

Given these points of correspondence between the case of thin-slab casting and the conditions that favor early adoption of process innovations by incumbents, the fact that Nucor, an entrant, was the first to adopt the new technology appears anomalous. The next section considers ways of rationalizing the pattern of adoption of thin-slab casting in game-theoretic terms and elaborates on one of them.

6.3   Theoretical Analysis

The models discussed in the previous section notwithstanding, the pattern of adoption of thin-slab casting might be rationalized game-theoretically in at least half a dozen different ways. Closer analysis of the case suggests, however, that not all these rationalizations are equally appealing. The ability to help separate out good rationalizations from bad ones is precisely one of the ways in which knowledge of the particulars of a case helps address the common complaint about game theory that was cited in chapter 1: that the degree of modeling discretion is often so significant that a model can be devised to explain almost any fact.

Possible Rationalizations

A particularly simple way to rationalize first-adoption by an entrant rather than an incumbent is to assert that the primary cost savings afforded by the new process technology pertains to capital rather than operating costs. The idea is that if an incumbent's capital costs are already sunk, it might rationally refrain from adopting the new technology even though entrants find it attractive. But this line of reasoning fails to explain why an incumbent might chose to upgrade its old ingot-casting capacity to conventional continuous casting at much higher capital outlays per ton than would be required to adopt thin-slab casting, as in the case of U.S. Steel, which is described below.

Second, it might be suggested that there were several incumbents in flat-rolled sheet rather than just one, which would invalidate the application of monopolist-entrant models. A problem with this argument is that modifying the basic Fudenberg and Tirole model (1986b, pp. 36–40), which assumes nondrastic innovation, deterministic adoption, and Bertrand competition, to allow multiple incumbents (or for that matter, multiple entrants) does not by itself reverse their prediction that the first-adopter will be an incumbent.

Third, it might be argued that steel casting was subject to continuing technological progress, in terms of improvements in potential operating performance, as well as declining adoption costs. As Schumpeter (1942, p. 98) pointed out, continuing technological progress can weaken the incentive for incumbents to lead in the adoption of interim technologies. Though the prospect of continuing progress *might* explain why U.S. Steel and other incumbents let Nucor move first, it is not a compelling explanation. Nucor's announcement that it would commercialize SMS's thin-slab casting process led to a cessation of other domestic efforts to commercialize another process for thin-slab casting, the Hazelett process. Research continued on direct casting of steel into sheet, but the impact of the leapfrogging possibilities afforded by direct casting was probably limited by significant lags and uncertainties in the development of the process, as well as by the relatively modest operating cost reductions it appeared likely to deliver compared to SMS's process.

Fourth, the fact that Nucor moved first might be rationalized by grafting asymmetric information onto the Fudenberg and Tirole (1986b) model cited earlier. More specifically, it is easy to build a model in which an incumbent rationally refrains from being the first to adopt a new process technology because successful adoption demonstrates to less-informed entrants that the new technology is workable, and thereby reduces the expected value of the assets the incumbent has precommitted to the old technology. But again there are problems with this explanation. For one thing, the utility of asymmetric information models is limited in the case being considered by the fact that information seems to flow relatively freely in the steel industry: Competitors regularly visit each others' plants, for example. In addition it is just as easy to build signaling models that point in the opposite direction: models in which the incumbent preempts a potential entrant purely in order to discourage entry by others. Finally, and most important, given the record of technological tardiness of integrated steelmakers in the United States, the supposition that a leading minimill would base its inferences about a new technology on their postures toward that technology strikes most industry observers as ludicrous.

A fifth expedient is to superimpose capacity constraints on the technology adoption problem. Precisely how this approach resolves the dilemma is described in the next subsection. For now, note that this approach is appealing on several a priori grounds. First, steel is very capital intensive and relatively undifferentiated, which magnifies the importance of physical capacity in that industry. Second, taking capacity levels seriously fits with an attribute of SMS's thin-slab casting process that Nucor's CEO, Iverson, regarded as central to his company's commitment to the process. Iverson had long wanted Nucor to enter the flat-rolled sheet segment but had rejected the use of conventional casting technology, which entailed a minimal efficient scale (MES) of as much as three million tons per year. By his own account he was attracted to thin-slab casting not only because of the operating cost reductions it offered but also because it reduced MES to less than one million tons per year. Since Oster's (1982) analysis of the diffusion of the basic oxygen furnace among U.S. steelmakers also flagged MES as an important consideration, it seems useful to construct a model in which innovation reduces MES as well as operating costs in order to check whether the reduction in MES affects the predicted order of adoption of a new process technology. That task is undertaken in the next subsection.

Before turning to that task, there is a sixth rationalization option that ought to be mentioned: the possibility that minimills, particularly Nucor, were simply more efficient at adopting the new technology than were incumbents, particularly U.S. Steel. This possibility could be handled, as in the previous chapter, by positing differences in efficiency and showing that if they are sufficiently large, the entrant should be expected to adopt first. It is not clear, however, that much value would be added in a deterministic context by doing so. Instead, the issue of differential efficiency is approached from an empirical rather than a theoretical perspective (see section 6.4).

A Theoretical Model

The effects of a reduction in MES on the diffusion of a process innovation cannot be examined without explicitly incorporating capacity constraints into models of the adoption of process technology. Because none of the received models of which I am aware attempts to do so, it is necessary to build and analyze a new one. The assumptions behind it reflect both the characteristics of the case studied and the need for tractability. The supply side of the present model is complicated, relative to the monopolist-entrant models reviewed in the last section, by the incorporation of capacity constraints. The demand side is therefore simplified in a way that nonetheless makes it possible to obtain closed-form expressions for expected operating profits.

More specifically, aggregate demand for the product is assumed to be price inelastic and mature: It equals Q at prices less than or equal to u, and it is zero otherwise. These assumptions can be justified in the context of flat-rolled steel by appealing, respectively, to the price elasticity of -0.27 estimated by Adams et al. (1985, p. 98) and to the fact that aggregate U.S. demand for flat sheet fluctuated very little between 45 million and 47 million tons per year from 1984 through 1989.

Demand is initially satisfied by an incumbent firm, firm 1. The assumption of a single incumbent can be rationalized, as in some of the previous chapters, in terms of the prevalent theoretical stratagem of specifying strong cases. The incumbent has the capacity to produce K_1 units of output at a marginal cost of $\bar{c}$ ($<$ u). To reflect the chronic excess capacity in flat-rolled sheet, it is assumed that $K_1 > Q$. A second firm, firm 2, could enter the market at the same scale with the same marginal cost but elects not to do so.

A possible gateway for entry by firm 2 is opened up by the arrival of a new process technology that reduces the marginal cost of entry to $\underline{c}$ ($< \bar{c}$), and the minimum scale required to enter to K_2 ($< K_1$). This new technology is and continues to be available to both firms; neither can purchase an enforceable patent on it. These assumptions reflect in obvious ways the features of thin-slab casting innovation that were discussed by way of background. In addition both firms are assumed to be equally efficient at exploiting the commitment opportunity that the innovation presents.[3]

The assumption of equal efficiency has a straightforward interpretation in terms of marginal costs: Adoption of the innovation assures either firm a marginal cost of $\underline{c}$ up to the level of the capacity it has fitted or retrofitted with the new technology. Such evenhandedness also extends to the fixed costs of adoption, which are assumed to be $C(t)$ per unit of new or refurbished capacity. Interesting dynamics are generated by assuming, as Fudenberg and Tirole (1986b) do, that $C(t)$ decreases with time but at a decreasing rate ($C'(t) < 0$; $C''(t) > 0$), that $C(0)$ is sufficiently high that neither firm would like to adopt at time 0, and that $C(t)$ eventually becomes so low that it is less than $(\bar{c} - \underline{c})/r$ (where r is the common discount rate) but continues to be greater than 0. In the context of thin-slab casting, these restrictions on the shape of $C(t)$ are most easily rationalized in terms of startup costs,

---

3. The next section will revisit this assumption of equal efficiency.

which added more than 20 percent to Nucor's total cost of constructing its first thin-slab casting plant but less than 10 percent to the cost of its second one. Letting SMS develop thin-slab casting further—for instance, by building a pilot plant capable of operating more than seven minutes at a time—would have reduced this element of adoption costs. Nucor actually considered waiting for this reason before it committed to commercializing thin-slab casting when it did.

A final set of assumptions pertains to the product-market competition that takes place if the new technology does induce entry by firm 2. As in chapters 2 and 3, the two firms each simultaneously announce a price, with the higher-priced firm experiencing demand only if its rival is capacity constrained and its own price is less than or equal to u. If the two prices tie, demand is split between the duopolists in proportion to their respective capacities.[4] Each firm is assumed to be risk neutral and therefore maximizes expected operating profits in the product-market game.

These assumptions about product-market competition reflect interactions in flat-rolled sheet, in which price seemed to be the key competitive variable over the short run (subject to capacity constraints). Although the modest value-to-weight ratio of the product did offer some possibilities for spatial differentiation, integrated steelmakers' efforts to exploit them through multiple-point basing systems had been constrained by imports and low domestic capacity utilization. And the likelihood that Nucor's entry would, as discussed earlier, further intensify competition in flat-rolled sheet suggests an additional reason for modeling short-run (capacity-constrained) interactions in relatively tough procedural terms: in terms of prices instead of quantities.

---

4. Because of price-inelastic demand, no additional assumption needs to be made about rationing rules.

To identify subgame-perfect outcomes of the technology adoption problem, it is necessary to begin by pinning down the profit flows to the two firms in the various pricing subgames that are possible.

Proposition 6.1 *Firms' expected operating profits at Nash equilibrium, Π_1 and Π_2, depend on whether they have adopted the new process technology or not.*

a. *If neither firm has adopted,*

$\Pi_1 = (u - \bar{c}) \cdot Q,$

$\Pi_2 = 0.$

b. *If firm 1 has adopted but firm 2 has not,*

$\Pi_1 = (u - \underline{c}) \cdot Q,$

$\Pi_2 = 0.$

c. *If firm 1 has not adopted but firm 2 has (at scale K_2),*

$\Pi_1 = (u - \bar{c}) \cdot \max(Q - K_2, 0),$

$\Pi_2 = (\bar{c} - \underline{c}) \cdot \min(K_2, Q) + (u - \bar{c}) \cdot \max(Q - K_2, 0) \cdot \min\left(\dfrac{K_2}{Q}, 1\right).$

d. *If both firms have adopted,*

$\Pi_1 = (u - \underline{c}) \cdot \max(Q - K_2, 0),$

$\Pi_2 = (u - \underline{c}) \cdot \max(Q - K_2, 0) \cdot \min\left(\dfrac{K_2}{Q}, 1\right).$

Proof   The proofs of parts a and b are trivial. The proofs of parts c and d, including characterizations of the pricing strategies that lead to these expected operating profits, can be found in Ghemawat (1993).   □

Parts c and d of proposition 6.1 correspond to cases in which there actually is product-market competition. In both cases, as in chapters 2 and 3, the larger firm's price schedule stochastically dominates the smaller one's (unless each of them has invested in enough capacity based on the new technology to satisfy aggregate demand by itself, in which case both firms' prices fall to $\underline{c}$). The larger firm's expected operating profits are limited, as a result, to its security level. The business-stealing effect is evident in the fact that the total operating profits expected by the industry are higher under part b of proposition 6.1 than under part c. Inspection also reveals that both firms' expected operating profits are continuous (although only piecewise differentiable) functions of Q, K_1, and K_2.

Parts c and d of proposition 6.1 also assume that firm 2 enters at the minimal scale possible, K_2. This assumption should not be taken to imply that K_2 is the *optimal* scale of entry. It is intended instead to facilitate the next subsection's treatment of K_2 as a shift parameter in a way that simplifies analysis of the effects of minimal scale on the order in which process innovations are adopted.

Proposition 6.1 does not by itself settle this order. It turns out that there is no blanket answer to this question because of the added complexity associated with capacity constraints. It is possible nonetheless to analyze extreme cases in order to assess Nucor's intuition about the importance of a relatively small MES—K_2 in the model—to its efforts to enter the flat-rolled sheet segment. The two extreme cases considered here are the limits as K_2 approaches, respectively, Q from below and 0 from above.

Proposition 6.2 *As K_2 approaches Q, the incumbent, firm 1, is predicted to adopt first.*

Proof Consider the limit point at which $K_2 = Q$ ($\leq K_1$). Given such a large MES, if firm 1 has already adopted, firm 2 will refrain from doing so because part d of proposition 6.1 implies that if it did, price competition would push operating profits for both firms down to zero. The less obvious case is the one in which firm 2 has adopted the new technology, but firm 1 has not. One might be tempted to conjecture that the subgame equilibrium then yields both firms strictly positive expected operating profits. Part c of proposition 6.1 implies, however, that in such a case firm 2 will announce a price of $\bar{c}$, and firm 1 will employ a mixed strategy in which it names $\bar{c}$ as its infimum, but without positive probability, obtaining zero operating profits. As noted earlier, firm 1 cannot improve its payoff by following suit and adopting the new technology because both firms would then make zero operating profits. As a result, when K_2 equals Q, the "follower," irrespective of whether it is firm 1 or firm 2, will never adopt. Because of the continuity of the payoff functions in K_2, that result continues to hold for values of K_2 sufficiently close to Q.

The rest of the proof follows along the lines described in detail by Fudenberg and Tirole (1986b) and is therefore simply sketched here. Because adoption by one firm constrains the other to earn zero profits thereafter, there is vigorous competition between the two to adopt first. The date at which firm 1 is indifferent between adopting the new technology first and "following" (staying put and making zero profits after adoption by its rival) turns out to be earlier than the corresponding date for firm 2 because of the business-stealing effect. As a result firm 1 adopts the new technology just before the indifference date for firm 2, t_2^1, which is implicitly defined as follows:

$$\int_{t_2^I}^{\infty} (\bar{c} - \underline{c})e^{-rt}dt \equiv C(t_2^I)e^{-rt_2^I}.$$ □

Proposition 6.3   *As K_2 approaches 0, the entrant, firm 2, is predicted to adopt first.*

Proof Consider the limit as K_2 approaches 0. From parts c and d of proposition 6.1, firm 2 expects to obtain a profit flow of $(u - \underline{c})$ per unit of new capacity, regardless of how much capacity firm 1 operates or whether it has already modernized that capacity. Therefore the dominant strategy for firm 2 is to adopt the new technology at a date t_2^*, defined by

$$\int_{t_2^*}^{\infty} (u - \underline{c})e^{-rt}dt \equiv C(t_2^*)e^{-rt_2^*}$$

and firm 1 follows at a date that turns out to coincide with the t_2^I date defined earlier. The continuity of the payoff functions in K_2 ensures adoption in the same order as when K_2 is sufficiently low, although strictly positive values of K_2 do alter the adoption dates relative to the limiting case in which K_2 equals 0.   □

While proposition 6.2 highlighted the business-stealing effect, proposition 6.3 highlights what is variously described as judo economics and the puppy dog ploy (see Gelman and Salop 1983 and Fudenberg and Tirole 1984). Taken together, these two propositions illustrate the importance of technological lumpiness in driving the pattern of adoption of new process technologies in a way that models that ignore capacity-related considerations cannot. Specifically the propositions imply that the decision-theoretic (cannibalization-based) and game-theoretic predictions from the previous subsection correspond to the limit points of a game-theoretic model of technology adoption that is parameterized in terms of the MES required for entry. MES matters in the model because if affects the ability of the "follower" to adopt at a later date and therefore affects competition to be the "leader."

Thin-slab casting can be interpreted in this light as a technology that lowered the MES required to enter the flat-sheet segment—from 6 to 8 percent of the total U.S. demand for flat sheet down to 2 to 3 percent—enough to tip the balance in favor of early adoption by an entrant. In other words, the model developed in this section *does* supply a game-theoretic rationale for why "an entrant" was the first to adopt the thin-slab casting process.

6.4   Empirical Analysis

While the idea that an entrant into flat-rolled sheet was more likely to adopt the thin-slab casting innovation than an incumbent has been rationalized game-theoretically, an important question remains. Why was Nucor, rather than other competitors, the one that adopted first? Answering this question requires a detailed look at the strategy and organization of Nucor and of competitors that might have considered adopting but did not. Two competitors would seem to figure toward the head of the queue: Chaparral, which was widely regarded as Nucor's leading minimill rival in terms of its organizational capabilities, and U.S. Steel, which as the largest U.S. integrated steelmaker was therefore disproportionately affected by Nucor's adoption of thin-slab casting in order to enter the last bastion of integrated steelmakers, namely flat-rolled sheet. Consider these three steel producers in turn.[5]

Nucor

The most obvious reason for Nucor's adoption of thin-slab casting before other minimills is that it seems to have been more

---

5. Ghemawat (1995) provides a much more detailed comparison of Nucor, Chaparral, and U.S. Steel.

efficient than average. The best evidence on this point is supplied by Neiva de Figueiredo (1993), who used stochastic production function methods (the procedure proposed by Battese and Coelli 1988) and a proprietary data set to estimate the technical efficiency of seventeen minimills: four operated by Nucor, another four by Florida Steel, and one each by other firms. One Nucor plant ranked first among the seventeen on this measure, another ranked fifth, and the others ranked eighth and ninth. In contrast, Florida Steel's plants ranked third, sixth, thirteenth, and sixteenth. The unweighted average measures of technical efficiency equaled 84 percent for Nucor's plants, 79 percent for Florida Steel's plants, and 77 percent for all non-Nucor plants in the sample. Note that in the absence of firm-level differences in efficiency, the odds that the most efficient Nucor plant would beat the most efficient Florida Steel plant, and so on, down to the two firm's least-efficient (fourth) plants, would be only $1/16$. The fact that Florida Steel was more efficient on average than minimill competitors other than Nucor further lengthens the odds against the null hypothesis of zero efficiency differences between Nucor and its minimill competitors. Given such differences in efficiency, a project that might look attractive to Nucor might appear unattractive to its minimill rivals.

To establish the existence of efficiency advantages is one thing; to account for them is another (and far more interesting) matter. Nucor's efficiency advantages can partially be accounted for by its management of its human resources. Nucor assembled workers into groups performing some discrete task (under a supervisor) and based most of each group's compensation on the extent to which production surpassed preset standards. Nucor's production incentives were higher powered than at most other minimills (consult exhibit 6.1 for some cross-sectional data assembled by Arthur 1992, 1994); they were also explicit, objective, output

Exhibit 6.1
Comparative Human Resource Variables

	Nucor		Other minimills		
	Number of plants	Mean value	Number of plants	Mean value	*t*-statistic
Number of production workers per supervisor	4	10.37	26	6.05	3.43
Total employment cost per production/maintenance worker ($/hr)	4	21.69	24	19.34	1.27
Bonus or incentive payments as a % of total employment cost	4	56.25	22	15.52	7.27
Turnover rate of production/maintenance workers (%/yr)	4	2.66	25	5.82	0.98

Source: Adapted from Arthur (1994) on the basis of a private communication.

based, and linear, as is often stressed in microeconomic models of efficient incentive contracting. Their most heterodox feature was reliance on group instead of individual incentives. This appeared to increase "peer pressure" that effectively substituted for supervision, as evinced by Nucor's higher ratio of production workers to supervisors (again consult exhibit 6.1).

Another ingredient of Nucor's efficiency advantage that is likely to have been even more important is its management of its capital resources, a fact recognized by Nucor's CEO, Iverson. Steel is a very capital-intensive industry, and the bulk of Nucor's estimated efficiency advantage (Neiva de Figueiredo 1993) reflected its lower capital recovery costs—costs that continued to be lower after the imposition of controls for vintage effects, numbers of products and grades, and aggregate levels of plant output. To see what might account for differential efficiency along this dimension, consider Nucor's capital investment policies.

Nucor tried to build or rebuild one plant per year—a very high frequency, compared to other large minimills as well as to steelmakers in general. Nucor acted, again atypically, as its own general contractor on plant-level projects. Engineers with experience at implementing such greenfield/greening investments were regarded as scarce resources to be transferred from plants where they were no longer needed to ones that were being built or rebuilt. Significant amounts of their know-how may be conjectured to have rubbed off on the construction workers with whom they worked, many of whom were retained as production workers, in part, for that very reason, once a plant had come (back) on line. This strategy seemed to have led to substantially superior capital efficiency: Nucor was able to build and start-up its first thin-slab caster at Crawfordsville, Indiana, for less than three-quarters of the cost reportedly estimated by two competitors and to achieve operating break-even a year and a half earlier

Exhibit 6.2
Capital Efficiency at Nucor

Construction		Startup	
Groundbreaking to First Melt		*First Melt to Break-even*	
Estimated Cost	$225m	Estimated cost	$30m
Actual Cost	$257m	Actual Cost	$60m
Others' Estimates	$400m+	Hickman Cost	$30m
Time Elapsed	23 months	Time Elapsed	10 months
Industry Average	36+ months	Industry Average	12 months
Hickman Estimate	17 months	Hickman Estimate	7 months

Source: Nucor, industry observers

than usual, effectively pushing its relative capital cost down toward the two-thirds level (see exhibit 6.2). Learning at Crawfordsville also helped reduce lags and start-up costs for Nucor's second thin-slab caster at Hickman, Arkansas. So both labor and capital contributed to Nucor's above-average efficiency.

Chaparral

For another part of the answer as to why Nucor was the first adopter of thin-slab casting, consider Chaparral, another celebrated U.S. minimill that has yet to commit to that technology. My interviews with Chaparral's top management team suggest that the decision not to innovate or imitate quickly was due primarily to the strategy to which they had precommitted rather than to lower levels of efficiency. Chaparral actually outscored Nucor at operating efficiency: Its one plant ranked fourth in efficiency among the seventeen compared by Neiva de Figueiredo (1993) and, at 86 percent, beat the 84 percent average for the four Nucor plants. And while Chaparral, as a single-site operation lacked Nucor's experience at building or refurbishing entire plants, research by Leonard-Barton (1992), among others, indicates that it too had developed superior capabilities at learning and innovation.

On being interviewed about Chaparral's nonadoption decision, its CEO, Gordon Forward, and other top managers tended to cite the strategy to which they had precommitted. Chaparral apparently pursued a more differentiated competitive strategy that placed more emphasis on high margins and less on high volumes than did Nucor's strategy. From Chaparral's perspective, SMS's thin-slab casting technology did not offer a large enough cost advantage over conventional methods for making flat-rolled sheet to be used to enter that large segment. Chaparral began instead to work on a proprietary process for thin-slab casting which would allow it to enter attractive but smaller niches with more substantial cost advantages.

The interviews at Chaparral indicated that its competitive strategy influenced not only its decision not to adopt SMS's thin-slab casting technology but also the activities that the firm performed. Chaparral's top management had a harmonious relationship with the company's production workers and paid them about as much on average as did Nucor, but without output-based bonuses. Production incentives appeared inconsistent with the relatively differentiated strategy (since quality was harder to meter than quantity) and its top managers' personal values. In terms of capital investment, Chaparral emphasized building up technological capabilities that were supposed to buffer the company from an intensification of rivalry in steelmaking. Its top managers professed no interest in propelling themselves down the experience curve by pursuing the "cookie cutter" approach of building the same basic plant over and over again at new sites. So Chaparral did not imitate Nucor at either thin-slab casting or in terms of the activities it performed—apparently not because of an inability to do so but because it was pursuing a quite different strategy.

U.S. Steel

Among the integrated steelmakers that failed to adopt thin-slab casting, the U.S. Steel division of USX is of particular interest. As the largest of the large integrated incumbents, U.S. Steel might have been predicted to have the greatest incentive to provide the collective good of entry deterrence through early adoption of the new technology (Olson 1965). As the healthiest financially, it was well positioned to do so. A specific nonadoption decision on its part provides a useful perspective. The decision concerns the modernization of its casting operations in the Monongahela River Valley (henceforth Mon Valley). U.S. Steel had agreed to the modernization as part of a settlement to a six-month strike at all of its plants that was negotiated in early 1987. After comparing the suitability of thin-slab casting and conventional continuous casting for more than two years, U.S. Steel settled on the latter in early 1990. Its executives described their decision as the last major casting investment they were likely to make in the twentieth century. Fortunately they were willing to discuss their reasoning.[6]

Perhaps the most important reason U.S. Steel selected conventional continuous casting instead of thin-slab casting was that its precommitment to modernizing the Mon Valley plant constrained it to work with a site that consisted of a steelmaking facility and a rolling mill located about ten miles apart. The distance between the two presented no problem for conventional continuous casting because slabs cast via that process were

---

6. The account that follows is based on Christensen and Rosenbloom (1990).

supposed to be cooled anyway prior to further processing. But the implications for thin-slab casting were dramatic, since that process was meant to be continuously coupled. It was deemed impractical to transport either molten steel or 150-foot-long thin slabs over that distance. Building a new furnace next to the existing rolling mill to make steel from scrap, or building a new rolling mill next to the existing furnace, was expected to raise the capital costs of thin-slab casting above those associated with conventional continuous casting.

The implementation of thin-slab casting also looked less attractive to U.S. Steel than to Nucor on operating criteria. Mon Valley's target capacity of 3 million tons per year meant that several thin-slab casters would have to be placed in parallel, and their output continuously merged into a single stream passing through the rolling mill. In addition, the labor savings SMS was promoting as an important advantage of thin-slab casting would be limited by the inflexible work rules built into U.S. Steel's contract with the United Steel Workers. Overall, U.S. Steel estimated that once workers had managed to master the unfamiliar, inflexible thin-slab casting process, the company might reduce operating costs at Mon Valley by 2 to 6 percent relative to conventional continuous casting—an inadequate amount given the higher capital and start-up costs associated with the new technology.

Another, more subtle reason for U.S. Steel's reluctance to implement thin-slab casting at Mon Valley is related to its customer base, which was dominated by appliance manufacturers. These large customers had resisted U.S. Steel's first installations of continuous casters in the 1960s by explicitly ordering ingot-cast steel instead of continuously cast steel because of concern about minute internal differences between the outputs of the two processes. The difference between steel produced via continuous casting and thin-slab casting was much more dramatic and pertained principally to surface quality, implying that appliance manufacturers would be unwilling to use thin-slab cast steel for surface applications right away. Nor did U.S. Steel not expect them to be patient with, or even tolerant, of its efforts to improve the quality of flat sheet produced via thin-slab casting over time.

These precommitments—to modernization at the Mon Valley mill, to a particular target capacity for it, to a contract with inflexible work rules, and to the mill's existing customer base—can all be interpreted in economic terms as constraints that increase the likelihood that cannibalization effects would dominate business-stealing effects in U.S. Steel's comparison of thin-slab casting and conventional casting. What is less clear is whether U.S. Steel's policy of investing only at its existing sites, which also depressed the profitability of adopting process innovations, can be rationalized in value-maximizing terms as well, or whether it reflected unwarranted strategic rigidity. See Ghemawat (1993) for additional discussion.

6.5   Reflections

Section 6.3 used game-theoretic modeling to analyze why a potential "entrant" into flat-rolled sheet, such as a minimill, might have been expected to adopt thin-slab casting more quickly than an integrated incumbent. Section 6.4 took an empirical tack: It explained the ability of Nucor to adopt the new technology more quickly than other minimills in terms of its greater efficiency, but also suggested that two potentially formidable competitors were held back by various precommitments. Taken together, these analyses suggest that the power of predictions about business interactions is likely to be maximized by integrating game-theoretic analysis of incentives with organization-theoretic competitor analysis that encompasses competitors' precommitments and predispositions as well as their efficiency levels. The desirability of such an integration will be discussed further in the next two chapters.

What warrants further discussion in this chapter is an issue that is even more fundamental than the question of why other minimills did not imitate Nucor's adoption of thin-slab casting more quickly: If Nucor's strategy and organization (particularly its management of human and capital resources) were responsible for its superior efficiency, why didn't other minimills imitate it along those dimensions? This latter question gets at the heart of sustained differences in the performance of competitors within the same industry.

Two generic answers have been proposed to the question of sustained profit differences among competitors. The differences between them can be highlighted by referring to them as the longitudinal and the cross-sectional theories about sustainability. The longitudinal theory is the one to which most scholars in strategic management as well as game-theorists seem to subscribe. It treats resources or capabilities that can only be varied in the long run as the roots of sustained superior performance on the grounds that they determine the menu of activities that it is economical (or even feasible) for a business to consider performing in the short run. The cross-sectional theory is a revisionist one, implicit in earlier work on strategy such as Andrews (1971), and most recently elaborated by Porter (1996). Porter maintains that sustained competitive advantage is based on tailoring systems of activities to a unique competitive position, that attempts at imitation are often ineffective because they require systematic rather than piecemeal changes, and that imitation may not even be attempted because competitors are pursuing different positions or are too weak-willed to make the activity-related trade-offs that successful positioning requires.

Attempts to compare the cross-sectional and the longitudinal theories of sustainability have been limited and generally bereft of empirical content (except for one- or two-paragraph caselets that, given their length, cannot even begin to get into interpretations different from the one being espoused). Fortunately the case of Nucor's sustained success provides more grist for this debate. Consider its implications.

It is clear that there were significant complementarities between Nucor's product-market strategy and the activities that it performed. Nucor's low-cost competitive strategy/position complemented its management of its human resources, particularly its production incentive plan, because quantity is easier to measure than quality, because the high capacity utilization implied by low costs narrowed the scope for divergence between output- and profit-maximization, and because expansion opportunities encouraged workers to suggest labor-saving cost-reducing changes in production methods, which they might have been loath to do in a context of stagnant or shrinking output. Nucor's low-cost strategy/position also complemented its management of its capital resources. Healthy operating cash flows from its low-cost position helped prevent Nucor's investment programs from getting stalled in midstream (as at many integrated steelmakers) and the regular addition or refurbishment of plants provided a mechanism for the transmission of experience from one plant to the next that drove down capital costs and implementation lags over time.

What is harder to argue is that these complementarities consisted exclusively of cross-sectional linkages among activities at a given point in time as opposed to linkages over time between the capabilities that had been built up and the activities they permitted (which fed back into them). It also seems implausible to assert that the cross-sectional complementarities that *did* exist among Nucor's activities were the primary deterrent to imitation because they rendered piecemeal as opposed to systematic attempts to change unprofitable. Imitation of Nucor's production incentive plan, for example, could be expected to benefit competitors following low-cost strategies irrespective of whether they also managed to imitate Nucor's management of its capital resources.

The two other sorts of explanations for nonimitation cited by Porter, differences in targeted competitive positions and a reluctance to make trade-offs that results in competitors being "stuck in the middle," seem to be limited in their explanatory power as well. Thus, while Chaparral appeared to be attempting to be more differentiated than Nucor, cluster analysis by Arthur (1992) indicates that it was an exception in this regard: A rather larger number of minimill competitors appeared to be targeting the same kind of low-cost position that Nucor had successfully managed to create for itself. And Porter's contention (in his presentations to executives) that Nucor followed a focused low-cost strategy does not fare much better. Product market data based, once again, on Arthur's work suggest that other minimills targeting low costs were at least as focused as Nucor. Thus, while the plants in the low-cost cluster reported significantly lower numbers of product types, sizes, and grades than the remainder, Nucor did not stand out along these dimensions: Its plants reported about the same number of product types and significantly higher number of product sizes and grades as the other low-cost plants.

These cross-sectional explanations of why competitors failed to imitate Nucor can be contrasted with simpler and, to my mind, more satisfying longitudinal explanations. Imagine a minimill that had historically paid its workers straight salaries (like Chaparral) but that wanted to emphasize the incentive-related component of their compensation (like Nucor). The management of such a minimill might have some trouble persuading workers to accept a large cut in their base pay in return for an assurance that they could make it up (and perhaps even earn slightly more) if they met more ambitious production targets. A particular source of difficulty, in light of the frequent failure of attempts to institute production incentive plans like Nucor's, is workers' fear that management will unfairly ratchet up production targets over time. Clearly the sort of reputation for dealing fairly with workers that Nucor's top management, particularly Iverson, its CEO for three decades, had developed would take a long time for another minimill to match. Just as clearly, it would be unnatural to explain this barrier to imitation in cross-sectional as opposed to longitudinal terms.

A similar story can be told about Nucor's management of its capital resources, particularly its policies of building or rebuilding one plant per year and of acting as its own general contractor. While other minimills, particularly ones that operated multiple plants, could imitate these arrangements, the initial payoffs to their doing so would presumably be limited—not so much as the result of cross-sectional effects but because of their limited base of experience. If the competitors were too far behind, they might, in line with classical experience curve theory, not even want to try to compete with Nucor on this basis. Once again interpretation of this longitudinal story in terms of cross-sectional effects would be artificial.

The implications of this discussion extend beyond controversies in strategic management to the rash of recent work by microeconomists on cross-sectional complementarities, beginning with Milgrom and Roberts' (1990b) application of lattice theory to such problems. If the past is any guide, the evolution of microeconomic modeling in this area may be driven more by opportunities to apply ever more advanced mathematical techniques than by any evidence that such a wholesale redirection of efforts is indeed warranted. Alternatively put, while some additional work on the cross-sectional approach is warranted, there is a risk that the expanded view of the firm that has been developed since the 1980s (see exhibit 1.2) may be collapsed back into consideration of just product market activities and the complementarities among them. Some concern is in order if one's primary interest is in business problems rather than in technique for its own sake.

6.6 Summary

This chapter on the steel industry, like the previous one on the PBX industry, looked at an apparent instance of incumbent failure to lead technologically but focused on process innovation rather than on product innovation. This choice of focus reflected differences in industry context: PBXs represented a very R&D-intensive industry in which (manufacturing) capacity was relatively cheap; steel, in contrast, represented an industry in which R&D-intensity was much more modest, but capacity costs much higher. As a result process innovation was the more natural focus in steel, and an appropriate characterization of interactive incentives required the imposition of capacity constraints. A game-theoretic model that captured this and other case-specific features helped explain why one might have expected the thin-slab casting innovation to be adopted first by an "entrant" (e.g., a steel minimill) rather than an "incumbent" (an integrated steelmaker).

This theoretical analysis was effectively conducted at the level of strategic groups. Empirical analysis at the firm level helped supplement it. Detailed empirical analysis of Nucor, a minimill, elucidated the efficiency advantage that was undoubtedly part of the reason why it was the first to adopt the new process technology. Empirical analyses of Chaparral, another successful minimill, and U.S. Steel, the largest integrated steelmaker, indicated that key competitors' nonadoption decisions may also have been influenced by a wide range of precommitments: to strategies, resources, contracts, and relationships.

The last section of this chapter also looked at the deeper issue of why other minimills targeting low-cost positions did not imitate the organizational arrangements that accounted for Nucor's extraordinary efficiency. The discussion suggested that longitudinal explanations of the sustainability of Nucor's competitive advantage fared much better than cross-sectional ones, even though the latter have become more fashionable of late.

7   Entry and Deterrence in British Satellite Broadcasting

The first three case studies in this book focused on models of competition with fixed product characteristics and production technologies.[1] The next two featured, respectively, competition over new products and processes. This final detailed case study fixes on an even more fluid situation: competition to monopolize a new product market made possible by a process innovation in broadcasting technology.

To be more specific, the analysis in this chapter is motivated by a war of attrition between British Satellite Broadcasting (BSB) and Sky Television over the market for satellite TV in the United Kingdom. Like the two preceding cases, this one could be read as yet another instance of incumbent failure: BSB entered the market first, with an up-to-date broadcasting technology, was surprised by Sky's fast-second entry with an older but cheaper technology, and eventually collapsed into Sky's arms on less-than-equal terms. That is not, however, the principal point of this chapter. Rather, it is to probe, with the case as an anchor, two foundational questions about game theory: Can firms be treated,

---

1. This chapter is a substantially rewritten revision of Brandenburger and Ghemawat (1994). I am solely responsible for all changes.

as per usual practice, as unitary players out to maximize their own payoffs, and if so, should their interactions be expected to lead to Nash equilibria?

I begin by describing the BSB-Sky interaction and then work backward (as is customary in game theory) through these two questions in the context of product-market wars of attrition. The implications for game theory turn out not to be innocuous; for researchers in strategic management, there are also nontrivial implications concerning the content of effective competitor analysis.

7.1 Case Background

Satellite television involves the transmission of television signals from the ground to a satellite and back down to receivers. The satellite serves as a giant television tower, and the greater its power, the smaller is the size of the receivers required.

The World Administrative Radio Conference of 1977 reserved for each country several high-powered television broadcast channels that could be picked up by satellite dishes small and inexpensive enough to be installed at individual homes. In April 1986 the British government invited applications to provide a commercial service on the U.K. channels and received five serious bids. In December of that year, it awarded a fifteen-year franchise for high-powered direct broadcast by satellite (DBS) to British Satellite Broadcasting (BSB), a consortium of five companies formed to bid on the project.

By July 1987 BSB had completed a first round of equity financing that raised a total of £222.5 million from eleven companies. The bulk of this money was earmarked for buying and launching two high-powered satellites (one for redundancy). BSB estimated that it would install 400,000 satellite dishes by the end of its first year of broadcasting (fall 1990), 2 million by 1992, 6 million by 1995, and 10 million by the year 2001. Operating break-even was expected at the 3 to 4 million mark in 1993, but the cost structure would continue to be dominated by mostly fixed (per-period) costs, such as program production and acquisition, marketing, and overhead. As a result the venture's economics would be very sensitive to the size of its customer base and its total start-up costs to its rate of market penetration. Total start-up costs were estimated at approximately £500 million and a second round of financing was scheduled for close to the commencement of broadcasting operations.

BSB's pursuit of these plans was disrupted in June 1988 by News Corporation's announcement that it would launch its own DBS venture in the United Kingdom, to be called Sky Television. News Corporation was a conglomerate, mostly in English-language media, that had recorded sales of about £3 billion and a return on sales of 7.8 percent in the preceding year. Its DBS service, Sky, was meant, like BSB, to be multichannel but was to be broadcast via a medium-powered satellite, Astra. Because of technological improvements, Astra could be received by acceptably small and inexpensive satellite dishes (although they would have to be somewhat larger than the dishes required to receive BSB's high-powered broadcasts).

The target launch date for Sky was in February 1989. News Corporation forecast that if this schedule could be met, Sky would install 1 million satellite dishes by the end of its first year of broadcasting and 5 to 6 million by the end of 1994. Operating breakeven was expected in late 1991 or early 1992 and total start-up costs, which would be shouldered by News Corporation, were estimated to be approximately £100 million. This estimate was substantially smaller than the corresponding figure for BSB because Sky did not need to launch its own satellites and because it was counting on cheaper programming, lower over-head, and a quicker roll-out.

In response to Sky's entry announcement, BSB revised its sales projections to 5 million satellite dishes by 1993 and 10 million by 1998. It planned to accelerate sales by increasing advertising and promotion levels, mostly closer to its planned launch date. More immediate in its effects was the bidding war that broke out between BSB and Sky for exclusive British television rights to Hollywood films, which were seen as key to each service's economics because of their ability to generate significant subscription revenues. By the end of 1988, BSB and Sky had committed a total of about £670 million to Hollywood film rights, including up-front payments of about £150 million. Both figures appear to have been more than twice as large as anticipated.

Sky went on the air first, in February 1989, as planned. Dish sales proved disappointing, however: Sky's cumulative total at the end of its first year of broadcasting was less than 600,000 and was not increasing nearly as rapidly as had been projected. Reasons that were invoked included shortages of receiving equipment, Sky's patchy programming, negative advertising by BSB, rising interest rates, and atypically nice weather.

This period proved, in many respects, even more difficult for BSB. Higher-than-expected costs necessitated a supplementary first round of financing in January 1989 that raised £131 million and a second supplementary later that year involving £70 million. In May 1989, BSB announced that it would miss its fall launch date because of delays in developing a complicated new semiconductor chip required for its satellite dish receivers. Finally in February 1990, it concluded a second round of financing that ensured £450 million in debt from banks, conditional on the timely achievement of operating targets and a matching £450 million from shareholders. This money was meant to fund

"Operation Fastburn," which involved increasing marketing expenditures to levels unprecedented in Britain. By then, BSB's billion-pound-plus capitalization made it the second costliest start-up in British history, behind the Channel Tunnel.

BSB finally went on the air in April 1990, with the target of installing at least 3 million dishes in its first three years. BSB's cumulated sales between April and October 1990 came to 175,000 dishes. Sky out-installed BSB two to one over that period, adding more than 350,000 dishes and bringing its total to 950,000. But BSB beat it by roughly the same margin in the last three months of the period, installing 125,000 dishes to Sky's 58,000. At the end of October 1990, BSB was losing money at the weekly rate of £6 to £7 million and Sky at a rate of about £2 million. Sky's parent, News Corporation, was facing a cash crunch and renegotiating several billion dollars of debt with bankers, who were insisting, among other things, that something be done to staunch the cash outflows from Sky.

On November 2, 1990, BSB and Sky announced that they would merge into BSkyB, with control to be split fifty-fifty between BSB's shareholders and Sky's parent, News Corporation. As an apparent response to News Corporation's cash constraints, it was supposed to receive its "half" of the first £1.2 billion of positive operating cash flow from the merged entity somewhat earlier than BSB's financial successors. It would also shoulder less than half of any immediate cash transfusions that the merged entity might require. Another implication of the merger was emphasized by its official description as "a combination of Sky's commercial acumen with the financial resources of BSB's major shareholders." In practical terms, top managers from Sky Television/News Corporation took charge of the merged entity and fired most of its employees, most of whom had been inherited from the old BSB operation.

7.2   Theoretical Background

BSB and Sky collectively lost £1.25 billion in their war of attrition before they decided to merge; they then suffered several hundred million pounds of additional losses before reaching break-even. These are large numbers, especially in light of the much smaller start-up costs initially envisaged for both operations. Is such a bitter fight consistent with the use of Nash equilibrium strategies by players out to maximize their respective profits?

This broad question has been addressed the most explicitly in the context of labor strikes. By the end of the 1980s, a consensus seemed to be emerging that the observed length of strikes could not entirely be accounted for by received game-theoretic models of bargaining over a shrinking pie (e.g., Hart 1989). Since then, however, theorists have managed to figure out better ways of explaining the delayed resolution of strikes (e.g., Cramton 1992). These divergent conclusions are due to differences in informational conditions and, by implication, to uncertainty. Instead of probing strikes at greater length however, these informational issues will be pursued in the context of product-market wars of attrition, with the BSB-Sky case affording an anchor.

Received theory tells us that whatever the context, fighting in wars of attrition has to be fraught with uncertainty: that with perfect and complete information, the pure strategy equilibria in a duopolistic context, for example, involve immediate concession by one of the two players. Of course there are also mixed-strategy equilibria that involve fighting even when all else is certain, but they are subject to several problems. First, arbitrarily long fights occur with arbitrarily small probability. Second, each player is expected to be indifferent in every phase of the war between fighting and conceding because its expected payoff is invariant to that choice. Third, the idea of conscious randomization by players (which is linked to payoff invariance) is hard to swallow in the context of long-run entry-or-exit decisions (as opposed to, say, short-run pricing decisions).

The simplest way of adding uncertainty (beyond that associated with the realizations of mixed strategies) to wars of attrition is to assume imperfect information about one or more structural parameters. It is easy, in such situations, to generate pure strategy equilibria that involve "fighting." Thus one might explain the war of attrition in U.K. satellite television in terms of imperfect information about the size of that market. In particular, one might stipulate that both BSB and Sky initially overestimated market size, leading them to expect to be profitable as duopolists and that they gradually came to their senses and decided to merge their interests.[2]

This is a conceptually coherent explanation of the war of attrition between BSB and Sky, and one whose attractiveness is increased by the fact that independent estimates of (medium- to long-run) market size fell over the period of that war. Still this explanation suffers from two significant limitations. First, the two competitors' dish-installation targets (and comparisons with the rate of penetration of the U.K. market by similar products such as VCRs) indicate that both ventures were initially aiming for a (near) monopoly. Second, even if this explanation did ring true, it would not "really" involve fighting: Both competitors would be willing to stay in as long as their (common) estimate of market size implied that they could operate profitably as duopolists, but as soon as the demand estimate drifted below that level (adjusted, perhaps, for option value), they would be back to the pure strategies of the perfect information world that involve immediate concession by one player.

---

2. Of course such an explanation fails, like the other discussed in this section, to explain why BSB and Sky did not merge at the very beginning of their interaction.

To "really" induce pure strategies that involve fighting, incomplete information is (as implied by the literature on the length of strikes) imperative. In its two-sided version, this would involve each of the two players being one of several possible "types," with each player knowing its own type but able only to guess at the other's. Each player's probability distribution over the other's type can be used to pin down a "Bayesian equilibrium" for a game of incomplete information of this sort (Harsanyi 1967, 1968a, 1968b). In the context of wars of attrition in growing (as opposed to declining) product markets, the leading example of such a model, cited in chapter 4, is Fudenberg and Tirole's (1986a).

In Fudenberg and Tirole's model, each player is uncertain about the other's level of fixed costs. The Bayesian equilibrium involves each player selecting a time, dependent on its beliefs about how its fixed costs stack up against its rival's, until which it will persist but after which it will withdraw if its rival remains active. With suitable boundary conditions, stopping times are greater than zero: It pays both players to lose money in order to be able to infer whose fixed costs are higher. And because information is revealed gradually, fighting goes on for a while.

This is, once again, a conceptually coherent explanation of the war of attrition between BSB and Sky but is subject, yet again, to a significant limitation. In Fudenberg and Tirole's (1986a) model, delayed selection requires ambiguity about relative cost levels. In the case being considered, however, there was public agreement that BSB's costs were significantly higher than Sky's because of its dedicated satellites, more expensive movie contracts, and sybaritic operating style. Selection should therefore have been relatively swift.

The line of analysis advocated by Harsanyi and implemented by Fudenberg and Tirole could perhaps be rescued, in the BSB-Sky context, by shifting the locus of incomplete information to some other structural parameter. But instead of doing so, Brandenburger and Ghemawat (1994) found it more plausible to shine the spotlight on strategic as opposed to structural uncertainty: on the idea that there might have been irreducible uncertainty about how "tough" one's rival could be expected to be. Such uncertainty, while assumed away by Harsanyi's (and Nash's 1951) formulation of equilibrium, seemed on the basis of both press accounts and interviews to have been a salient feature of the war of attrition between BSB and Sky. The question that is addressed in the next section is whether such uncertainty is adequate, given common belief in rationality, to account for lengthy wars of attrition in product markets.

7.3   Theoretical Analysis

To analyze the difference strategic uncertainty can make, consider a stripped-down version of the two-player war of attrition with zero structural uncertainty that unfolds in discrete time (indexed by $t = 0, 1, 2, \ldots$). At the beginning of each period t, each player must choose between two actions: fighting and conceding. A player who, at the start of some period, chooses to fight incurs a cost of c that period, but a player who chooses to concede bears no costs. As long as at the start of each period both players continue to choose to fight, neither secures a monopoly. If, however, at the start of some period, one player chooses to fight while the other chooses to concede, then the first player secures a monopoly, which is worth V. If at the start of some period both players choose to concede, each player obtains the amount $V/2$. To ensure that the game is worth the candle, it is assumed that $V > 2c$. Players discount future costs and benefits at a common discount factor δ.[3]

---

3. These and the other assumptions of symmetry that follow are made in the interest of parsimony.

A player's choice of strategy in this war of attrition consists in choosing a stopping time, that is, a time at which to concede if the other player has not yet done so. Denote the two players as A and B, respectively. Then the set of possible strategies for player A can be written as $\{a_0, a_1, a_2, \ldots, a_\infty\}$, where a_t, for $t = 0$, 1, 2, $\ldots$, denotes the strategy of conceding at the start of period t (given that player B has not yet conceded), and a_∞ denotes the strategy of never conceding (always choosing to fight). The set of possible strategies for player B can be written in analogous fashion as $\{b_0, b_1, b_2, \ldots, b_\infty\}$.

What are the possible outcomes to this game when players are rational (i.e., act to maximize their respective payoffs), each believes the other to be rational, each believes that the other believes that the first is rational, and so on ad infinitum? Answering this question requires a formal framework in which statements like "Player A ascribes probability 1 to player B's ascribing probability 1 to player A's being rational" can be written down and studied. Aumann and Brandenburger (1995, sec. 2) offer such a formalism, which they term an *interactive belief system*. This formalism enriches Harsanyi's treatment of types in a way that can be illustrated with exhibit 7.1, which presents a particular interactive belief system for the war of attrition.

In exhibit 7.1 a particular type of a player is associated with a probability distribution over the set of possible types of the other player, *and* (unlike Harsanyi's formulation) with a choice of strategy for the first player. Each row corresponds to a different type of player A and is labeled by the strategy that type chooses. Similarly each column corresponds to a different type of player B and is labeled by the strategy that type chooses.[4] The probability

---

4. In general, this is not an adequate way of labeling types, since more than one type of a given player may choose the same strategy. (These types would then differ in the probability distributions held.) It suffices here because no two types of a player

Exhibit 7.1
An Interactive Belief System

Each cell contains an upper-right entry (player B distribution) and a lower-left entry (player A distribution).

	b_0	b_1	b_2	b_3	...	b_l	...	b_∞
a_0 (UR)	0	$1-\varepsilon$	$1-\varepsilon$	$1-\varepsilon$		$1-\varepsilon$		$1-\varepsilon$
a_0 (LL)	0	0	0	0	...	0	...	1
a_1 (UR)	0	0	$\varepsilon(1-\varepsilon)$	$\varepsilon(1-\varepsilon)$		$\varepsilon(1-\varepsilon)$		$\varepsilon(1-\varepsilon)$
a_1 (LL)	$1-\varepsilon$	0	0	0	...	0	...	ε
a_2 (UR)	0	0	0	$\varepsilon^2(1-\varepsilon)$		$\varepsilon^2(1-\varepsilon)$		$\varepsilon^2(1-\varepsilon)$
a_2 (LL)	$1-\varepsilon$	$\varepsilon(1-\varepsilon)$	0	0	...	0	...	ε^2
a_3 (UR)	0	0	0	0		$\varepsilon^3(1-\varepsilon)$		$\varepsilon^3(1-\varepsilon)$
a_3 (LL)	$1-\varepsilon$	$\varepsilon(1-\varepsilon)$	$\varepsilon^2(1-\varepsilon)$	0	...	0	...	ε^3
$\vdots$								
a_l (UR)	0	0	0	0		0		$\varepsilon^l(1-\varepsilon)$
a_l (LL)	$1-\varepsilon$	$\varepsilon(1-\varepsilon)$	$\varepsilon^2(1-\varepsilon)$	$\varepsilon^3(1-\varepsilon)$	...	0	...	ε^l
$\vdots$								
a_∞ (UR)	1	ε	ε^2	ε^3		ε^l		0
a_∞ (LL)	$1-\varepsilon$	$\varepsilon(1-\varepsilon)$	$\varepsilon^2(1-\varepsilon)$	$\varepsilon^3(1-\varepsilon)$	...	$\varepsilon^l(1-\varepsilon)$	...	0

distribution associated with a particular type of player A is depicted by the lower-left entry in each cell of that row. Likewise the probability distribution associated with a particular type of player B is depicted by the upper-right entry in each cell of that column. In these distributions the parameter ε should be thought

make the same choice. Notice also that in the interactive belief system of exhibit 7.1, every strategy appears; that is, for each strategy, there is a type of player that chooses it. This need not be so in general.

of as some fixed number between 0 and 1. While different ε's could be allowed in different cells, this representation is particularly simple and implies that the different types' distributions are "natural." The first type of either player (type a_0 or type b_0) thinks that the other player is a "fighter" and so throws in the towel immediately. The second type (a_1 or b_1) thinks that the other player may well concede immediately but, if the other player does not do so, gives up hope, concluding that the other player is a fighter and throwing in the towel. And so on. There is also a type of either player (a_∞ or b_∞) who is an "eternal optimist"—always of the view that the other player is going to concede and accordingly always choosing to fight.

To continue, a *state of the world* is simply a pair of types, one for each player. Specification of an interactive belief system for a game, together with the selection of a state in that system, constitutes a complete description of the strategies the players choose, the players' conjectures, their beliefs about other players' conjectures, and so on ad infinitum.

To see how this works, choose a specific state in exhibit 7.1, say (a_2, b_1). This state describes a situation in which player A chooses the strategy a_2 and player B chooses the strategy b_1. What is A's conjecture about B? It can be read immediately from the probability distribution held by A's type: Player A assigns a probability of $1 - \varepsilon$ to B's choosing the strategy b_0, a probability of $\varepsilon(1 - \varepsilon)$ to B's choosing the strategy b_1, and a probability of ε^2 to B's choosing the strategy b_∞. Similarly player B assigns a probability of $1 - \varepsilon$ to A's choosing the strategy a_0 and a probability of ε to A's choosing the strategy a_∞. What are A's beliefs about B's conjecture? These too can be read from the exhibit. Player A assigns (1) a probability of $1 - \varepsilon$ to B's type being b_0, and hence to B's assigning a probability 1 to A's choosing a_∞; (2) a probability of $\varepsilon(1 - \varepsilon)$ to B's type being b_1, and hence to B's assigning a probability of $1 - \varepsilon$ to A's choosing a_0 and a probability of ε to A's choosing a_∞; and (3) a probability of ε^2 to B's type being b_∞, and hence to B's assigning a probability of $\varepsilon^t(1 - \varepsilon)$ to A's choosing a_t for $t = 0, 1, 2, \ldots$. Player B's beliefs about A's conjecture can be read off in similar fashion. Indeed, it should be clear that all beliefs about beliefs about . . . one or another player's conjecture about its rival can be read from the exhibit in this way.[5]

What have been described so far are the players' choices, conjectures, beliefs about conjectures, and the like. But what about the players' rationality, their beliefs about each other's rationality, and so on? The interactive belief system describes that as well. Call a type of a player *rational* if that type's choice of strategy maximizes the player's expected payoff, calculated using that type's conjecture.

Type a_0 of A is clearly rational, since that type's conjecture ascribes a probability of 1 to B's never conceding. What about type a_1 of player A? Type a_1 assigns a probability of $1 - \varepsilon$ to B's choosing b_0 (conceding immediately) and a probability of ε to B's choosing b_∞ (never conceding). Given this conjecture, the operative choices for A come down to choosing between a_0 (conceding immediately) and a_1 (fighting once and then conceding). The expected payoff from choosing a_0 is $(1 - \varepsilon)V/2$, while the expected payoff from choosing a_1 is $-c + (1 - \varepsilon)V$. The strategy a_1 yields player A at least as high an expected payoff as a_0 provided that $-c + (1 - \varepsilon)V \geq (1 - \varepsilon)V/2$ or $\varepsilon \leq 1 - 2c/V$. In this case, type a_1 is indeed rational. A little thought shows that in fact every

---

5. In using the interactive belief system in this manner, there appears to be an implicit assumption that the system itself is in some sense "transparent" to the players. This is not in fact an assumption but a tautology. By design the interactive belief system already describes all the uncertainty facing the players.

type a_t of player A, for $t = 1, 2, \ldots , \infty$, is rational exactly when the preceding inequality holds. And because of the symmetry of the interactive belief system in exhibit 7.1, the conditions for the various types of player B to be rational are the same as those just derived for the corresponding types of player A.

In what follows, it shall be assumed that $\varepsilon \leq 1 - 2c/V$. All types of either player are then rational, which can be illustrated by reconsidering the state (a_2, b_1). It has already been established that at this state both players are rational. But what probability does A ascribe to B's being rational? Type a_2 assigns a positive probability to B's type being b_0, b_1, or b_∞. Since each of these types of B is rational, A in fact assigns a probability of 1 to B's being rational. Indeed, it is not difficult to see that since all types of either player are rational, there is common belief in rationality at (a_2, b_1). That is, each player assigns a probability of 1 to the other's assigning a probability of 1 to . . . the rationality of one or another player.[6] This observation leads directly to the first of two propositions developed in this section.

Proposition 7.1 *Consider the discrete-time war of attrition. There is an interactive belief system for this game such that, given any number T, there is a state in the system at which:*

a. *the players are rational,*

b. *there is common belief in rationality,*

c. *each player has a strictly positive expected payoff, and*

d. *the players fight in each of the periods 0, 1, 2, . . ., T − 1 and then concede in period T.*

Proof Exhibit 7.1 itself is a suitable interactive belief system. Choose ε to satisfy $0 < \varepsilon < 1 - 2c/V$, and pick the state (a_T, b_T).

---

6. In fact there is common belief in rationality at every state in the interactive belief system.

Given the choice of ε, all types of either player are rational; a fortiori, types a_T and b_T are rational, and there is common belief in rationality at (a_T, b_T). The expected payoff of either of the types a_T and b_T is readily calculated to be $[-c + (1 - \varepsilon)V](1 - \varepsilon^T\delta^T)/$ $(1 - \varepsilon\delta)$, which is strictly positive.   □

Proposition 7.1 implies that in the discrete-time war of attrition, a fight of any duration whatsoever is possible when the players are rational and there is common belief in rationality. That is, these two assumptions do not in any way restrict the possible outcomes of the game. Moreover both players can have strictly positive expected payoffs, even though they may both end up incurring overall losses.

Proposition 7.1 is not entirely satisfactory, however, because rationality and common belief in rationality obtain ex ante at the start of period 0: The players' expected payoffs are computed at the start of the game. The next question concerns what happens if rationality and common belief in rationality are required—in a sense to be made precise—to hold throughout the game, not just at the start. Analogously one might ask whether it is possible for the players to have strictly positive expected payoffs (calculated looking forward) throughout the course of the game.

Answering this second question requires incorporation of whatever the players learn as the game progresses into the interactive belief system. In fact that is readily done. Revert to some particular state of the interactive belief system in exhibit 7.1. Suppose that at this state the game lasts at least one period; that is, both players choose to fight in period 0. Consider now the situation at the start of period 1. Intuitively it is common belief at this point that player A did not adopt the strategy a_0 and player B did not adopt the strategy b_0. The updated belief is captured formally by crossing out the first row and column of the interactive belief system and renormalizing each type's truncated probability distribution.[7] The situation at the start of period 1 is fully described by this updated interactive belief system, with the actual state being identified with that at the start of the game. If both players choose to fight in period 1 as well, the situation at the start of period 2 is described by crossing out the a_1 row and b_1 column of the updated interactive belief system and again renormalizing. And so on.

It is now possible to give formal content to statements like "player A is rational in period t," or "player A assigns a probability of 1 in period t to player B's being rational in period t." Such statements are true if the corresponding condition holds at the given state in the t-times updated interactive belief system. And this leads directly to the second proposition of this section.

Proposition 7.2 *Consider the discrete-time war of attrition. There is an interactive belief system for this game such that, given any number T, there is a state in the system at which:*

a. *the players are rational in each of the periods 0, 1, 2, . . . , T,*

b. *there is common belief in rationality in each of the periods 0, 1, 2, . . . , T,*

c. *each player has a strictly positive expected payoff (calculated looking forward) in each of the periods 0, 1, 2, . . . , T − 1, and*

d. *the players fight in each of the periods 0, 1, 2, . . . , T − 1 and then concede in period T.*

Proof Exhibit 7.1 is once again a suitable interactive belief system. As in the proof of proposition 7.1, choose ε to satisfy $0 < \varepsilon < 1 - 2c/V$ and pick the state (a_T, b_T). In this state the players are known to be rational, to have positive expected payoffs, and to

---

7. Alternatively expressed, the distribution associated with any given type of A is now a conditional distribution, calculated by conditioning on the event that B's type is not b_0. The updated distribution associated with any given type of B is likewise a conditional distribution, conditioned on the event that A's type is not a_0.

exhibit common belief in rationality at the start of period 0. Next observe that the updated interactive belief system, obtained by crossing out the first row and column in the exhibit and renormalizing, is isomorphic (up to the relabeling of types) to the original interactive belief system. It follows that at the identified state (a_T, b_T), the players are rational, have strictly positive expected payoffs, and there is common belief in rationality at the start of period 1. The argument repeats. □

To summarize the two propositions, there can be arbitrarily long fights in wars of attrition, even with common belief in rationality and without structural uncertainty. This conclusion, which is at odds with standard equilibrium reasoning, is due to strategic uncertainty and the "fog of war" that it can induce. Thus we have reached a negative answer to the second of the two foundational questions posed in the introduction to this chapter: Even if firms are treated as unitary players out to maximize their own payoffs, their interactions need not lead to Nash equilibrium.

7.4   Case Analysis

It is time to work back to the first of the two foundational questions about game theory raised at the beginning of this chapter: Can firms in fact be treated as unitary players who maximize their respective profits? This question is anathema to true-blue economists, who tend to treat (constrained) profit-maximization as axiomatic, but it is of intense interest to other researchers. The details of the BSB-Sky case provide some empirical perspective.

Available information, while far from complete, indicates that BSB was taken unawares by Sky's entry and reacted by digging in its heels. The first point will be dealt with summarily by citing BSB's treasurer, Richard Brooke: "We were not concerned about competitive threats until Sky came along. Murdoch's announcement came from left field and took everybody by surprise." On the second point, it is instructive to look at how BSB altered its initial business plan in response to Sky's entry.

As noted above, BSB's initial business plan called for a customer base of 400,000 satellite dishes by fall 1990, 2 million by 1992, 6 million by 1995, and 10 million by 2001. Sky's entry prompted a revision of this plan, to a customer base of 5 million dishes by 1993 and 10 million by 1998. BSB now planned to accelerate penetration by increasing its marketing expenditures. This revised plan, like the initial one, was not communicated widely, suggesting that it was more than just "cheap talk" intended to influence potential customers' adoption decisions.

Upon closer examination the revision embodies an assumption that is curious at least in the context of the satellite case: that the transition from thinking that one has zero competitors to thinking that there is indeed one will lead to an increase in advertising expenditures large enough to lift optimal (own) volume with competition higher than optimal volume without it. One reason this assumption is curious is that the aggregate demand for satellite television in Britain was perceived to be relatively inexpansible: a fixed pie, according to an industry observer. Another, more subtle but perhaps even more significant reason is due to the fact that the two competitors' technologies were incompatible, in the sense that their satellite dishes could not receive each other's programming. Potential British adopters of satellite television were reported to be concerned about being stranded with the wrong technology: Many of them had also been early adopters of VCRs (which had penetrated Britain relatively quickly) and quite a few had chosen Sony's Betamax standard—only to watch the VHS standard capture most of the market, limiting the availability of programming for their Betamax machines. Their concerns regarding satellite television were intensified by significant hardware costs (£200 to £250 per dish) and by heavy advertising by BSB and Sky that, particularly on BSB's side, highlighted the issue of incompatibility. Thus competition may, by inducing potential adopters to defer their adoption decisions until they could see which technology was winning out, have shrunk the size of the pie instead of merely failing to expand it much.

This line of reasoning is easily formalized in terms of a simple model related to Butters (1977) and Grossman and Shapiro (1984) that is explicit about how advertising affects customer behavior. Assume that advertising conveys information about the existence of a particular television service (a network of TV channels) and the consumer surplus it may afford to S potential adopters, each of whom will sign on with at most one of the two services. The potential adopters differ from each other only in terms of the advertising messages that they hear: The probability of reaching a particular potential adopter with a particular message is assumed to be r (where $0 < r \ll 1$) and to be independent of the probability that he/she will see another message sent by the same company, or for that matter by its rival. A potential adopter who receives no messages is unaware of the existence of the two television services and therefore purchases neither; a potential adopter who receives messages from just one of the two competitors is willing to pay up to u for that competitor's service; and a potential adopter who receives messages from both competitors responds by purchasing neither (or, if we were to be a bit more realistic, by deferring his adoption decision).

Firm i's profit function can then be written:

$$\Pi_i = (u - c) \times S \times [1 - (1 - r)^{N_i}] \times (1 - r)^{N_j} - aN_i,$$

where the term in square brackets represents the probability that a representative potential adopter has seen at least one of firm i's N_i advertisements, the term that follows it is the probability that he/she hasn't seen any of rival firm j's N_j advertisements, and c and a denote, respectively, variable production costs and the cost per advertising message. The first-order condition for interior maximization of profits by choosing the *optimal* advertising level, N_i^*, is

$$(1 - r)^{N_i} = -a/[(u - c) \times S \times \ln(1 - r) \times (1 - r)^{N_j}].$$

It is easy to check that the reaction functions slope downward: as N_j^* increases, N_i^* decreases. Therefore as firm i shifts from thinking that it has a monopoly (implying $N_j = 0$) to recognizing that it must compete against another firm which will advertise at positive levels (implying $N_j^* > 0$), that recognition decreases its optimal level of advertising, N_i^*, as well as its optimal penetration level (the optimized value of the product of two probabilistic terms in the profit function). The fact that BSB ratcheted up its plans for both advertising and penetration in response to Sky's entry is therefore doubly troubling.

Finally BSB's aggressive response is also troubling because Sky's entry announcement seemed to turn BSB into the underdog. BSB would launch several months (actually more than one year) later than Sky. BSB's dishes would be priced a bit higher, at £250 versus £200 (plus a £40 installation charge). BSB could count, at the time, on just three channels, compared to four for Sky, which might also benefit from television broadcasting on some of Astra's twelve other channels. Unlike News Corporation, BSB did not own a film library nor have experience with television broadcasting. BSB was also clearly the operation with the (much) higher overhead costs. And although BSB's transmission technology would enhance the sight and sound performance of new television sets equipped to take advantage of it, there were indications that the incremental benefits would not be enough to justify the added costs (and risks). Perhaps the most telling sign was the withdrawal from the BSB consortium of Amstrad, a marketer and distributor of consumer electronics, that was supposed to ensure availability of the satellite dishes and other hardware. Amstrad's founder and top manager, Alan Sugar, appeared alongside his counterpart at News Corporation, Rupert Murdoch, when the latter announced the launch of Sky and, in his new role as Sky's principal supplier of dishes, dismissed BSB's technology as "a lot of nonsense which requires a lot of redundant components."

For all these reasons, BSB's response to Sky's entry—ratcheting up its planned advertising and penetration levels—is hard to rationalize with profit maximization. According to industry observers, it more plausibly reflects a chief executive officer, Anthony Simmonds-Gooding, who was personally committed to making BSB an unqualified success in order to cap off a distinguished career in marketing, as well as a governance structure, consisting of an unwieldy consortium of BSB's shareholders, which was unable to rein him in until much later on.

Devout profit-maximizers may not be convinced by this interpretation. Indeed, they may even be able to seize upon features of the British satellite broadcasting industry (e.g., network externalities) to concoct stories that make attempts to accelerate penetration the optimal response to the emergence of competition. Although it is difficult to anticipate, let alone address, all the stories that might be devised to protect the postulate of profit maximization in this particular case, more general questions can be raised about the efficacy of such immunizing stratagems. A large body of empirical evidence indicates that individuals and firms often irrationally escalate commitment to losing courses of action in competitive situations because of the sunk cost fallacy, attempts to justify past choices, selective perception, autistic hostility, and various other biases and distortions.[8] A pure faith in the prevalence of profit maximization throughout wars of attrition would appear therefore to be misplaced.

7.5   Reflections

In addition to the perspective that it provides on the foundations of game theory, the BSB-Sky case also sheds light on an important topic in strategic management: competitor analysis. Begin with what game theory itself suggests in this regard: using the interplay of competitors' incentives and, in particular, the concept of strategic equilibrium, to pin down the outcomes of competitors' interactions. While this approach is subject to its own limitations, as noted in the last two sections of this chapter, explicitly strategic (self-consciously interactive) analysis along the indicated lines *can* be fruitful if the cases discussed earlier in this book, particularly in chapters 2 through 4, are any guide. Such interactive analysis is nonetheless absent from received frameworks for competitor analysis in strategic management (e.g., Porter 1980, ch. 3).

More recent contributions to strategic management can be read as identifying some of the ways in which the "no-fat" models preferred by game-theorists need to be enriched to illumine interactions among actual firms. Thus the resource-based view (RBV) of the firm (Wernerfelt 1984) suggests that firms' resource precommitments should be expected to have a major influence on their behavior. A recent extension by Teece and Pisano (1994) focuses on the variability of firms' resource endowments in the operational long run (the RBV focuses on the operational short run), and suggests that differences in "dynamic capabilities" (the

---

8. Consult, for instance, Bazerman and Neale (1992, ch. 2) and Rubin, Pruitt, and Kim (1994, ch. 7).

efficiency with which new product market opportunities can be exploited or resource endowments upgraded) drive the course of competitor interactions. Based on past form, we may yet be subject to an even more dynamic story in which the flexibility to shift capability thrusts is asserted to be the key strategic advantage. And so on.

These dissimilarities mask an important similarity in recent thinking in strategic management: the idea that at any given point in time, competitors' opportunity sets can be taken to differ because of resource/capability/flexibility constraints. Recognition of such differences in opportunity sets significantly enriches "no-fat" competitor analysis. But it is still not rich enough because it ignores a key principle of evolutionary economics: that performance relative to competitors depends not just on opportunity sets but also on the strategies that are actually tried. To make the same point in other words, resource/capability/flexibility constraints can, in principle, be reconciled with conventional microeconomic analysis, which presumes profit maximization, by postulating constrained profit maximization instead.[9] Nonoptimal choices from opportunity sets, in contrast, cannot be assimilated in this fashion but can still have a major influence on the course of interactions. For instance, would it have been rational for Sky to enter, in spite of all its competitive advantages, if it had anticipated that BSB's response would be to increase rather than decrease its commitment, through an incompatible technology, to a market that appeared likely to prove a natural monopoly? To ask this question is to wonder whether deviations from profit maximization contami-

9. Tirole (1988, pp. 50–51) has articulated the hope that even when competitors do not manage to maximize their respective profits, their organizational inefficiencies might be separable (in terms of third-party observation) from their product market interactions.

nated the whole play of the game, in the sense of being responsible for the fact that there was any fight at all.

By implication, if competitor analysis is to be useful in the real world, it should supplement the economic analysis of incentives, capabilities and precommitments with behavioral analysis of predispositions. Numerous factors that shed light on such predispositions, as well as influences on their strength, have been identified in the literature on strategic management. Thus strategies are likely to persist, particularly if past performance has been satisfactory. The personal motivations of managers are likely to matter as well, particularly if governance-related restraints or incentives are weak. And so on.

To make the requirements for and rewards to expanded competitor analysis concrete, reconsider News Corporation from BSB's perspective. BSB was, as noted above, apparently blindsided by News Corporation's entry. It might have been more likely to identify News Corporation as a potential competitor ahead of time had it used an expanded framework for competitor analysis that looked at resources, capabilities, strategies, and personalities as well as the sorts of interactive considerations highlighted by the "no-fat" theoretical model analyzed earlier.

Preexisting resources that made News Corporation a particularly threatening potential entrant included not just the fact that it was already the second-largest media conglomerate in the world but, more specifically, its ownership of the film library and production capabilities of Twentieth Century–Fox, a major Hollywood studio, and of newspapers that accounted for one-third of British daily circulation (which could be—and were—used to promote Sky), as well as the political goodwill of British Prime Minister Margaret Thatcher and her Conservative party (which was important because of gray areas in the regulation of satellite TV).

Capabilities are a fuzzier category, but one can cite News Corporation's previous experience with satellite television, particularly the pan-European Sky Channel, and perhaps also its history of skirting regulatory loopholes and beating competitors to the air, which can be traced back to its entry into television in Australia. In the late 1950s, when the Australian government allotted News Corporation one of two commercial television broadcasting licenses for Adelaide rather than the monopoly its founder, Rupert Murdoch, had campaigned for, News Corporation successfully raced to be the first to begin broadcasting. And in 1962, when News Corporation was denied a stake in the new license for Sydney, it threatened to broadcast to the city anyway by buying an unprofitable station in a town sixty miles away as well as access to some U.S. television programming. The competitor that had won the Sydney franchise conceded a 25 percent stake to News Corporation.

Numerous aspects of News Corporation's revealed strategy—patterns in its past choices—further amplified the threat of its entry. At a corporate level, News Corporation was shifting its emphasis from print to electronic media and, within the latter category, was focusing on satellite, as opposed to cable, transmission. It was also focusing on English-speaking markets, and while it owned significant newspaper and television interests in Australia and the United States (where its Fox Broadcasting Company appeared to be succeeding as the fourth television network), its interests in the second-largest English-speaking market, Britain, were confined to newspapers. News Corporation had indicated its general interest in British television by purchasing a 7.5 percent stake in the ailing Independent Television (ITV) franchise for London in the mid-1970s (which it divested a few years later, reportedly because it felt that it did not have enough influence on the station's positioning). A recent, more specific indicator of its interest in direct broadcast by satellite (DBS) to Britain was its participation in one of the losing consortia that bid for the British high-powered DBS franchise which BSB won.

Finally personalities may have mattered at News Corporation as well as at BSB, particularly the personality of Rupert Murdoch who had founded News Corporation and continued to control it financially and managerially. Murdoch, originally an Australian, was widely reputed to have a chip on his shoulder against Britain and its media establishment. As he himself put it at the press conference at which he announced the launch of Sky, "My contention is that broadcasting in this country has too long been the preserve of the old establishment and is deeply elitist in its thinking and approach to programming." It is conceivable that Murdoch derived nonpecuniary personal benefits from challenging BSB's upmarket "establishment" approach with a disestablishmentarian, downmarket one. From BSB's perspective Murdoch's widely broadcast attitudes could arguably have helped predict ahead of time that he would prove one of the more dangerous of the competitors that bid for but lost the British high-powered DBS franchise to BSB.

As far as the rewards to expanded competitor analysis are concerned, BSB might have behaved rather differently had it taken potential competitors more seriously, with important implications for its positioning at the time News Corporation announced the launch of Sky. In terms of programming, BSB might have moved earlier to tie up the British rights to the films of the major Hollywood studios: At the time of Sky's entry, it was close to signing agreements with most of the major studios but was holding out for access to films within six months of their release on video instead of the customary twelve months. In addition BSB might have reconsidered the minimal differentiation from the BBC that was implicit in the high-quality programming that it was planning: Sky subsequently pursued a more differentiated position. The British government might have been dealt with differently as well: Rules could have been clarified, regulatory loopholes (e.g., indirect entry via a medium-powered satellite, as well as the possibility of cross-owning and cross-promoting British newspapers and television channels) could have been closed off, and better terms could have been bargained for because of potential competition (e.g., insistence on the rights to all five rather than just three high-powered channels). To deal more directly with potential competitors, BSB might have prepositioned itself better by accelerating its launch date and slimming down a cost structure that was widely viewed as bloated. It could also have been less exuberant in its forecasts about the demand for satellite television in Britain. While some of these steps could still have been taken after Sky's entry, and were, the delay generally reduced their effectiveness, confirming the rewards to anticipating rather than merely reacting to competitors.

To summarize this section, use of an expanded framework for competitor analysis might have helped BSB to assign News Corporation a position toward the head of the queue of potential entrants. If BSB had registered ahead of time the threat from News Corporation in particular and from potential competitors in general (it was aware, after all, of the planned launch of the Astra medium-powered satellite), it might have taken a host of actions that could either have deterred Sky's entry or positioned BSB better to deal with postentry competition. Instead, BSB appeared to ignore potential competition and to preposition itself as an inefficient "fat cat." Note the implication that careful competitor analysis—including but extending beyond the theoretical analysis of no/low-fat models—can have implications for internal organization as well as for external interactions.

7.6 Summary

Compared to the preceding chapters, this chapter has placed more emphasis on the limits of game theory than on its uses. Two principal difficulties arise. The first difficulty, which was flushed out by the empirical analysis, is that it may not always be possible to treat competitors as unitary actors out to maximize their own payoffs. This is partly due to the fact that organizations are not monadic; they consist, instead, of various constituencies with diverse interests (e.g., shareholders vs. managers in the case of BSB). It may not always be possible, let alone likely, for organizational rules to aggregate such diversity into a well-behaved objective function. In addition there is always the possibility of idiotic behavior, pure and simple. Scouting both possibilities requires a detailed analysis of internal organization and is aided by Selznick's (1957) observation that commitments to acting in particular ways are built into organizations.

The second difficulty with standard game theory, which was flushed out by the theoretical analysis, is that even if competitors can, to a first appromixation, be treated as unitary, payoff-maximizing players, the concept of strategic equilibrium may unduly restrict the set of possible outcomes by ruling out strategic uncertainty. Once one grants the existence of strategic uncertainty, the scope of the probability assessments that are in order extends to encompass rivals' strategies as well as the structural parameters of their payoff functions. The expanded framework for competitor analysis described in the last section of this chapter is meant to help with such direct assessments of competitors' strategies. While economic incentives cannot be ignored, neither can behavioral considerations—a topic that will be revisited in the next chapter.

8   Conclusions

Chapter 1 of this book proposed using the case method to probe the uses (and limits) of game-theoretic reasoning about business strategy. The six chapters that followed took on this task in the context of a wide range of business commitments. It is time to summarize the conclusions from the cases considered. That was, after all, one of the principal reasons for assembling the individual case studies into a book.

I read the case studies as suggesting that game theory can be useful to business strategy and that the case method can help the two to connect. Much of this chapter will elaborate this reading and review the reasons that the cases already presented in this book support it. But given the modesty of the case sample, it will be supplemented with a minicase, on the recent spectrum auctions by the U.S. Federal Communications Commission (FCC), that provides extrasample leverage.

The principal reason for looking at the spectrum auctions is the unprecedented extent to which they were informed by game-theoretic reasoning. They therefore represent a crucial case for assessing the uses and limits of game theory—one that can significantly strengthen *or* weaken the conclusions derived from the other cases in this book. Assessments of the spectrum auctions along this dimension are aided by the fact that a number of game theorists who were involved in advising the FCC on auction design or competitors on their bidding strategies have written up their experiences.[1] While their inferences (like anyone else's) have in-built biases, they do facilitate the cross-checking of my own inferences based on the other cases considered in this book.

A second reason for looking at the spectrum auctions is related to the type of industry involved. Some of the competitive settings surveyed in this book, particularly in the earlier chapters (which tend to cover chronologically earlier events), have been discounted by students of strategic management on the ground that they deal with a golden age of oligopoly that is now past or that they are, for some other reason, too simple to present much of a strategic challenge.[2] While I disagree with this characterization, it does seem useful to seek out another case to which it cannot be misapplied. Few competitive arenas could be more fluid, as of the mid-1990s, than the evolving digital space.

This chapter therefore begins by describing the design of and developments in the spectrum auctions that were initiated in 1994 and 1995. The next two sections review conclusions from the earlier case studies about the uses of the case method and of game theory and cross-check them against this minicase. The section that follows discusses the application of game theory to business situations in order to help managers (rather than researchers) with the games that they play. The focus of the discussion shifts from the uses of the case method, which researchers,

---

1. The game theorists whose written accounts I have relied on are Ausubel and Cramton (1996), Chakravorti et al. (1995), Cramton (1995), McMillan (1994), McAfee and McMillan (1996), Milgrom (1996), and Salant (1996). I also had access to several more traditional management consultants' perspectives on the auctions, and to a large company which was active in the MTA broadband auction.
2. Consult, for instance, Hamel and Prahalad (1994) or D'Aveni (1994).

particularly in IO, are more apt to question, to the uses of game theory, about which researchers in strategic management and practitioners are more likely to have questions.

8.1 A Minicase: The PCS Auctions

In August 1993 the U.S. Congress authorized the FCC to auction slices of the radio spectrum for personal communications services (PCS) instead of simply giving them away. The FCC issued a Notice of Proposed Rule Making and invited comments on it from industry. More than two hundred firms and lobbying groups, many of whom were advised by leading game theorists, responded. Proposals by game theorists Paul Milgrom and Robert Wilson for Pacific Bell (a Regional Bell Operating Company, or RBOC) and Preston McAfee for AirTouch (a cellular telephone company) proved instrumental in steering the FCC toward a nontraditional auction format.

Milgrom, Wilson, and McAfee advocated, and the FCC largely adopted, a *simultaneous, multiple-round, ascending* format. According to the proposed format, all the licenses of a particular type would go on sale together, bidders might, subject to eligibility limitations, bid for any collection of licenses, and bidders could raise one another's bids by at least a minimum increment or, perhaps, withdraw after prices at the end of the previous round were announced. This process would continue, round after round, until no new bids on any license were forthcoming.

This design was explicitly driven by game-theoretic reasoning. The choice of a simultaneous format rather than an administratively simpler sequential one was based on complementarities among nonoverlapping licenses—the ability to spread fixed costs, minimize interference at license interfaces and standardize on one of several incompatible technologies—as well as substitutability between overlapping licenses. The multiple-round, ascending bid format was meant to improve information about rivals' valuations and thereby soften the effects of the winner's curse—a staple of auctions in which values are uncertain but correlated and winning is "bad news" because it increases the likelihood that the winner has overestimated the value of the object at stake.

The simultaneous, multiple-round design was first applied by the FCC to "narrowband" licenses, which covered relatively thin slices of the spectrum that would support paging and messaging services (see exhibit 8.1). The nationwide narrowband auction raised roughly ten times as much in the way of revenues for the U.S. Treasury as some preauction estimates. The net prices for comparable amounts of spectrum were even higher in the subsequent regional narrowband auction despite 40 percent discounts for small businesses and female/minority-owned bidders in one-third of the spectrum bands on offer. Four of the bidders, including one minority bidder, won the same band in each of the five regions (two-thirds of the regional licenses offered), creating four new nationwide competitors.

The two auctions that followed were for "broadband" licenses that covered enough of the spectrum to permit wireless telephony, in competition with the two existing cellular companies in each local market (who were barred from bidding there) as well as RBOCs (Regional Bell Operating Companies) that provided local wireline service. Ninety-nine licenses, two per major trading area (MTA), were offered in the first of the two broadband auctions.[3] The three biggest bidders, in the end, were WirelessCo (a consortium of the long-distance carrier, Sprint, and

---

3. While there are 51 MTAs in the United States, one of the two licenses in three of them—New York, Los Angeles–San Diego, and Washington–Baltimore—was allocated outside the auction, to technological pioneers.

Exhibit 8.1
Simultaneous, Multiple-Round PCS Auctions

License type	Licenses	Dates	Rounds	Qualified bidders	Winning bidders	Revenues ($m)
National narrowband	10	July 1994	47	29	6	617
Regular narrowband	30	October–November 1994	105	28	9	395
MTA broadband	99	December 1994–March 1995	112	30	18	7,034
BTA broadband	493	December 1995–May 1996	184	255	89	10,217[a]

[a]Reauction of the 18 licenses on which winners defaulted reduced net revenues to $10,102 million.

three cable TV companies, TCI, Comcast, and Cox), which won 29 licenses for $2.1 billion, AT&T, the long-distance carrier, which won 21 for $1.7 billion, and PCS PrimeCo (a consortium of Air-Touch and three RBOCs, Bell Atlantic, U.S. West, and NYNEX), which won 11 for $1.1 billion. The big three managed to fill most of the gaps in their cellular holdings: of the 46 contiguous MTAs in the continental United States, AT&T ended up owning cellular or PCS licenses in 40, WirelessCo in 39, and PrimeCo in 38. In addition other RBOCs generally won licenses in the areas in which they already had wireline service. The total proceeds prompted journalists to describe this as the biggest auction ever.

The second broadband auction offered one license each for 493 Basic Trading Areas (BTAs) and was reserved for small businesses. The three biggest bidders were NextWave, which won 56 licenses for $4.2 billion, and seven of the 18 that were reauctioned because of defaults for another $0.5 billion, DCR Communications, which won 43 for $1.4 billion, and General Wireless, which won 14 for $1.1 billion. Each of these big bidders had large backers, including Asian companies. The net proceeds, even after allowing for installment payments at subsidized interest rates, exceeded those from the MTA broadband auction, although only half as much spectrum (chopped into smaller geographic chunks) was at stake.

Game theorists' accounts of these auctions tend to concentrate on the FCC (i.e., on design issues) and to claim that game theory stood it in good stead in light of several sorts of evidence: the revenues the auctions raised; their apparent efficiency in assigning licenses to the bidders expected to value them the most and in allowing nationwide aggregations to form; and the subsequent adoption of the simultaneous, multiple-round format for spectrum auctions in other countries, including Canada, Mexico, and Australia. My objective here is substantially broader: I intend to relate this minicase to the other cases studied in this book to see if any general lessons emerge. As noted earlier, the focus of the discussion will shift from the uses of the case method to the uses of game theory.

8.2   The Uses of the Case Method

The cases studied in this book suggest that the case method can be useful in three different ways. First of all, the case method can help to generate examples (or counterexamples) of stipulated theoretical effects—in the case of game theory, "strategic" behavior. This is important because our collective stock of examples is generally agreed to be small, even when thinly researched and therefore potentially misleading examples are included.[4] Case examples also ease the communication of theoretical ideas to practitioners or would-be practitioners. The PCS auctions, for instance, have been widely cited in the business press as evidence that game theory has finally come of age.[5]

Second and more important, the case method supplies clues about how to add to, advance, or alter existing theory. Consider the last six chapters one by one. The case on the large turbine generator industry surfaced a competitive variable, backlogs, that had not previously been looked at through a game-theoretic lens. The case on the titanium dioxide industry prompted a reassessment of the dependence of capacity expansion patterns on differences in efficiency. The cases on declining chemical pro-

---

4. The oft-cited example of De Beers, which was analyzed more carefully than is customary in chapter 1, is a case in point.
5. Consult, for instance, the citations in McAfee and McMillan (1996, p. 159).

cessing industries suggested a new parametric assumption: modeling the effects of negative rather than positive market growth rates on industry structure. The cases on the PBX and steel industries highlighted important interrelationships between variables: between product innovation and customer bases in PBXs and process innovation and minimal efficient scale of production in steel. The case on British satellite television raised foundational questions about game theory. And most of the cases studied, particularly the later ones, called attention to differences in competitors' efficiency in particular and to organizational embeddedness in general, as well as to the importance of information/uncertainty—issues that will be discussed at greater length later on in this chapter.

The PCS auctions conform to this pattern. The large prior literature on auctions was, in the words of a leading contributor to it (Milgrom 1996, p. 16), "largely irrelevant for the FCC's [design] problem." Or as Vice-President Albert Gore remarked at the opening ceremony for Auction 4, "They couldn't just look it up in a book." Since then, however, there has been a spate of theoretical work on simultaneous, ascending auctions with interdependencies: McAfee and McMillan (1996) cite half a dozen recent contributions in this vein as well as a comparable number of issues that remain to be explored. Thus the PCS auctions have already begun to redirect auction theory.

A third use of the case method is that it can help test theories in addition to exemplifying and helping build them. This assertion is apt to be controversial: The usual argument against it is that cases, as samples of one, cannot be used to establish proof (or disproof). But consider, once again, the last six chapters. The case on the large turbine generator industry showed that a case study typically generates more than one observation—sometimes even a number adequate for regression analysis. But in the titanium dioxide case, an attempt to apply sophisticated regression models overlooked the main event, Du Pont's start-up of a large new plant. More insight into whether that start-up was preemptive in intent was afforded by looking at Du Pont's own calculations than by relying on unverifiable conjectures about competitors' interactions. In the cases on declining chemical industries, order statistics were used to test models of shrinkage and exit, reminding us that statistical analysis does not always require the running of regressions. The analyses of product innovation in PBXs and process innovations in steel were what political scientists call "configurative idiographic": They started with the phenomenon of incumbent failure to innovate and tried to piece together a comprehensive picture (relying in part on regression analyses by others) of the structural and firm-specific factors responsible for it. In the case of British satellite television, the empirics revolved around comparative static analysis of BSB's plans before and after Sky announced its entry.

The PCS auctions add to our catalog of the empirical methods that can be employed in case-based tests of theory. Obviously assessments of how well the auctions performed supply a direct take on the theoretical models—in this case actually a melange of theoretical predictions—that guided auction design.[6] This is exactly the sort of opportunity that many consulting assignments offer, although most of them cannot be reported on in detail because of confidentiality constraints. For a dramatization, consider the report that one organization involved in the PCS auctions fired a group of researchers for writing up and circulating their analysis of the auctions without receiving full clearance.

---

6. While systematic statistical analysis can help with such assessments—and with the two additional empirical modes of analysis discussed in the next paragraph—it has been largely absent from the academic assessments of the PCS auctions that have been offered to date despite the large number of observations that are available.

Abstracting away from confidentiality constraints, there is yet another problem with depending on the actual outcomes of decisions to test their theoretical base: Such analysis is retrospective rather than prospective. In the case of the PCS auctions—as in most real-world applications—protagonists wanted to validate theoretical predictions about the effects of auction design ahead of time. Two other modes of empirical analysis, experiments and simulations, were widely used to meet this demand. Pacific Telesis, for example, relied on experiments by Charles Plott to help evaluate Milgrom and Wilson's theoretical recommendations about the auction design that it ought to support (Milgrom 1996, p. 16). And GTE, which was concerned about the complexity and time requirements of a thorough experimental approach, pretested the theoretical implications of the simultaneous, multiple-round design by working through simulations that pitted different bidding strategies against (one another Salant 1996).

To summarize the discussion so far, the arguments that cases can be used to illustrate and influence theory should be fairly uncontroversial. The argument that they can also be used to test theory tends to be more controversial, largely because it is fashionable (at least in applied IO) to believe that regression analyses are the touchstone for all meaningful empirical work. The cases considered in this book suggest that regressions are sometimes the preferred mode of empirical analysis (large turbine generators and declining chemical processing industries), that they may sometimes play an adjunct role (PBXs and steel), and that they may sometimes be impossible to implement in any sensible way (titanium dioxide and British satellite TV?).

Another way of making the same point is to note that the case method focuses on a unit of analysis that is commonly employed by scholars ranging from historians to the hegemonists of the

"New Empirical Industrial Organization" and that it is correspondingly eclectic in the empirical approaches that it can accommodate. When data are dense, it often makes sense to run regressions. But data frequently lack that desirable attribute. Even the dataset that has perhaps been milked the most assiduously by the new empirical IO—on the prices posted by a U.S. railroad cartel in the 1880s (sic)—may be a case in point: It has been said to exhibit too few price wars to permit fulfillment of the purpose to which it was originally applied, estimation of the triggers of such wars (Bresnahan 1989). If a dearth of data can be asserted to be a problem with the "best" dataset, one closer to average is more likely to lend itself to simple yet inventive uses of sparse data than to implementation of ever more advanced econometric techniques. That is why the cases in this book deliberately touched on a number of quantitative and qualitative alternatives to regression analysis.

8.3   The Uses of Game Theory

The cases studied in this book also shed light on the different ways in which game theory can be useful. First, it obviously provides a language and a set of logical tools for analyzing situations in which interactions are potentially important. The interactive effects identified by game-theoretic analysis often formalize preexisting intuitions, but they can also be unanticipated and even counterintuitive: Plausible candidates for one of the latter two appellations include the price-buffering effect identified in chapter 2, the capacity-preemption effect (due to buffering in the pricing subgame) in chapter 3, and the size-hurts-survivability effect (in declining capacity-driven industries) in chapter 4. In a somewhat different vein, the two chapters on product and process innovation (chapters 5 and 6) took the business-stealing effect identified by modern game theory and flushed out some of the structural conditions that can be predicted to affect its size relative to the opposed cannibalization effect, identified by earlier decision-theoretic analysis, in influencing incentives to innovate by incumbents versus entrants. And chapter 7, with its illustration of why the war of attrition can be such a dangerous game to play, suggested that theoretical analysis of a game can lead to a useful understanding of the underlying forces at work even when one does not count on equilibrium to arise.

Reports from the PCS auctions reinforce these inferences. For example, game theorists helped identify a subtle "displacement" effect that was particularly important in interactions among "national" bidders: The idea that the marginal cost of raising a rival's bid on a particular license was not confined to that license but included the likelihood that that rival would subsequently bid more aggressively on other licenses if it was interested in maintaining its overall eligibility level or intent on using up its budget.

A second use of game theory, explicit in this book's empirical focus, is that it may help explain actual patterns of interaction. Look, in particular, at the relative explanatory power of interactive considerations and differences in efficiency in each of the cases considered in detail in the previous chapters.

The first three detailed cases supply evidence of the importance of interactive considerations in how competitive interactions play out, independently, and even despite differences in efficiency that might, taken alone, point in different directions. Relative pricing patterns in large turbine generators can readily be rationalized in interactive terms but run counter to what one would expect on the basis of efficiency effects. In titanium dioxide the preemptor, Du Pont, *was* the most efficient producer, but interactive considerations (specifically, its anticipation that greater product market concentration would permit higher prices) seem to have been critical to its commitment to add a large new plant. And study of declining chemical processing industries suggests that capacity may not always be unwound in the (socially) efficient order: that interactive considerations can sometimes outweigh differences in efficiency.

The next two case studies (chapters 5 and 6) indicate that interactive considerations complement considerations of differential efficiency in explaining why "outsiders" were able to lead "insiders" in the adoption of particular innovations. They also highlight the importance of unbundling difference in efficiency to gain deeper insight into the causes and consequences of such interfirm differences. Thus the case on a product innovation in the PBX industry calls attention to variations in the efficiency of different ways of organizing product development efforts. The case on a process innovation in the steel industry sparks an even broader consideration of the sources of differences in efficiency. And the final case study (chapter 7) reinforces the complementarity between interactive considerations and differential efficiency: The latter can explain the eventual outcome (the high-cost competitor folded) but the losses en route to that outcome seem to require the power of the former. In all cases interactive considerations seem to pack some explanatory power, even when outcomes are dominated by differences in efficiency. Taken together, the detailed case studies in this book strongly suggest that researchers in strategic management should increase their (currently low) level of attention to game theory instead of simply focusing on differential efficiency.

The PCS auctions also exhibit several types of behavior that are, to varying degrees, difficult to explain without recourse to the sorts of interactions that game theory emphasizes. The adoption of "demand-reduction" strategies in response to the displacement effect is perhaps the clearest example (Ausubel and Cramton 1996).[7] Thus, in the nationwide narrowband auction, PageNet dropped out of the bidding for a third license of a particular type at a price well below its estimated value in order to avoid driving up the prices of the two other licenses that it was seeking.[8] Similar behavior has been ascribed to the three biggest bidders in the MTA broadband auction and is backstopped by the observation that Barry Nalebuff, a consultant to PrimeCo, and Adam Brandenburger devoted all of an appearance on the MacNeil-Lehrer Newshour during the MTA auction to explaining the logic of demand reduction. At the conclusion of the BTA broadband auction, the president of the second-largest bidder, DCR Communications, made the following statement:

About three or four weeks ago, we stopped trying to expand our footprint. Our analysis was that if we tried to buy any other significant markets we'd be displacing someone who would use the money to do something someplace else, and it was going to be a continuous round-robin with the prices going up, so we just said the hell with it, let's stop.[9]

To summarize the discussion so far, it should be clear that game theory can be useful in *analyzing* the interactions among rational competitors and in *describing* (some of) the interactions that actually take place among real competitors. But there is also a third perspective, neither wholly analytical nor descriptive,

---

7. The PCS auctions also featured attempts to signal commitment in a number of different ways, but their efficacy seems in general to have been limited, as discussed in the next section.

8. This perspective on PageNet's decision draws on the description by Cramton (1995), who was a member of PageNet's bidding team.

9. *PCS Week*, May 8, 1996, p. 3.

that is worth scouting: the *prescriptive* one of helping real decision-makers improve the quality of the decisions that they make.[10]

The lines between these three perspectives are of course blurred, implying that analytical and descriptive contributions can also help with prescription. To focus just on the PCS auctions, the displacement effect identified by game-theoretic analysis presumably encouraged the adoption of demand-reduction strategies by PageNet and other bidders, and the simulations undertaken by GTE helped it validate the strategy of "lying low" in the initial rounds of the MTA auction by bidding on licenses other than the ones in which it was most interested, Atlanta and Seattle. But while purely analytical or descriptive contributions provide broad, qualitative insights into interactive possibilities, they do not fully address the managerial craving for more precise guidance about what to do. Can game theory be of more help to managers? This question deserves to be discussed in some detail in a separate section.

8.4   Game-Theoretic Prescriptions

It is useful to begin this section on the prescriptive uses of game theory by calibrating the extent to which it actually *is* used in business. Since we lack systematic evidence on this score, I mounted an exploratory effort that involved interviewing the heads of strategic planning or the chief financial officers of a dozen large companies that tend to operate in concentrated markets and to have a reputation for successfully using other sophisticated analytical techniques (e.g., conjoint analysis, Monte Carlo

---

10. For elaborations of this trichotomy, see chapter 2 of Raiffa (1982), and the introduction and chapter 1 of Bell, Raiffa and Tversky (1988).

simulations, and option pricing theory). Despite these company attributes most of the managers I interviewed had not even heard of game theory. One thought he had but was confusing game theory with "wargaming." The remaining companies mostly turned out to be applying the (not very game-theoretic) structure-conduct-performance paradigm of old IO to their own situations. The few genuinely game-theoretic applications, including two that I had worked on with different clients, tended to focus on short-run pricing interactions—with the prisoner's dilemma supplying a particularly popular structure—but without looking at the feedback effects from short-run outcomes to long-run competition.

My interviews suggest therefore that limited managerial awareness of game theory may be one of the principal problems constraining its practical applications. The PCS auctions can be seen as the exception that proves this rule. According to Milgrom (1996) most of the prospective bidders had not heard of game theory until they read the FCC's Notice of Proposed Rule Making which carefully footnoted the literature on auction theory. Although that literature turned out to be largely irrelevant to the auction format that was adopted, the curiosity of the telecommunications companies was aroused: They began to track down the names cited in the footnotes. And that is how so many game theorists came to be involved in the PCS auctions.

The problem of generally limited awareness of game theory will not disappear any time soon, but it can be and is being fixed. The PCS auctions and, in particular, glowing descriptions in general business periodicals of the role that game theorists have played in them have prompted a number of large companies that had not used game theory in the past to start taking an interest in it. Academic specialists are available to advise them and consulting firms are gearing up to do so as well. Perhaps even more important, many of the top business schools are now equipping their MBA students with some understanding of the uses (and limits) of game theory. Finally advances in information technology may be of some help as well.

My interviews also suggest, however, that there are several difficulties with pushing game theory to the next level of usefulness, in which managers might be able to assess the importance of interactive effects as well as identify their existence. Interestingly enough, the problems that my respondents cited in this regard are different from the ones which academic game theorists most often agonize about: too many game-theoretic models to choose from, and too many equilibria within a significant number of them. Managers seem, at least on the basis of my small sample, to think that grounding game-theoretic analysis in the particulars of their situations—the case method—helps address the problems wrought by multiplicity.[11] This section will focus therefore on the (related) problems that *do* concern managers: that competitors' internal organization (and objectives) may be more complex than assumed by game theory and that uncertainty plays a more important and rather different role in the real world than is generally contemplated in game-theoretic models. Both of these problems can be illustrated with reference to the cases discussed in detail in the earlier chapters of this book as well as the minicase on the PCS auctions.

The Role of Internal Organization

Game-theoretic IO tends to focus on external interactions, particularly with competitors. Yet considerations of internal organiza-

---

11. The ways in which the case method may help with model selection have already been illustrated in this book. For a discussion of one way in which it may help with equilibrium selection, reconsider Schelling's (1960) classic discussion of focal points.

tion, broadly defined, were evident in all the cases discussed in detail in this book, particularly the later ones. In large turbine generators changes in General Electric's pricing policies required, among other things, changes in the degree of decentralization of pricing decisions. In titanium dioxide Du Pont used its knowledge of competitors' internal organization to set prices at a level that would deter them from expanding; in addition internal cashflow constraints nearly blocked its implementation of a strategy to add a large new plant preemptively. In antiknock lead additives the order of closure of Ethyl's two U.S. plants may have been influenced by its divisional structure. Differences in organizational capabilities and the organizational choices that underlay them were evident in the case on product innovation in PBXs and were explored in much more depth, along with other precommitments, in the case on process innovation in steel. Governance structures and personalities appeared to take a hand as well in the case on British satellite television.

The PCS auctions also provide numerous examples of competitors actually paying considerable attention to rivals' resources, objectives, and even personalities in planning their moves. In the broadband MTA auction, for example, GTE, as described from the inside by Salant (1996), recognized that rivals with particularly high private value components for particular licenses were likely to include long-distance carriers intent on bypassing the local exchange carriers, the local exchange carriers themselves who already had infrastructure that could be used to reduce the costs of providing wireless services, and cable television operators who were interested in converting their one-way systems into switched two-way networks. Another related source of private-value differences was suggested by the inference that the big three—AT&T, PCS PrimeCo, and WirelessCo—would be willing to pay additional premia in order to fill the gaps in their existing cellular operations and create (near-)national networks. GTE also attempted to gain a sense of the budgets that rivals were likely to have available to them and to build in consideration of the key people that would influence their decisions. Thus it regarded ALAACR as a wildcard because of the financial resources and the personality of the man behind it, Craig McCaw, and American Portable Telecommunications as a particularly "strategic" bidder because of the long relationship between its parent and Robert Weber, an eminent auction theorist.

This swarm of organizational effects supports the inference that traditional "no-fat" game-theoretic modeling cannot be counted on to illuminate competitor interactions all by itself. Attention must usually be paid not only to the interplay of incentives among competitors trying to maximize profits but also, as suggested in the last three chapters, to competitors' capabilities, contractual commitments, strategies, personalities, and organizational structures. In addition such enriched analysis must sometimes extend beyond direct competitors to indirect ones (potential entrants, substitutes, complements, buyers, and suppliers). The specificity wrought by the case method often helps to focus the analysis of this plethora of factors. A game-theoretic perspective further narrows the field by suggesting that the critical internal factors are the ones that affect external interactions.

What is apt to be more controversial is whether the critical factors identified by enriched competitor analyses can always usefully be boiled down into analytical models of interactions among optimizing agents. I have two practical doubts in this regard. First, even when the relevant differences among competitors can largely be summarized in terms of payoff asymmetries, as in the PCS auctions, the resultant models quickly become too difficult to solve analytically. Auction theorists, for example, have had trouble coming up with analytical characterizations of the strategies of bidders with asymmetric valuations (although some numerical methods are available). Second, to the extent that competitor behavior is affected by predispositions as well as economic precommitments, the centrality of the concept of game-theoretic equilibrium is compromised. From a practical perspective, at least, if predispositions drive a wedge between profit maximization and actual behavior, it makes more sense to figure out what competitors will do rather than what they would do if they were sophisticated and single-minded about maximizing profits.

For these reasons my own preferred approach to analyzing cases in the course of research and consulting assignments is to supplement "low-fat" models—which raise incentive issues that are ignored in conventional discussions of competitor analysis (e.g., Porter 1980, ch. 3)—with separate, detailed competitor profiles that provide clues as to the ways in which competitors' choices may diverge from profit maximization. This will fail to satisfy theorists who crave completely game-theoretic approaches (see Kreps 1990, pp. 114–16), but it does seem to make sense to managers.

The Role of Uncertainty

Additional content analysis of the game-theoretic IO articles published in the leading general-interest economics journals since the mid-1970s, as discussed in chapter 1 and elaborated in appendix A, indicates that the overwhelming majority of them ignore the effects of uncertainty by assuming perfect information. Yet my interviewees seemed to regard uncertainty as the single biggest obstacle to practical applications of game theory.

The cases discussed in detail in this book tend to bear out their concerns about uncertainty. Participants in the large turbine generator industry had trouble—prior to General Electric's institution of a new pricing policy in 1963—figuring out their rivals' strategic intent. In the titanium dioxide case Du Pont's preemption strategy ran into, and was nearly derailed by, unexpectedly weak aggregate demand. In the antiknock lead additives case Ethyl's top management seemed uncertain about the cost positions of its two U.S. plants in deciding which one to close first. In the cases on innovation in the PBX and steel industries, there was uncertainty about how well particular technological approaches would work. And the case on British satellite television featured uncertainty about aggregate demand, the viability of different technologies, and rivals' strategies.

The PCS auctions were arguably suffused with an even broader range of uncertainties. Attempts to value MTA broadband licenses, for example, were clouded by significant uncertainties concerning the terms at which additional licenses would be awarded later on, the rate of market penetration, the evolution of wireless technology (which might, among other things, expand the transmission capacity of a given amount of spectrum), the toughness of eventual price competition, and the prospects for new types of services—to focus just on common value components. Yet these and other uncertainties were essential to understanding the auction: Menezes (1995) has showed that with perfect or even complete information, what is perhaps the most natural equilibrium in a simultaneous ascending auction involves sales taking place at the opening bids!

To understand the implications of uncertainty for the practical uses and limits of game theory, it is useful to begin by classifying

Exhibit 8.2
Types of Uncertainty

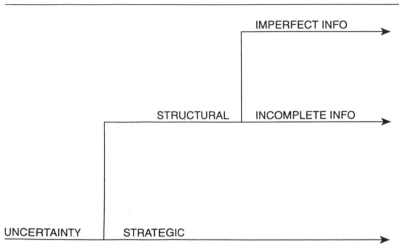

the kinds of uncertainties that are possible into the three categories depicted in exhibit 8.2. Working from top to bottom, uncertainties deepen. The least invasive way of injecting uncertainty
into game-theoretic models is to assume complete but imperfect
information so that uncertainty concerns a structural variable
about which there is no private information. This was, for example, the approach taken in the analysis of capacity preemption
in the titanium dioxide industry and of product innovation in the
PBX industry. When the assumption of imperfect but complete
information is tolerably accurate, equilibrium-based reasoning
can, subject to the caveats of the previous subsection, be applied
in relatively straightforward ways to practical problems. The major additional complication, relative to the perfect information
case, is the possibility of reducing uncertainty by acquiring additional information. While option-theoretic methods have recently
been applied to the problem of commitment under imperfect information in the nonstrategic cases of monopoly or perfect competition, formal integration with game-theoretic models that

cover the intermediate case of imperfect competition is rare[12]—and practical applications presumably rarer still. So for the moment considerations of "flexibility value" have to be jury-rigged onto game-theoretic applications.

The second node of exhibit 8.2 involves structural uncertainty and incomplete (private) information. Such situations have been modeled rather extensively by game theorists, mostly under the rubric of signaling (or reputational) games. Effects of this sort were noted in some of the cases considered in detail in this book, but the motive forces seemed to be somewhat different from those usually modeled. Du Pont's limit pricing in titanium dioxide, for example, apparently reflected an attempt to manipulate competitors' mechanical decision rules about new investments, as opposed to a conventional "separating" equilibrium (in which no one would be fooled by the signal of low prices). And reputations such as USX's (for technological tardiness) often appear to have been created inadvertently rather than deliberately.

The PCS auctions raise additional concerns about signaling models. While there were several sorts of attempts to stake out licenses by signaling commitment, their efficacy seems to have been quite limited. Thus, while "jump bids" significantly greater than the required minimum (increment) were common in the narrowband auctions, they did not seem to have much of an effect on final prices and were employed far less frequently in the broadband auctions. And the attempt by Pacific Telesis to stake out the MTA broadband license for Los Angeles through news-

---

12. For example, approximately 1 percent of Dixit and Pindyck's (1994) authoritative text on investment in real assets under uncertainty deals with imperfectly competitive situations. That is because the technical challenges associated with characterizing option values in models of strategic interaction are formidable. When (and if) progress is made on this front, it is likely to counteract the "waiting-to-invest" bias of much of the nonstrategic option-theoretic literature. The reason is that with imperfect competition and exclusionary opportunities, the "lock-in" risk of investing has to be balanced against the "lock-out" risk of not investing. See Ghemawat (1991a), especially chapter 6, for additional discussion.

paper advertisements and other public statements of interest apparently backfired: Craig McCaw's ALAACR exploited Pacific Telesis' declared interest to push up prices and make it pay more for Los Angeles than any bidder did for any other MTA license. Indeed, concerns about such exploitation led GTE (and apparently WirelessCo) to engage in signal-jamming rather than signaling by adopting the strategy of lying low and concealing its interest in particular licenses in the early rounds of the MTA auction. According to David Salant, who worked for GTE during the auction, the value of signaling was compromised by a high level of ambient noise that made it difficult to figure out whether a particular bid had a signaling component, and if so, what it was supposed to mean.

From a more general perspective, the practical utility of formal models of signaling tends to be compromised by their sensitive dependence on unobservables (information sets), their ability to rationalize virtually any type of behavior, and signal-to-noise ratios that seem to be lower in the real world than in textbooks. Thus, while considerations of signaling do crop up in practical applications of game theory, the usefulness of the concept of informational equilibrium itself seems to be nugatory. Managers seem, at least in my own consulting experience, to be more comfortable stepping beyond equilibrium-based analysis of pure structural uncertainty (the second node of exhibit 8.2) to direct consideration of the strategic uncertainty (the third node of the exhibit): the possibility that even after enriched competitor analysis, there may be irreducible uncertainty about the strategies competitors will select.

Strategic uncertainty has, aside from the problem of multiple Nash equilibria and a limited amount of work on rationalizability, been almost entirely ignored by game theorists. The case of BSB versus Sky and the theoretical model associated with it suggest, however, that it can be important. In practical applications, taking strategic uncertainty seriously typically means that equilibrium-based analysis must be supplemented with consideration of "countertheoretical" actions by competitors and, more generally, of multiple possible scenarios. Once again the PCS auctions supply an example. In advising clients about how to value broadband licenses and what to do with the ones that they win, the management consulting firms of whose work I am aware have not attempted to forecast a particular competitive equilibrium. Instead, they have tended to specify and work through the implications of a number of different scenarios parameterized by the toughness of price competition.[13]

The theoretical implications of allowing for strategic uncertainty are, as noted above, largely unexplored. But experience incorporating such uncertainty into consulting projects does suggest a number of useful heuristics. For one thing, it generally encourages an emphasis on strategic robustness rather than exact optimization: See exhibit 8.3 for a case example. For similar reasons strategic uncertainty raises questions about strategies that involve extremes of brinkmanship. It also leads managers to cross-check their assessments of the payoffs to various courses of action with prior beliefs derived from experience, such as whether a particular action fits a company's distinctive competence.[14] Obviously these insights are partial and incomplete, which is one of the reasons the business of applying game theory to business remains an art rather than a science—and is likely to continue to do so.

---

13. For example, analyses presented by Mercer Management Consulting at a well-attended preauction conference considered an array of possible outcomes ranging from a "son-of-cellular" scenario with moderate rivalry to an "airline-industry" scenario with intense rivalry.

14. See chapter 7 of Ghemawat (1991a) for additional discussion.

Exhibit 8.3a
Payoffs in the Production of Compact Discs ($ millions)

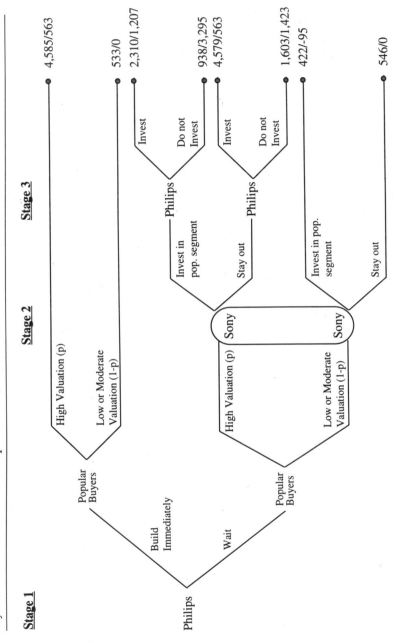

Exhibit 8.3b
Uncertain Listenership: The Case of CDs

A good illustration of the importance of robustness in the presence of strategic uncertainty is provided by McGahan's (1994) case on Philips's commitment to compact-disc (CD) pressing capacity in the United States. At the end of 1982 Philips faced a decision about whether to commit immediately to a U.S. plant for start-up in late 1983 or to wait for a year and test demand, particularly in the large popular-music segment, by importing CDs from a plant already built to Europe. The risk of building immediately was that popular demand would fail to materialize, saddling Philips with excess capacity; the risk of waiting was that Philips's leading competitor, Sony, could, if it chose, build a plant at the same time—although Sony would have to make its choice under uncertainty under the assumption that Philips could keep information about the results of importing popular-music CDs proprietary.

Based on detailed information about this situation, McGahan estimated the present values to Philips and Sony under the various scenarios as indicated in the game tree shown above. This payoff structure has interesting implications. Solving the game backward, if Philips has not already invested, it will do so at stage 3 if buyers of popular music are revealed to have a high valuation for CDs but will not if they have a low valuation. At stage 2 Sony must condition its choice on its assessment of the probability p that popular buyers place a high valuation on CDs. Specifically it will invest as soon as it can if and only if

$$1207p - 95(1 - p) > 563p.$$

According to McGahan, Philips "put the probability of quick acceptance in the popular segment at about 5 percent. And there was no reason to believe that Sony's managers would not make the same assessment." With p equal to 5 percent (or even 10 percent), the inequality given above is violated, implying that Sony should *not* invest. Armed with this conclusion, we can now work through Philips's choice in stage 1. Philips should build immediately if and only if

$$4585p + 533(1 - p) > 4579p + 546(1 - p).$$

With p equal to 5 percent, the left-hand side of the inequality comes to 735.6 and the right-hand side to 747.7, suggesting that Philips stands to gain an extra \$12 million by waiting in stage 1 rather than building immediately. So, abstracting away from risk aversion, the

Exhibit 8.3
Continued

> logic of equilibrium analysis implies that Philips should wait to build
> in stage 1 because it can count on Sony waiting to build in stage 2.
>   Consider how this analysis changes, however, in the presence of
> strategic uncertainty, which implies that Philips cannot count on Sony
> waiting in stage 2 if Philips waits in stage 1. If Sony *does* deviate from
> the equilibrium strategy calculated above, Philips expects to make
> 516.4 ($2310p + 422(1 - p)$) rather than 747.7 by waiting. Since the
> difference is large, even a small probability of deviation by Sony ($>$
> 5.3 percent) makes it worth Philips's while to build immediately in-
> stead of waiting. As a result, in discussions of the Philips-Sony case
> that I have led, MBA students tend to vote for the robust alternative
> of building immediately.

8.5 Summary

The diffusion of game-theoretic concepts in the study and practice of business still does not seem to have reached a steady state.
Researchers can help push this process along by grounding their
game-theoretical models to a greater extent in empirical contexts
than in theoretical conundra, by reallocating some of their time
from theoretical to empirical research and, on the latter front, by
making the case method rather than regression analysis per se
the centerpiece of their efforts. The individual rationality of the
last prescription depends, in large part, on the acquiescence of
the editors of leading journals.[15]

From a managerial perspective, game-theoretic trees already
offer low-hanging fruits. But more efficient exploitation of game

---

15. While a number of editors of IO/management strategy journals, notably Daniel
Spulber of the *Journal of Economics and Management Strategy,* have begun to encourage
case research that need not involve regressions, the future publishability of such
research is far from settled if other business subfields are any guide. Thus *Marketing
Science* started a "field research" effort in the late 1980s but has since discontinued it.

theory will require deeper understanding of the theory and its limitations. Companies that have already cultivated a degree of commitment to the idea that sophisticated general analytical techniques can help with strategy—that strategy is not just about leaping nimbly from one fad to the next—are better placed to make progress in this respect.

Appendix A: Content Analysis of Economics and Management Journals

The evidence presented in chapter 1 on game theory's dominance of the literature on industrial organization (IO) since the late 1970s and its virtual absence from the literature on business strategy is based on content analysis of the articles published in five leading journals in economics and in strategic management.

To select the five economics journals, I relied on Laband and Piette's (1994) rankings, and excluded the *Journal of Financial Economics* (ranked first) and the *Journal of Monetary Economics* (ranked fourth) as special-interest journals that publish very few articles on industrial organization (IO). In keeping with the focus on general-interest journals, I also resolved a tie for seventh place between the *American Economic Review* and the *RAND Journal of Economics* in favor of the former (although I excluded the *AER*'s annual *Proceedings* issue). The *RAND* offers interested readers an opportunity for extra-sample validation.

Classification of the articles (and notes) published in the selected journals into the categories of IO and non-IO was complicated by the fact that IO itself is a portmanteau. My working definition of the field largely followed the selection of topics in Tirole's (1988) authoritative textbook, implying the exclusion, inter alia, of work on bargaining, auctions, and the economics of regulation. I also excluded contributions to the theory of the firm and to pure (as opposed to applied) game theory. While each of these exclusionary principles can be challenged, I did try to implement them consistently by classifying all the articles in these journals myself, over a concentrated period of time.

I also subclassified the IO articles in the economics journals in two ways. The subclassification into articles that focused on developing or testing game-theoretic models versus those that did not was relatively straightforward, at least in comparison with the classification exercise described above. As far as the subclassification into theoretical versus empirical contributions was concerned, I counted all articles that contained original empirical work as empirical, irrespective of whether they also developed new theory. This procedure resulted in roughly 27 percent of the total corpus of IO articles being categorized as empirical, which is not too far from Peltzman's (1991) estimate, based on rather different procedures and a sample consisting of all the IO articles abstracted in the *Journal of Economic Literature* in 1989, of 30 percent.

The content analysis of five leading strategic management journals was substantially simpler given its more modest objectives and the sparseness of contributions motivated by game theory. The leading journals were selected on the basis of the article impact rates cited by Park and Gordon (1996), who in turn drew on *Journal Citation Reports* (1991). I went through these journals with the assistance of Patricio del Sol. We took a fairly expansive view of articles that focused on developing or testing game-theoretic models, although I did exclude articles that merely referred to the prisoners' dilemma or discussed action-response cycles without imposing the consistency requirements of game-theoretic equilibrium on them.

Appendix B: Game-Theoretic Teaching Cases

Case	ICCH number
De Beers Consolidated Mines Limited (Ghemawat and Lenk)	391-076
General Electric versus Westinghouse in Large Turbine Generators (A) (Porter and Ghemawat)	380-128
General Electric versus Westinghouse in Large Turbine Generators (B) (Porter)	380-129
General Electric versus Westinghouse in Large Turbine Generators (C) (Porter)	380-130
Du Pont in Titanium Dioxide (A) (Ghemawat)	390-112
Du Pont in Titanium Dioxide (B) (Ghemawat)	390-114
Du Pont in Titanium Dioxide (C) (Ghemawat)	390-115
Du Pont in Titanium Dioxide (D) (Ghemawat)	390-116

References

Abernathy, W. J., and K. B. Clark. 1985. Innovation: Mapping the winds of creature destruction. *Research Policy* 14:3–22.

Abernathy, W. J., and J. M. Utterback. 1978. Patterns of industrial innovation. *Technology Review* 80:2–9.

Adams, F. G., T. Alleyne, C. Bell, R. Koss, B. Punto, and M. Puhakka. 1985. Industrial-policy impacts on the U.S. steel industry: A simulation study. In *Industrial Policies for Growth and Competitiveness*, vol. 2, F. G. Adams, ed. Lexington, MA: D.C. Heath.

Allen, B. T. 1976. Tacit collusion and market sharing: The case of steam turbine generators. *Industrial Organization Review* 4:48–57.

Andrews, K. R. 1971. *The Concept of Corporate Strategy*. New York: Dow Jones-Irwin.

Arrow, K. J. 1962. Economic welfare and the allocation of resources. In *The Rate and Direction of Inventive Activity*, R. Nelson, ed. Princeton, NJ: Princeton University Press.

Arthur, J. B. 1992. The link between business strategy and industrial relations systems in American steel minimills. *Industrial and Labor Relations Review* 45:488–506.

Arthur, J. B. 1994. The effects of human resource systems on manufacturing performance and turnover. *Academy of Management Journal* 37:670–87.

Arvan, L. 1985. Some examples of dynamic Cournot duopoly with inventory. *RAND Journal of Economics* 16:569–78.

Aumann, R., and A. Brandenburger. 1995. Epistemic conditions for Nash equilibrium. *Econometrica* 63:1161–80.

Ausubel, L. M., and P. C. Cramton. 1996. Demand reduction and inefficiency in multi-unit auctions. Working paper 96–07. Department of Economics, University of Maryland.

Bain, J. S. 1956. *Barriers to New Competition*. Cambridge: Harvard University Press.

Barnard, C. I. 1938. *The Functions of the Executive.* Cambridge: Harvard University Press.

Barney, J. B. 1986. Strategic factor markets: Expectations, luck, and business strategy. *Management Science* 32:1231–41.

Barney, J. B. 1991. Firm resources and sustained competitive advantage. *Journal of Management* 17:99–120.

Barney, J. B. 1997. *Gaining and Sustaining Competitive Advantage.* Reading, MA: Addison Wesley.

Barzel, Y. 1968. Optimal timing of innovations. *Review of Economics and Statistics* 50:348–55.

Battese, G. E., and T. J. Coelli. 1988. Prediction of firm-level technical efficiencies with a generalized frontier production function and panel data. *Journal of Econometrics* 38:387–99.

Baumol, W. J., J. C. Panzar, and R. D. Willig. 1982. *Contestable Markets and the Theory of Industry Structure.* New York: Harcourt Brace Jovanovich.

Bazerman, M. H., and M. A. Neale. 1992. *Negotiating Rationally.* New York: Free Press.

Bell, D. E., H. Raiffa, and A. Tversky, eds. 1988. *Decision Making: Descriptive, Normative, and Prescriptive Interactions.* Cambridge: Cambridge University Press.

Blaug, M. 1980. *The Methodology of Economics.* Cambridge Surveys of Economic Literature. Cambridge: Cambridge University Press.

Blinder, A. S. 1993. Why are prices sticky: Preliminary results from an interview study. In *Optimal Pricing, Inflation and the Cost of Price Adjustment,* Eytan Sheshinski and Yorarn Weiss, eds. Cambridge: MIT Press.

Brandenburger, A. M., and P. Ghemawat. 1994. Preliminary notes on the war of attrition between British Satellite Broadcasting and Sky Television. Mimeo. Harvard Business School.

Brandenburger, A. M., and B. Nalebuff. 1996. *Coopetition.* New York: Doubleday.

Brandenburger, A. M., and H. W. Stuart, Jr. 1996. Value-based business strategy. *Journal of Economics and Management Strategy* 5:5–24.

Bresnahan, T. F. 1989. Empirical studies of industries with market power. In *Handbook of Industrial Organization,* vol. 2, R. Schmalensee and R. D. Willig, eds. New York: North-Holland.

Butters, G. R. 1977. Equilibrium distributions of sales and advertising prices. *Review of Economic Studies* 44:465–91.

Camerer, C. F. 1991. Does strategy research need game theory? *Strategic Management Journal* 12:137–52.

Caporaso, J. A. 1995. Research design, falsification, and the qualitative-quantitative divide. *American Political Science Review* 89:457–60.

Carlton, D. W. 1989. The theory and the facts of how markets clear: Is industrial organization valuable for understanding macroeconomics? In *Handbook of Industrial Organization*, R. Schmalensee and R. D. Willig, eds. New York: North-Holland.

Caves, R. E. 1984. Economic analysis and the quest for competitive advantage. *American Economic Review* 74:127–32.

Caves, R. E. 1994. Game theory, industrial organization, and business strategy. *Journal of Business Economics* 1:11–14.

Chakravorti, B., W. W. Sharkey, Y. Spiegel, and S. Wilkie. 1995. Auctioning the airwaves: The contest for broadband PCS spectrum. *Journal of Economics and Management Strategy* 4:345–73.

Christensen, C. M. 1992. The innovator's challenge: Understanding the influence of market environment on processes of technology development in the rigid disk drive industry. Unpublished DBA dissertation. Harvard Business School.

Christensen, C. M., and J. L. Bower. 1996. Customer power, strategic investment and the failure of leading firms. *Strategic Management Journal* 17:197–218.

Christensen, C. M., and R. S. Rosenbloom. 1990. Continuous casting investments at USX corporation. Case service 9–391–121. Harvard Business School.

Coase, R. H. 1972. Durability and monopoly. *Journal of Law and Economics* 1:143–50.

Cooper, A. C., and D. Schendel. 1976. Strategic response to technological threats. *Business Horizons* 19:61–69.

Cramton, P. C. 1992. Strategic delay in bargaining with two-sided uncertainty. *Review of Economic Studies* 59:205–25.

Cramton, P. C. 1995. Money out of thin air: The nationwide narrowband PCS auction. *Journal of Economics and Management Strategy* 4:267–343.

Cyert, R., P. Kumar, and J. Williams. 1995. Impact of organizational structure on oligopolistic pricing. *Journal of Economic Behavior and Organization* 26:1–15.

D'Aveni, R. A. 1994. *Hypercompetition: The Dynamics of Strategic Maneuvering*. New York: Free Press.

De Vany, A. 1976. Uncertainty, waiting time, and capacity utilization: A stochastic theory of product quality. *Journal of Political Economy* 84:523–41.

De Vany, A., and G. Frey. 1982. Backlogs and the value of excess capacity in the steel industry. *American Economic Review* 72:441–51.

Deily, M. E. 1985. Capacity reduction in the steel industry. Ph.D. dissertation. Department of Economics, Harvard University.

Deily, M. E. 1988. Investment activity and the exit decision. *Review of Economics and Statistics* 76:595–602.

Dixit, A. K. 1980. The role of investment in entry deterrence. *Economic Journal* 90:95–106.

Dixit, A. K., and R. Pindyck. 1994. *Investment under Uncertainty*. Princeton, NJ: Princeton University Press.

Dudey, M. P. 1992. Dynamic Edgeworth-Bertrand competition. *Quarterly Journal of Economics* 107:1461–77.

Edgeworth, F. Y. [1897] 1925. The pure theory of monopoly. Trans. of the *Giornale degli Economisti* in *Papers Relating to Political Economy*, vol. 1, sec. 2. London: Macmillan.

Fellner, W. 1949. *Competition among the Few*. New York: Sentry Press.

Fine, C., and L. Li. 1989. Equilibrium exit in stochastically declining industries. *Games and Economic Behavior* 1:40–59.

Fishman, A. 1990. Entry deterrence in a finitely-lived industry. *RAND Journal of Economics* 21:63–71.

Freeman, C. 1982. *The Economics of Industrial Innovation*. Cambridge: MIT Press.

Friedman, M. 1953. *Essays on the Methodology of Positive Economics*. Chicago: University of Chicago Press.

Fudenberg, D., and E. Maskin. 1986. The folk theorem in repeated games with discounting and with incomplete information. *Econometrica* 54:533–54.

Fudenberg, D., and J. Tirole. 1984. The fat cat effect, the puppy dog ploy and the lean and hungry look. *American Economic Review, Papers and Proceedings* 74:361–68.

Fudenberg, D., and J. Tirole. 1986a. A theory of exit in duopoly. *Econometrica* 44:943–60.

Fudenberg, D., and J. Tirole. 1986b. *Dynamic Models of Oligopoly*. Chur, Switzerland: Harwood Academic Publishers.

Gelman, J. R., and S. C. Salop. 1983. Judo economics: Capacity limitation and coupon competition. *Bell Journal of Economics* 14:315–25.

Ghemawat, P. 1984. Capacity expansion in the titanium dioxide industry. *Journal of Industrial Economics* 32:145–63.

Ghemawat, P. 1985. Concentration in decline. Working paper. Harvard Business School.

Ghemawat, P. 1986. Capacities and prices: A model with applications. Working paper. Harvard Business School.

Ghemawat, P. 1987. Investment in lumpy capacity. *Journal of Economic Behavior and Organization* 8:265–77.

Ghemawat, P. 1990. The snowball effect. *International Journal of Industrial Organization* 8:335–51.

Ghemawat, P. 1991a. *Commitment: The Dynamic of Strategy*. New York: Free Press.

Ghemawat, P. 1991b. Resources and strategy: An IO perspective. Unpublished draft. Harvard Business School (May).

Ghemawat, P. 1993. Commitment to a process innovation: Nucor, USX, and thin-slab casting. *Journal of Economics and Management Strategy* 2:135–61.

Ghemawat, P. 1995. Competitive advantage and internal organization: Nucor revisited. *Journal of Economics and Management Strategy* 3:685–717.

Ghemawat, P., and A. McGahan. 1996. Order backlogs and strategic pricing: The case of the U.S. large turbine generator industry. Working paper. Harvard Business School.

Ghemawat, P. and B. Nalebuff. 1985. Exit. *RAND Journal of Economics* 16:184–94.

Ghemawat, P., and B. Nalebuff. 1990. The devolution of declining industries. *Quarterly Journal of Economics* 105:165–86.

Ghemawat, P., and M. D. Whinston. 1987. The Ethyl Corporation in 1979. Case services 388–075. Harvard Business School.

Gilbert, R. J., and R. G. Harris. 1984. Competition with lumpy investment. *RAND Journal of Economics* 15:197–212.

Gilbert, R. J., and D. M. G. Newbery. 1982. Preemptive patenting and the persistence of monopoly. *American Economic Review* 72:514–26.

Goldschmid, H. J., H. M. Mann, and J. F. Weston, eds. 1974. *Industrial Concentration: The New Learning.* Boston: Little, Brown.

Grant, R. M. 1991. The resource-based theory of competitive advantage: Implications for strategy formulation. *California Management Review* 33:114–35.

Green, D. P., and I. Shapiro. 1994. *Pathologies of Rational Choice Theory.* New Haven: Yale University Press.

Griesmer, J. H., and M. Shubik. 1963. Toward a study of bidding processes. Part II: Games with capacity limitations. *Naval Research Logistics Quarterly* 10:151–73.

Grossman, G. M., and C. Shapiro. 1984. Informative advertising with differentiated products. *Review of Economic Studies* 51:63–81.

Hall, E. A. 1985. An analysis of preemptive capacity expansion in the titanium dioxide industry. Ph.D. dissertation. Boston College.

Hall, E. A. 1990. An analysis of preemptive behavior in the titanium dioxide industry. *International Journal of Industrial Organization* 8:469–84.

Hall, R. E. 1986. Chronic excess capacity in U.S. industry. Working paper 1973. National Bureau of Economic Research.

Hall, R. E. 1988. The relation between price and marginal cost in U.S. industry. *Journal of Political Economy* 96:921–47.

Hamel, G., and C. K. Prahalad. 1994. *Competing for the Future.* Boston: Harvard Business School Press.

Harrigan, K. R. 1980. *Strategies for Declining Businesses.* Lexington, MA: Lexington Books.

Harsanyi, J. 1967. Games with incomplete information played by "Bayesian" players. Part I. *Management Science* 14:159–82.

Harsanyi, J. 1968a. Games with incomplete information played by "Bayesian" players. Part II. *Management Science* 14:320–34.

Harsanyi, J. 1968b. Games with incomplete information played by "Bayesian" players. Part III. *Management Science* 14:486–502.

Hart, O. 1989. Bargaining and strikes. *Quarterly Journal of Economics* 104:25–44.

Henderson, R. M. 1993. Underinvestment and incompetence as responses to radical innovation: Evidence from the photolithographic alignment equipment industry. *RAND Journal of Economics* 24:248–70.

Henderson, R. M., and K. B. Clark. 1990. Architectural innovation: The reconfiguration of existing product technologies and the failure of established firms. *Administrative Science Quarterly* 35:9–30.

Hotelling, H. 1931. The economics of exhaustible resources. *Journal of Political Economy* 39:137–75.

Hounshell, D. A., and J. K. Smith, Jr. 1988. *Science and Corporate Strategy: Du Pont R&D, 1902–1980*. Cambridge: Cambridge University Press.

Huang, F. C., and L. Li. 1986. Continuous stopping time games. Working paper. Sloan School of Management, MIT.

Hunsaker, J., and D. Kovenock. 1995. The pattern of exit from declining industries. Working paper. Krannert Graduate School of Management, Purdue University.

Jones, N. 1996. When incumbents succeed: A study of radical technological change in the private branch exchange (PBX) industry. DBA dissertation. Harvard Business School.

Journal Citation Reports. 1991. Institute for Scientific Information, Philadelphia.

Jovanovic, B. 1982. Selection and the evolution of industry. *Econometrica* 50:649–70.

Judd, K. L. 1985. Credible spatial preemption. *RAND Journal of Economics* 16:153–66.

King, G., R. O. Keohane, and S. Verba. 1994. *Designing Social Inquiry*. Princeton, NJ: Princeton University Press.

Kreps, D. M. 1990. *Game Theory and Economic Modeling*. Oxford: Oxford University Press.

Kreps, D. M., and J. A. Scheinkman. 1983. Quantity precommitment and Bertrand competition yield Cournot outcomes. *RAND Journal of Economics* 14:326–37.

Kreps, D. M., and A. M. Spence. 1987. Modeling the role of history in industrial organization and competition. In *Contemporary Issues in Modern Microeconomics*, G. Feiwel, ed. London: Macmillan.

Krishna, V. 1992. Learning in games with strategic complementarities. Working paper 92–073. Harvard Business School.

Kuhn, T. 1962. *The Structure of Scientific Revolutions.* Chicago: University of Chicago Press.

Kwoka, J. E., Jr. 1982. Regularity and diversity in firm size distributions in U.S. industries. *Journal of Economics and Business* 34:391–95.

Laband, D. N., and M. J. Piette. 1994. The relative impacts of economics journals: 1970–1990. *Journal of Economic Literature* 32:640–58.

Law, J. 1705. *Money and Trade Considered with a Proposal for Supplying the Nation with Money.* Edinburgh: Andrew Anderson.

Lean, D. F., J. D. Ogur, and R. P. Rogers. 1982. Competition and collusion in electrical equipment markets. Bureau of Economics Staff Report to the Federal Trade Commission.

Leonard-Barton, D. 1992. The factory as a learning laboratory. *Sloan Management Review* 33:23–38.

Levin, R. C., A. K. Klevorick, R. R. Nelson, and S. G. Winter. 1987. Appropriating the returns from industrial R&D. *Brookings Papers on Economic Activity* 3:783–831.

Lieberman, M. B. 1990. Exit from declining industries: "Shakeout" or "Stakeout"? *RAND Journal of Economics* 21:538–54.

Londregan, J. 1990. Entry and exit over the industry life cycle. *RAND Journal of Economics* 21:446–58.

Mansfield, E. 1968. *Industrial Research and Technical Innovation.* New York: Norton.

Mansfield, E., M. Schwartz, and S. Wagner. 1981. Imitation costs and patents: An empirical study. *Economic Journal* 91:907–18.

McAfee, R. P., and J. McMillan. 1996. Analyzing the airwaves auction. *Journal of Economic Perspectives* 10:159–75.

McGahan, A. M. 1994. The incentive not to invest: Capacity commitments in the compact-disc introduction. In *Research on Technological Innovation, Management and Policy,* vol. 5, R. A. Burgelman and R. S. Rosenbloom, eds. Greenwich, CT: JAI Press.

McMillan, J. 1994. Selling spectrum rights. *Journal of Economic Perspectives* 8:145–62.

Menezes, F. 1995. Multiple-unit English auctions. Draft. Australian National University.

Milgrom, P. 1996. Auctioning the radio spectrum. Draft. Stanford University.

Milgrom, P., and J. Roberts. 1990a. Rationalizability, learning and equilibrium in games with strategic complementarities. *Econometrica* 58:1255–77.

Milgrom, P., and J. Roberts. 1990b. The economics of modern manufacturing: Technology, strategy, and organization. *American Economic Review* 80:511–28.

Milgrom, P., and J. Roberts. 1992. *Economics, Organization and Mangement.* Englewood Cliffs, NJ: Prentice Hall.

Moorthy, K. S. 1984. Marketing segmentation, self-selection, and product line design. *Marketing Science* 3:288–307.

Mullin, W. P. 1995. Agency costs, distortion costs, and the deterrence of corporate crime. Mimeo. Department of Economics, Michigan State University.

Nash, J. 1951. Non-cooperative games. *Annals of Mathematics* 54:286–95.

Neiva de Figueiredo, J. 1993. Determinants of efficiency in steel minimills: A comparative Study. Mimeo. Harvard Business School.

Neumann, J. von, and O. Morgenstern. 1944. *The Theory of Games and Economic Behavior*. Princeton, NJ: Princeton University Press.

Norton, J. A., and F. M. Bass. 1987. A diffusion theory model of adoption and substitution for successive generations of high-technology products. *Management Science* 33:1069–86.

Olson, M. 1965. *The Logic of Collective Action*. Cambridge: Harvard University Press.

Oster, S. 1982. The diffusion of innovation among steel firms: The basic oxygen furnace. *Bell Journal of Economics* 13:45–56.

Park, S. H, and M. E. Gordon. 1996. Publication records and tenure decisions in the field of strategic management. *Strategic Management Journal* 17:109–28.

Peltzman, S. 1991. The handbook of industrial organization: A review article. *Journal of Political Economy* 99:201–17.

Peteraf, M. A. 1993. The cornerstones of competitive advantage: A resource-based view. *Strategic Management Journal* 14:179–91.

Pisano, G. P. 1996. *The Development Factory: Unlocking the Potential of Process Innovation*. Boston: Harvard Business School Press.

Porter, M. E. 1980. *Competitive Strategy*. New York: Free Press.

Porter, M. E. 1981. The contributions of industrial organization to strategic management. *Academy of Management Review* 6:609–20.

Porter, M. E. 1991. Towards a dynamic theory of strategy. *Strategic Management Journal* 12:95–117.

Porter, M. E. 1996. What is strategy? *Harvard Business Review* (November–December):61–78.

Porter, M. E., and A. M. Spence. 1982. The capacity expansion process in a growing oligopoly: The case of corn wet milling. In *The Economics of Information and Uncertainty*, J. J. McCall, ed. Chicago: University of Chicago Press.

Postrel, S. 1991. Burning your britches behind you: Can policy scholars bank on game theory? *Strategic Management Journal* 12:153–155.

Prahalad, C. K., and G. Hamel. 1990. The core competence of the corporation. *Harvard Business Review* 68:79–91.

Raiffa, H. 1982. *The Art and Science of Negotiation*. Cambridge: Belknap Press of Harvard University Press.

Reinganum, J. F. 1983. Uncertain innovation and the persistence of monopoly. *American Economic Review* 73:741–48.

Rosenbloom, R. S., and C. M. Christensen. 1994. Technological discontinuities, organizational capabilities, and strategic commitments. *Industrial and Corporate Change* 3:655–85.

Rotemberg, J. J., and G. Saloner. 1989. The cyclical behavior of strategic inventories. *Quarterly Journal of Economics* 104:73–97.

Rubin, J. Z., D. G. Pruitt, and S. H. Kim. 1994. *Social Conflict: Escalation, Stalemate, and Settlement*. New York: Random House.

Rumelt, R. P., D. Schendel, and D. Teece. 1991. Strategic management and economics. *Strategic Management Journal* 12:5–29.

Salant, D. J. 1996. Up in the air: GTE's experience in the MTA auctions for personal communication services licenses. Draft. Charles River Associates.

Saloner, G. 1991. Modeling, game theory, and strategic management. *Strategic Management Journal* 12:119–36.

Schelling, T. C. 1960. *The Strategy of Conflict*. Cambridge: Harvard University Press.

Scherer, F. M. 1980. *Industrial Market Structure and Economic Performance*. Chicago: Rand McNally.

Schmalensee, R. 1987. Collusion versus differential efficiency: Testing alternative hypotheses. *Journal of Industrial Economics* 35:399–425.

Schmalensee, R., and R. D. Willig, eds. 1989. *Handbook of Industrial Organization*. New York: North-Holland.

Schorsch, L. L. 1996. Why minimills give the U.S. huge advantages in steel. *McKinsey Quarterly* 2:45–55.

Schumpeter, J. A. 1942. *Capitalism, Socialism and Democracy*. New York: Harper.

Selten, R. 1975. Reexamination of the perfectness concept for equilibrium points in extensive games. *International Journal of Game Theory* 4:25–55.

Selznick, P. 1957. *Leadership in Administration*. New York: Row, Peterson.

Shapiro, C. 1989. The theory of business strategy. *RAND Journal of Economics* 20:125–37.

Smith, A. [1776], 1937. *An Inquiry into the Nature and Causes of the Wealth of Nations*. Edwin Cannan, ed. New York: Modern Library.

Spence, A. M. 1977. Entry, capacity, investment, and oligopolistic pricing. *Bell Journal of Economics* 8:534–44.

Spence, A. M. 1979. Investment strategy and growth in a new market. *Bell Journal of Economics* 10:1–19.

Spulber, D. F. 1993. Editorial: Do firms differ? *Journal of Economics and Management Strategy* 2:121–34.

Stalk, G., P. Evans, and L. E. Shulman. 1992. Competing on capabilities: The new rules of corporate strategy. *Harvard Business Review* 70:57–69.

Stobaugh, R. 1988. *Innovation and Competition: The Global Management of Petrochemicals.* Boston: Harvard Business School Press.

Stokey, N. 1981. Rational expectations and durable goods pricing. *Bell Journal of Economics* 12:112–28.

Sull, D. N. 1996. Organizational inertia and adaptation in a declining market: A study of the U.S. tire industry. DBA dissertation. Harvard Business School.

Sull, D. N., R. S. Tedlow, and R. S. Rosenbloom. 1997. Managerial commitments and technological change in the U. S. tire industry. Forthcoming in *Industrial and Corporate Change.*

Sultan, R. 1974. *Pricing in the Electrical Oligopoly,* vol. 1. Boston: Division of Research, Harvard Business School.

Sultan, R. 1975. *Pricing in the Electrical Oligopoly,* vol. 2. Boston: Division of Research, Harvard Business School.

Sutton, J. 1991. *Sunk Costs and Market Structure.* Cambridge: MIT Press.

Teece, D., and G. Pisano. 1994. The dynamic capabilities of firms: An introduction. *Industrial and Corporate Change* 3:537–556.

Tirole, J. 1988. *The Theory of Industrial Organization.* Cambridge: MIT Press.

Tushman, M. L., and P. Anderson. 1986. Technological discontinuities and organizational environment. *Administrative Science Quarterly* 31:439–65.

Utterback, J. M. 1994. *Mastering the Dynamics of Innovation.* Boston: Harvard Business School Press.

Ware, R. 1985. Inventory holding as a strategic weapon to deter entry. *Economica* 52:93–101.

Wernerfelt, B. 1984. A resource-based view of the firm. *Strategic Management Journal* 5:171–80.

Whinston, M. 1988. Exit with multiplant firms. *RAND Journal of Economics* 19:568–88.

Williamson, O. E. 1991. Strategizing, economizing, and economic organization. *Strategic Management Journal* 12:75–94.

Wilson, C. 1983. Games of timing with incomplete information: An application to oil exploration. Mimeo. Department of Economics, New York University.

Womack, J., D. Jones, and D. Roos. 1990. *The Machine That Changed the World.* New York: Rawson.

Zarnowitz, V. 1962. Unfilled orders, price changes, and business fluctuations. *Review of Economics and Statistics* 44:367–94.

Index